FOREIGN NEWS AND THE
NEW WORLD INFORMATION ORDER

FOREIGN NEWS AND THE NEW WORLD INFORMATION ORDER

ROBERT L. STEVENSON ● **DONALD LEWIS SHAW** / EDITORS
School of Journalism, University of North Carolina, Chapel Hill

LOVE, PEACE + Good SEX

THE IOWA STATE UNIVERSITY PRESS ● AMES

© 1984   The Iowa State University Press
All rights reserved

Composed by University of North Carolina Printing Department
Chapel Hill, N.C. 27514

Printed by The Iowa State University Press
Ames, Iowa 50010

First edition, 1984

Library of Congress Cataloging in Publication Data
Main entry under title:

Foreign news and the new world information order.

  1. Foreign news—Addresses, essays, lectures.
I. Stevenson, Robert L.   II. Shaw, Donald Lewis.
PN4784.F6W64   1984   070.4′33   83-12988
ISBN 0-8138-0706-9

CONTENTS

FOREWORD

THOSE INVOLVED in the debate over improved systems of information and communications in the world will be challenged and aided by the analyses in this book. They are needed in this country and abroad. We can hope that more thoughtful studies of this nature will follow from American and foreign observers and institutions.

This book confirms what we have suspected about ourselves and others. The availability of news from outside national borders has grown, but its distribution is unbalanced and its utilization is limited and "spotty." All societies appear at fault in this respect. The authors pose challenges to the conventional wisdom on both sides of the "new order" debate. They provide a healthy reminder of our reluctance to bother about how we report the world to ourselves and others.

Professors Robert L. Stevenson and Donald L. Shaw, who with the collaboration of Dean Richard R. Cole, conceived, organized, and supervised the original analyses that are described in Part I and that led to the essays in Parts II and III, deserve our thanks. The world is provided here with rigorous, quantitative analyses of foreign news content in a variety of media systems, analyses that have not been available with such coverage and quality heretofore.

Part of the international debate deals with the question, Who controls the movements of information, particularly that segment of the flows that we call news? The nature of information may not have changed, but its organization, access, and transmission have evolved greatly in the last fifty years. These are being questioned today. But underlying discussions of a political and economic nature is the question, Do our modern means of communications aggravate or alleviate the obvious lack of understanding between cultures and nations? Communications do not always aid communication.

Every year brings an increase in the volume of information flows around the world, using all means, with and without the amazing modern technologies, which we only dimly appreciate. Thus it seems natural that all societies reexamine the selection of what small portions of those information flows are presented in the media, especially in print and electronic news systems. What little are we saying to ourselves about others? What little are they selecting to say about us? There has seldom been enough of that type of questioning, except perhaps by historians long after the fact.

It is often said that our world has shrunk because of modern technology and that we live in a global village. These are misleading images. The world in fact has expanded and exploded into great complexity. It can never be a "village," mine or yours. Then what should it be?

The complexity is presented to us with apparent detail and immediacy, in living color and from "corners" of the world formerly ignored. Should we not strongly question our daily news—while paying tribute to those enterprising and talented individuals who do wonders in bringing it to us? It may seem ephemeral, but that is not to say unimportant since it reflects what we have been: our collective and collected myths and images. It consists also of those images that others consciously or unconsciously transmit to us. It also subtly prepares us for what we shall be. Naturally, it must reflect a multidimensional, accelerating world of flowing patterns and speeding fragments—and many revolutions. But should it not also tell us of the range of mankind's efforts for survival and its search for wholeness?

It is not easy to take readings and to make assessments of the content of mass media and to do so with common coverage of several cultures. We have not exercised our capacities very much in that regard, in part because of the careful conceptualization and intellectual rigor required for studies.

The authors have proceeded with that care and rigor and have carried out pioneering analyses. They have called upon their associates and students at the School of Journalism, University of North Carolina at Chapel Hill, and at other institutions in a remarkable cooperative venture. Their work has properly attracted attention and has enabled them to solicit and here present a number of perspectives and essays that contribute to our understanding.

This is another valuable contribution by the United States to an international cooperative venture. We can be proud of that. We can be glad also that UNESCO offers so many possibilities for this country to share the knowledge and vision produced by this society and, in the process, to learn from others and to help in the building of the systems of world order.

JOHN E. FOBES

JOHN E. FOBES was deputy director general of UNESCO and chairman of the U.S. National Commission for UNESCO. He is now chairman of the U.S. Association for the Club of Rome.

PREFACE

THIS BOOK is the result of work by many people, some of whom we do not know. The ones we do know deserve the modest recognition we can give them.

The research project on which the book is based was originally a request from the United Nations Educational, Scientific, and Cultural Organization (UNESCO) to the International Association for Mass Communication Research (IAMCR) whose president, Prof. James D. Halloran, is director of the Center for Mass Communication Research in Leicester, United Kingdom. Halloran invited all members of IAMCR to participate in the study.

Richard R. Cole of the School of Journalism, University of North Carolina at Chapel Hill, expressed an interest in participating and was asked by Halloran to assume responsibility for analysis of the sample of United States media. We decided that we would collaborate in the project with colleagues at Indiana University who had also expressed an interest in the project. We also decided to expand our participation to include news agencies as well as national media and to extend the analysis to countries that would not otherwise be included.

Before the analysis got underway, Cole became dean of the School of Journalism at UNC-CH, and the editors of this volume assumed major responsibility for the completion of the project. We decided that David H. Weaver and G. Cleveland Wilhoit would concentrate their efforts at Indiana on the news agencies.

At about the same time, we approached the United States International Communication Agency for financial support and assistance in securing the requisite media samples. At USICA, we are grateful for the cooperation we received from Stanton Burnett, then director of the research service, and James P. MacGregor, the project officer who worked with us for the duration of the project. We are also grateful to the many people at ICA posts overseas who bought extra copies of newspapers and taped radio and television newscasts. In most cases, we do not know these people and cannot be certain even now that they are aware of the outcome of their efforts, but we acknowledge their invaluable contribution.

At Chapel Hill, we assembled a group of coders, keypunchers, and others who worked throughout the summer of 1979 and later. This team was directed by Thomas J. Ahern, Jr., who served as field director. He was assisted by Abdel el Mashat, Harriet McLeod, James Elliott, Jere Link, Anthony Hall, Zainul Biran, Antonio Simoes, Lily Montano, Elena Elms, Cristina Krasny, Worrapat Napaporn, and James Protzman.

Contributing on a voluntary basis were Halldor Halldorsson, William Roberts, and Susan Stiles. Professional colleagues Emmanuel E. Paraschos at the University of Arkansas at Little Rock and Christine Ogan at Indiana University contributed data on two additional countries.

In preparing this manuscript, we have been aided by Bill Newton, Jo-Lan Chi, Shailendra Ghorpade, Dulcie Murdock, Stan Wearden, Gary Gaddy, and especially by Jeanne Chamberlin.

Major financial support came from USICA. Additional assistance for the preparation of this manuscript came from two grants from the UNC University Research Council.

Some of the chapters in this book have appeared in different form elsewhere, primarily as scholarly papers. We have tried to remove repetition but otherwise leave the authors' original perspectives, conclusions, and styles.

Part I, "The Politics of Foreign News," originally was our report to USICA. It was distributed by the Office of Research at USICA in different form as a two-part report, "Foreign News and the 'New World Information Order' Debate," R-10-80, July 1, 1980.

Most of the chapters in Part II, "National News Systems," were presented as convention papers. " 'Contingencies' in the Structure of Foreign News" and "Friend or Foe? Egypt and Israel in the Arab Press" were presented to the Association for Education in Journalism in East Lansing, Mich., in 1981 where the latter was awarded first place in the International Communication Division student paper competition. "The Cultural Meaning of Foreign News," " 'Bad News' and the Third World," and "A Comparative Study of Third World Elite Newspapers" were presented to the International Communication Association in Boston in 1982. "Leaders and Conflict in the News in 'Stable' vs. 'Pluralistic' Political Systems" was presented to the Association for Education in Journalism in Athens, Ohio, in 1982. "Greece and Turkey Mirrored" was written for this volume.

The chapters in Part III, "International News Flow," are from diverse sources. "Foreign News in the Western Agencies" appeared as an appendix to the IAMCR report to UNESCO, "The World of the News; the News of the World." "A Test of the Cultural Dependency Hypothesis" was the second-place winner in the AEJ International Communication Division student competition in Athens, Ohio, in 1982. The last two chapters, "A Test of Galtung's Theory of Structural Imperialism" and "Determinants of Foreign Coverage in U.S. Newspapers," were written as master's theses at the University of North Carolina, the first in the Department of Political Science, the second in the School of Journalism. "Determinants of Foreign News Coverage in U.S.

Newspapers" was also presented to the International Communication Association in 1982.

All but one of the chapters, "The Cultural Meaning of Foreign News," use all or part of the 29-nation data set, although most are based on data from the 17 countries we supplied. Where the chapter is based on only part of the full data set, it is a function of either the author's purpose or availability of data at the time that particular analysis was undertaken.

We would like to say a word about the relationship between this project and the larger, multinational effort coordinated by IAMCR. This book represents our interpretation of our data, which is not always shared by other participants in the larger project. In presenting our analyses, we have tried to make clear that we were not speaking of the full project or for the group of researchers who contributed to the IAMCR report.

To date, only a small part of the results of the full project is widely available. This is a summary of the project with several comments and interpretations, which appears in *Journal of Communication* in 1983. The full report remains at UNESCO headquarters.

Scholars often differ on the meaning of research evidence. Some of our fellow researchers in other countries do not agree with our conclusions, and even in this book, authors often make different interpretations of essentially the same data. This does not represent a weakness of the project as much as an indication of the difficulty of applying scientific rigor to the essentially political issues of the international debate. We believe that the scholar's responsibilities include the illumination of public policy questions, however, and have proceeded with those responsibilities in mind.

ROBERT L. STEVENSON
DONALD LEWIS SHAW

The Politics of Foreign News

IT is surprising, Dr. Richard Hoggart, assistant director general of UNESCO from 1970 to 1975, has said, how many people hardly know of the debate over a new world information order and of its critical stage (Legum and Cornwell 1978, 17). The "critical" element of the debate may have ended with the unanimous approval of a declaration on mass media at the UNESCO General Conference in Paris in 1978. The resolution, although not a "victory" for any of what we see as three separate sides in the debate, was at least evidence of a spirit of compromise by most concerned and a collective determination to get on with the business of implementing the resolution's provisions. Much of the response to the report of the MacBride Commission, formed by UNESCO to deal with international communications issues, has emphasized the need to come up with specific recommendations to achieve what the UNESCO declaration calls a free *and balanced* flow of information.

A point that became clear early in the debate—back in the early 1970s—was the absence of adequate empirical data about the flow of news and information around the world. The few studies done since the pioneering research of the 1950s and 1960s were occasionally useful, but too often they were narrowly focused, sometimes irrelevant to the questions raised in the 1970s, and at best, small pieces in a very large puzzle.

It also became clear early in the debate that some of the charges were without empirical support or were based on research done a decade or two earlier. Because the Western media and news agencies have changed more in the past decade or two than is generally recognized—in most cases for the better—the absence of reliable, up-to-date data too often makes reasonable and reasoned argument difficult. This project was undertaken to fill in part of that gap.

Chapter 1 provides an overview of the "patchwork of confusing, often overlapping and sometimes contradictory charges" about the state of world communications and particularly the dominance of the United States in that field.

The authors identify two separate kinds of issues, one between East and West, that is, between the Western capitalist democracies and the industrialized socialist countries, and one between North and South, where "North" is defined as the industrialized Western nations and "South" is the world's vast less-developed region. East-West issues are essentially over the relationship between the news media and government. North-South issues cover some of the same ground and emphasize more the disparity—large and growing—between the information-rich countries of the North and the information-poor nations of the Third World.

In Chapter 2, the project that brought together researchers in a dozen countries to pursue the common quantitative analysis of foreign news is introduced and explained. It is, as the authors point out, probably the largest systematic study of foreign news coverage ever undertaken and certainly the only one that addresses the political issues in what approaches a systematic, global fashion.

Chapter 3 combines results of the project with findings of comparable research to address the questions raised in Chapter 1. The authors conclude that many of the complaints about Western coverage of and service to the Third World are not justified. But on the other hand, foreign news in Western media is spotty, narrowly defined, and uneven. Is this evidence of a need for a new world information order?

The authors answer with a theme that recurs throughout the entire book: the problems of world news flow are less problems of Western dominance than problems of journalism. The criticisms of the West can be applied to foreign coverage of every national system in the study, representing societies as diverse as the United States and the Soviet Union, and covering the spectrum of Third World countries from Algeria to Zambia. A remarkable similarity in the *quantitative* aspects of foreign news emerges that implies an almost universal definition of news: foreign news is politics, mostly in the immediate geographic region or in countries where the national interest is represented, and newsmakers are high government officials.

What is needed, the authors conclude, is not the mobilization of news media to support government objectives but improved professionalism and independence so that media can do better what they can do best.

REFERENCE

Legum, Colin, and John Cornwell. 1978. *A free and balanced flow.* Lexington, Mass.: Lexington Books.

Issues in Foreign News

Robert L. Stevenson and Richard R. Cole

THERE is a new worldwide concern about an old issue—communication. Communication is not a new concern for the United Nations and particularly not for the United Nations Educational, Scientific, and Cultural Organization (UNESCO) where efforts to restructure the world communication system have been underway for a decade.

The early efforts, which continued from the founding of the United Nations after World War II until the mid-1960s, emphasized the importance of a free flow of information among nations and the use of mass media in the Third World to build "modern"—i.e., Western—societies to overcome poverty, illiteracy and the heritage of colonialism.

By the middle of the 1960s, however, when so much of the postwar order came under challenge, a new idea began to take shape. This new idea criticized the overwhelming dominance of Western media and Western news agencies over the Third World. Talk of a new world economic order, incorporated in a resolution approved by UNESCO in 1974, was matched by discussions of a "new world information order."

The new world information order parallels the new economic order in that it calls for a more equitable distribution of resources between the advanced nations and the Third World, but it is equally vague about how to accomplish that task. Regional meetings sponsored by UNESCO as early as the 1960s identified problems with the inadequate flow of information within regions of the world, and a 1969 meeting of communications experts in Canada called for an increase in the flow of information from the Third World to the West. It also urged a "balanced circulation of news."

Both the 1974 and 1976 UNESCO General Conferences avoided a definitive declaration on the role of mass media because most of the Western nations —by then actively opposed to much of the gathering momentum for a call for a new information order—would not accept language that incorporated the idea of state responsibility for the mass media.

However, the 1976 General Conference in Nairobi did invite the UNESCO director general to appoint a commission to continue study of the problems that had split the conference. Amadou Mahtar M'Bow, the director general, appointed a 16-member commission and named as chairman Sean MacBride, an Irish statesman who had been awarded both the Nobel Peace Prize and the Lenin Peace Prize. The commission was to

> study the current situation in the fields of communication and identify problems which call for new action at the national level and a concerted, global approach at the international level. (International Commission for the Study of Communication Problems n.d., 4)

The commission's resulting report (International Commission for the Study of Communication Problems 1980) was a philosophical document open to multiple interpretations. It did not endorse clearly any of the competing views on the new world information order debate. The report recognized the need for improving the balance of international communication, but at the same time, it endorsed most of the traditional principles of a free flow of information, concepts that some would consider as antithetical.

Recent attention has shifted to a newly created UNESCO entity called the International Program for the Development of Communication (IPDC), which has been given responsibility for achieving the vaguely defined objectives of a new world information order. First efforts of the IPDC are mixed. On one hand, almost all of the projects funded by the entity are designed to improve information flow within and among Third World regions. All of the participants in the debate agree that these are worthwhile objectives. But on the other hand, several of the projects rely on the principle of government-operated mass media, to be used in support of government-defined national objectives. These projects will not get the support of Western nations, which are expected to supply the bulk of the resources for the IPDC.

If the new world information order debate has evolved from a shrill confrontation to a more pragmatic effort to cooperate in improving the world's communication resources, the issues that produced the debate have not changed. We will now consider them in detail.

INFORMATION ORDER ISSUES. The arguments in the debate are a patchwork of confusing, often overlapping, and sometimes contradictory charges. It can be argued that there are really two separate debates, sharing some arguments but quite different in nature. One issue is the flow of communication between East and West—between the dominant, industrialized countries of the capitalist West and the socialist countries of Eastern Europe and the Soviet Union. A different set of issues defines the debate about imbalances in the flow between North and South—the industrialized countries of the Northern Hemisphere and the developing, mainly nonaligned nations of the Third

World, located psychologically if not always geographically in the southern half of the globe.

The socialist countries figure in the latter debate only to a limited degree. The debate is mostly between the Third World of the South and the First World of industrialized capitalist countries, specifically the United States and Britain, which together account for much of the world of international news and information flow.

Within each of these two axes of contention—East-West and North-South —three areas of complaint can be defined (1) the imbalance of flow between East and West and between North and South (2) the content of the flow in each direction (3) and the control of the flow.

NORTH-SOUTH DEBATE. If one defines "cultural communication" to include all forms of communications between nations, the influence of Western nations, particularly the United States, is enormous. Commercial products, language, popular culture, and of course news in all parts of the Third World emanate in large part from the West. Recent critics of the West like Wells (1972), Schiller (1973), and Beltran (in Nordenstreng and Schiller 1979) have documented this influence and explained it as evidence of cultural imperialism, an effort by Western governments and multinational corporations to maintain the Third World in a state of economic, political, and cultural dependency.

The most visible targets of these charges are the four major Western news agencies and their broadcast equivalents. Three of the four news agencies are Anglo-American—Associated Press, United Press International, and Reuters —as are the three largest suppliers of newsfilm—Visnews, UPITN, and CBS.

Mustapha Masmoudi, the former Tunisian minister of information and a leading spokesman for the Third World on communication issues, contends that "almost 80 percent of the world news flow emanates from the major transnational agencies; however, these devote only 20 to 30 percent of news coverage to the developing countries, despite the fact that the latter account for almost three-quarters of mankind" (1979, 172-73).

SPECIFIC CHARGES. From this control of an overwhelmingly one-directional flow of news by a small number of Western organizations, it is argued, comes a set of distortions at both ends of the flow, and a cultural and information dependence that denies Third World countries the opportunity to address the world themselves or to listen to it except through these cultural filters of Western news agencies. These specific charges about the unbalanced flow of news between North and South are made:

1. World news is defined by the West and distorts or excludes authentic

but non-Western values of the Third World.

Masmoudi told the UNESCO commission that

> information is distorted by reference to moral, cultural or political values peculiar
> to certain states, in defiance of the values and concerns of other nations. The cri-
> teria governing selection are consciously or unconsciously based on the political
> and economic interests of the transnational system and of the countries in which
> this system is established. (1979, 174)

To the Third World, this means that the values imposed are the values of
the First World and, equally distressing, that their cultures and cultural evolution are seen in the rest of the world only through Western filters.

   2. This cultural filter excludes much of the world, especially that part
not of immediate interest to the West.

Several researchers have tried to identify characteristics of nations that
predict the amount and kind of news coverage that nations get in the international systems. These studies, however, have not discovered regularities that go
beyond those apparent to the casual observer and those that can be explained
by unique events.

   3. What little information from the Third World that does get into the
world news system emphasizes fragile aspects of the Third World.

This is surely the most common complaint about Western coverage of
underdeveloped areas. As in many of the arguments in the world information
order debate, a detailed and influential statement of the Third World indict-
ment is Masmoudi's statement to UNESCO:

> Moreover, [they often] present these communities—when indeed they show inter-
> est in them—in the most unfavorable light, stressing crises, strikes, street demon-
> strations, putsches, etc., or even holding them up to ridicule. . . . The present-day
> information system enshrines a form of political, economic and cultural colonial-
> ism which is reflected in the often tendentious interpretation of news concerning
> the developing countries. This consists in highlighting events whose significance,
> in certain cases, is limited or even non-existent; in collecting isolated facts and
> presenting them as a "whole"; in setting out facts in such a way that the conclu-
> sion to be drawn from them is necessarily favorable to the interests of the trans-
> national system; in amplifying small-scale events so as to arouse justified fears;
> in keeping silent on situations unfavorable to the interests of the countries of
> origin of these media. (1979, 174)

   4. Distorted, negative treatment of the Third World in the Western media
is transferred to the Third World itself because of the latter's dependence on
the Western news agencies.

"News from Botswana," Aggarwala argues (in Horton 1978, 197), re-
minding us of the days when the only telephone link between two neighboring
African countries was often via London and Paris, "more often than not,
reaches the people of Zambia through one of the four Western wire services."

By transmitting to the developed countries only news processed by them, that is, news that they have gathered, the transnational media impose their own way of seeing the world upon the developing countries.

5. Development news is lacking.

An important component of the argument about news reported from and supplied to the Third World is "development news," a somewhat ambiguous term that covers both special information developing countries need and the kind of information about events in the Third World that ought to be reported internationally but seldom is. The idea is not new. Lerner's early work on the passing of traditional society (1958) and on emerging of modern society recognized the mass media as a key element in the process of modernization. And one could argue that the idea goes back even to Lenin's concept of the press as collective organizer, propagandist, and agitator. In both definitions of development news, the media are important components in a government's efforts to develop a spirit of nationhood. A media system outside the control of government, even when it is mildly critical of the government but supportive of the social system in which it operates (as is the U.S. system), is intolerable, and a press that is aloof from government is a luxury that many Third World governments feel they cannot afford.

In this regard, developmental journalism is closely linked to the optimistic theories of communication and national development that offered the promise of rapid economic, social, and political development in the 1950s and 1960s. In those years, the view was that it was information Third World countries needed to help them in the slow and difficult climb toward prosperity and maturity. Now we know the relationship between "modern" and "traditional" values is more complex.

But sometimes developmental journalism has a definition that refers not to special information Third World countries need, but to information that describes the progress being made in the Third World in national development. It is the "good news" from the Third World that tells the rest of the world not about disasters, coups, poverty, and violence, but about the victories over disease and poverty about successes in piecing together nationhood from the patchwork quilt of diverse and often hostile cultural groups left to the Third World as the legacy of colonialism.

EAST-WEST FLOW. The second element of the world information order argument—the nature of the flow of news between East and West—has elements in common with the Third World complaints about the flow between the Third World and the industrialized countries of the Northern Hemisphere, but it is also different.

The flow of news between East and West, it can be noted at the beginning, is small in both directions (although smaller from East to West than vice versa) and generally controlled by the receiving country. The socialist countries of the Second World are the invisible part of the world, in the news at least. And it is this lack of visibility that is as striking in Latin America, Africa, Asia, and the Middle East as it is in the countries of Western Europe and North America.

At the slightly broader level of information exchange—television programs, movies, and the like—the flow is more like a trickle. An occasional children's TV program from the Soviet Union, an area in which Soviet television is generally given high marks for quality, appears on U.S. screens, and the Bolshoi's version of "The Nutcracker" is a staple of the holiday season in the West. But beyond these and similar irregular cultural productions, little exchange takes place. Soviet television makes use of Western newsfilm and occasionally even TV graphics, but with its own interpretation of them. In addition to snippets of Western news, a Western entertainment program or movie appears at infrequent intervals in the USSR, but for the most part, the two superpowers are almost invisible in each other's mass media. Cultural exchanges are carefully controlled. News media are a different matter.

The flow between the West and the nations of Eastern Europe is somewhat larger than the West to the USSR but is still weighted heavily from West to East. Western entertainment series appear regularly on some Eastern European television screens, and the news media seem to carry a larger amount of news about the West. A 1970 study by Gerbner and Marvanyi shows that a third of the foreign coverage of newspapers in Hungary and Czechoslovakia was from Western Europe or North America, compared to 1.3 percent from the Soviet Union. Our Eastern European colleagues report a somewhat larger percentage originating from the Soviet Union and Eastern Europe in the UNESCO/International Association for Mass Communication Research (IAMCR) study, but several of the countries use more news from Western Europe than their Eastern neighbors.

SPECIFIC CHARGES. The issues that divide East and West are less well defined than those in the North-South debate, but most have to do with the role of government in mass media. The most general issue is cultural sovereignty, an extension of political and economic sovereignty. An extension of this concept defines government responsibility for the activities of mass media and particularly the potential use of direct broadcast satellites to cross national boundaries.

Cultural Sovereignty. The main complaint from socialist countries in the world information order debate has been less about the flow of information than about the troublesome concept of information and cultural sovereignty.

This notion, like many of the ideas in the international debate, is double-edged.

On one hand, it incorporates the idea that nations ought to be able to speak to other nations directly, not through the intermediaries of the world news agencies. At this level, the argument is seconded by many Third World countries who argue that they are ignored or ridiculed by the powerful nations of the West.

But the argument also includes the right of nations to determine what will be said about them in the international marketplace and the responsibility of nations for newsgathering that operates under their flags.

This latter concept was contained in the draft resolution presented at the UNESCO General Conferences in 1976 in Nairobi and in Paris in 1978. More than anything else, it caught the attention of Western governments and particularly the Western news agencies and made them take seriously the information order debate. The compromise resolutions finally approved in Nairobi and Paris eliminated any reference to government rights and responsibilities in international news flow, but several regional meetings of UNESCO have supported the concept.

Governmental Responsibility. If national sovereignty were extended to information as envisioned in these resolutions and accepted as a principle of international relations, a government presumably could hold the U.S. government responsible for unflattering information carried by the Associated Press, the *New York Times*, or CBS. And presumably a government could demand as well that organizations like Visnews and Reuters report events with information provided by or at least approved by the government concerned. Details of operation are unclear, but the thrusting of responsibility upon government is not.

An important question in this argument is whether countries that demand the right to control information about them are also willing to accept the principle in reverse. The government of the Soviet Union, for example, presumably could insist that TASS or Novisti be the sole supplier of information about the Soviet Union around the world, but it is not clear whether the Soviet Union would also be willing to restrict its coverage of the United States to information supplied by or approved by the American embassy. It seems unlikely.

The question of reciprocity is also apparent in the area of international broadcasting, a part of the national sovereignty issue that looms large in the debate between East and West. Outside broadcasters—particularly the occasionally strident voices like Radio Free Europe and Radio Liberty—have annoyed the Soviet Union and Eastern Europe ever since they went on the air after World War II. Acceptance of the principle of cultural sovereignty might well be used to justify a demand that these broadcasts cease unless they receive the permission of the receiving nations.

As with the question of international print news flow, it is unclear whether supporters of the principle are willing to accept it in both directions. Radio Moscow, for example, is a major international broadcaster. It may be the largest broadcaster, depending on what stations are counted and how broadcast hours are calculated. While its broadcasts to the West have mellowed in the last decade or two, its tone to hostile neighbors like China is often strident. Even if Western governments were willing to give permission for Radio Moscow programs to continue broadcasts to the West in return for reciprocal privileges, one wonders how willing some of the Soviet Union's less friendly neighbors would be to accept broadcasts from the Soviet Union under the full weight of international law.

The problem is not limited to agreements between East and West. A crucial test of any nation's right to communicate under the color of information sovereignty might be its willingness to reciprocate with neighbors with whom relations are less than cordial. India's desire to communicate with a nation without going through third-party Western news agencies is understandable enough, but is India willing to accept, say, Pakistan's news version of Indian reality? What about exchanges between Ethiopia and Somalia? Israel and the Arabs? Iran and Iraq? This list could be quite long. The most vocal critics of information sovereignty are too often silent on the crucial question of reciprocal sovereignty.

Direct Satellite Broadcasting. A curious extension of the argument for cultural and information sovereignty is an effort by the Soviet Union over the last decade to obtain United Nations sanction for a prohibition on the use of direct satellite transmission of television without prior permission of target nations. The argument was partly behind the 1972 United Nations resolutions —supported only by the United States—asking the U.N. Committee on the Peaceful Uses of Outer Space to draft principles to regulate direct satellite broadcasting. It is curious both because no nation has shown any inclination to extend its international radio broadcasts to television and because it would be quite simple for any receiver nation to interfere with such a scheme.

The new generation of television in many countries—notably Western Europe, Japan, and Canada but not yet the United States—is taking the form of direct satellite broadcasting. The challenge, however, is one of keeping signals beamed more or less to one country and of keeping the signals, all broadcasting from the same geostationary orbit above the equator, from interfering with one another. A country that did not want its citizens to receive a "slopover" signal, whether intended or not, could easily modify its receivers or its own transmissions such as the Soviet Union did after importing conventional sets from Western Europe, to prevent them from picking up unwanted signals. And in the Soviet Union and Eastern Europe, where no direct satellite broadcasting system has been announced, the one-meter dish antennas necessary to receive satellite signals could easily be proscribed by law or detected if built and installed without government sanction.

RECONSIDERING THE ISSUES. Most of the studies that follow examine one or more of these specific charges in detail. However, before we turn to the data, we can reconsider the issues in general by examining other research. We will look at the availability of news sources other than the major Western agencies, whether the flow of information is as imbalanced as critics of the West contend, and whether the new generation of television in the United States has not already reversed the flow of programming. We also examine the values underlying the news.

Alternative Sources. The development of regional agencies received special attention in the latter part of the 1970s (Horton 1978). The principal Western agencies form the pinnacle of elite news services in the world. They are the largest, they transmit the most information, and they are used the most. But it is important to remember that below them is a tier of secondary agencies that provide additional information and perspective and, in fact, are widely used.

Several new regional agencies, most organized within the last few years, offer the promise of greater diversity of sources. ACAN, with assistance from the Spanish agency, EFE, operates in Central America, and Reuters has helped the development of LATIN, a Latin American regional service that relays information in Mexico and Central and South America. DEPTHnews (the first word stands for Development, Economics, and Population Themes) has operated in Asia since 1969 with a variety of services to media organizations.

Similar cooperative ventures have been organized in other parts of the world, some with modest but significant regional success. Others exist mostly either as hopeful blueprints for the future or as puffery for Third World governments with no exposure outside of the originating countries.

Other alternatives exist but without visible success. The Soviet agency TASS must be put into this category. Even though it operates as a world agency and makes its service available without cost to media and agencies in many parts of the world, TASS news appears in the world press only in a handful of countries with close ties to the Soviet Union. In our study of 17 countries outside of the Soviet Union, we could find no more than a handful of stories credited to the agency.

Another alternative is the Non-Aligned News Agencies pool, formed in 1975 specifically in response to complaints of the lack of alternatives in the Third World to the Western wire services. The pool, which transmits a file of items submitted by its member agencies through a radio network of existing national agencies, has yet to become visible as a news source, despite some optimistic claims by the head of Tanjug, the Yugoslav news agency, which has assumed prime responsibility for the pool. In our study we could find no evidence of pool material, and even the Yugoslav media apparently make little use of it.

In many cases it is difficult to ascertain the origin of news copy because national news agencies compile a file from various sources and either credit stories to themselves or, very often, to no source at all. The practice varies widely, but this illustrates an important point about the control that Third World countries exert over the world news that appears in their media: the media clients of the Western news services in Africa and parts of Latin America are not the media themselves but national agencies, operating with varying degrees of freedom from the government, which prepare a national file for exclusive distribution to media within the country.

Harris's critical (to the West) study of the Ghana News Agency for UNESCO (1977) indicated that the agency had facilities to receive 12 different wire services, ranging from Reuters (used mainly) and AFP to the Middle East News Agency (originating in Egypt) and Tanjug. The agency also had (in 1976 when the study was done) four of its own correspondents, two of whom, it should be noted, were stationed in London and New York. The agency also monitored radio broadcasts from other African countries and the international broadcasters beaming programs to Africa.

The "monopoly" that the four Western wire services are said to have on news to the Third World is incomplete. There are choices—if Third World editors are prepared to use them.

Values in the News. The assertion of the imposition of Western values on news to and from the Third World also must be carefully examined. An example that has become a classic cliché is the frequent reference to the use of "Marxist President Allende" by the Western wire services in the 1960s but the absence of any comparable reference to "Capitalist President Johnson." Another favorite example is UPI's story from New York in 1974 about a planned meeting of bauxite-producing countries that emphasized Washington's fears that the meeting might lead to the formulation of a cartel that "could set the United States' economy back more than 40 years" (Righter 1978, 36).

Such provincialism is not limited to the West. Harris's study of the Ghana News Agency illustrates what appears to be a common condition. Among the staff of the Ghana News Agency, there was, according to Harris, a consensus on the "usability" of material from Reuters and AFP, but a feeling that they still operated with too much of a cold war mentality, reflected in phrases like "Soviet-backed MPLA." Harris continues:

While the use of political adjectives annoyed the foreign staff the problem was not unsurmountable—all that was really involved was changing the adjective. One of the most common examples cited in this context was the substitution in stories about Rhodesia, South Africa, Angola, etc., of "nationalists" or "freedom fighters" for "guerrillas" or "terrorists." Another example was that stories about Ian Smith would generally be rephrased to describe him as the "racist Ian Smith." One minor reservation was made about such substitution by a few foreign editors, particularly with reference to changing "terrorist" to "nationalist" or to "freedom fighter"—this substitution would only be made if the editor believed that the "cause for which they are fighting is just—that is, in the African interest." This, in practice, meant that most stories would be amended. (1977, 236-37)

Press coverage of Ian Smith has not changed. The sample of our study covered part of the 1979 election in Rhodesia, which was referred to almost constantly in the Zambian press as the "sham, bogus election," while Smith was usually described as the "racist puppet Smith." It is hard to believe that this copy came off the AFP or Reuters wire with such adjectives already in place.

Our coders—working with material from the four major news services' coverage in Latin America, Africa, and the Middle East—could find little evidence of the use of ideological labels in describing newsmakers and, in fact, few adjectives of any kind. The policy of nonpartisan reporting is not new; such value statements began to disappear from the AP at least a century ago (Shaw 1967).

Are the media biased? Content analyses appear regularly after many political campaigns with varying degrees of competence and sophistication. And almost without exception, the conclusions are consistent: coverage is often superficial and too often uninformed; it is, however, "balanced" in the sense that both or all major sides are given more or less equivalent coverage. Sometimes coverage is forced into balance because editors insist on equivalent coverage even when, in the view of the reporters, it is not justified.

Stevenson and Greene (1977) recently tried to identify what it was that consumers have in mind when they see news bias. They concluded that bias in the news from the readers' and viewers' perspective is information that conflicts with the picture of reality readers already have in their minds: bias exists when the news disagrees with what you think is true. Apparently people seldom consider that they could be "wrong."

Of course, the superficially "objective" news—that is, deliberately balanced, detached style devoid of interpretation, implication, and too often even coherence—of the Western media and agencies lends itself easily to this kind of conflict between content and expectation. Any story that is balanced to include equivalent presentation of both sides of an issue will inevitably conflict with the expectations of almost any reader or viewer with an expectation of what the story should be. It's a no win situation.

Imbalanced Flow. One of the effects of the dominance of Western media and wire services, it is charged, is that the world is reported by Americans and Britishers and seen throughout the world through their cultural lens.

The news services deny this. Righter (1978, 33) summarizes the staffing patterns of the two American wire services by noting that AP's foreign

> stringers and reporters outnumber its foreign staff eight to one and the proportion is six to one where fulltime correspondents are concerned. Of 559 on AP's journalistic staff abroad, 478 are non-Americans. UPI, in a formal report to UNESCO in 1978, pointed out that the entire staff of its Latin American desk in New York was Latin American, as were one of the two top staff in every UPI bureau in that region. More than half of the bureau managers in Asia were Asian, and in Europe, they included eight nationalities. The chief editor of its International Desk was British—and more bureau staffs and stringers were "nationals" of the country in which they work.

An article (Massing 1979) critical of the Latin American services of AP and UPI complained that the New York staffs were dominated by Argentinians to the distress of other nationalities in Latin America. There is irony in this criticism: Latin Americans may complain because so much of their news is reported or edited by Argentinians or is about Argentina. But that is a very different complaint from the usual charge that it is the Yankees who are in control.

The dominance of the three world centers—New York, London, and Paris—through which news from and to the Third World is routed is also criticized. The new generation of information-processing equipment, which ties in electronic terminals worldwide via satellites, probably has increased centralization in these cities, but it has also put editors there in easier and faster contact with reporters around the world. Garbled copy can be clarified and questions about content sent to the point of origin more easily than in the earlier, simpler days when the editor too often had to act on what he or she thought the reporter meant.

The new equipment has also allowed the development of regional distribution of copy, a practice that goes a long way toward solving the problem of distributing information of interest only within a single region of the world. In our study, the only way we could get samples of AP copy from Latin America was to have it monitored for us at specific AP bureaus in the region. There is no single AP Latin American wire; news stories are tagged for routing to any or all of five separate files. Exchange takes place between Latin American bureaus as well, with copy moving only between the bureaus concerned and never reaching New York.

The range of material available internationally is often underestimated. Some measure of diversity is seen in a study of the newscasts (Boyd and MacKay 1978) directed toward Africa on one day in late 1977 by ten broadcasters, ranging from Radio Peace and Progress, ostensibly a nongovernment voice from the Soviet Union, to the BBC and the Voice of America. Two African services, Radio South Africa and the Voice of Nigeria were included. The percentage of material relating to Africa ranged from 100 percent on Radio Peace and Progress to 0 percent for Israeli Broadcasting Authority programs, but six of the voices used at least 40 percent of African material. More to the point here is the spread of topics covered on this one day in December, 1977. Twenty separate stories were used in the broadcasts, but not a single story was presented on all ten services. A visit by U.S. Secretary of State Vance to Jordan was carried by nine of the ten, but the average story appeared on only three of the ten services.

Schramm's cautions (1978, 15–16) about imagining that his "composite" wire service in Asia was anything more than a statistical summary are appropriate:

> Let us be careful, however, not to assume that the Composite Wire we have been describing is any more than an average. There are striking differences among the four wires, in addition to their variations in total length. Two wires carry a greater amount of non-Third World news than do the others. Two wires concentrate on international relations much more than do the others. One wire specializes in very short items. Actually 40 percent of the Third World stories on that particular wire were two inches or less in length, about twice as many as on the other wires. There are considerable differences in the stories they cover. The wires undoubtedly specialize in countries where they have the best resources and the most clients. An example of this is the coverage of the cricket match between Australia and India, in Brisbane. Two wires did not report it at all. The other two carried about 9,000 words on the match. The story filled 45 percent of the Indian news on one wire, 30 percent on the other. Obviously a great deal of this coverage was intended for India itself, and for a few other countries in which international cricket is of great interest.

Schramm also followed the news from India over the five-day sample period as it moved across the wires in 13 Asian daily papers. Of 11 stories from India, only four were carried on all four Western wire services, and none found its way into all 13 papers. The most widely used story, which was carried on three of the four wires, was used by six papers. It reported an explosion at the nuclear heavy water plant in India that had put the plant out of operation and raised suspicions of sabotage. A report on the Indian prime minister's plans to visit Nepal at the end of the week, which got 3,200 words on three of the four wire services, in contrast, was not reported in a single one of the 13 Asian papers outside of India.

It is clear that the flow of news and information is overwhelmingly from North to South, and from a handful of industrialized nations in the West to the developing nations. Most of the news is supplied by the four Western news agencies and their broadcast counterparts, although alternatives do exist. Most of the popular culture of mass media also has a strong Anglo-American look. But the aggregate data measuring the flow of information and entertainment around the world can be misleading. Many of the data are also out of date.

Wells's figure (1972), for example, that 80 percent of the Latin American television programming originates in the United States may have been true in the early 1960s when the research was carried out. But as Legum and Cornwell (1978) point out, Varis' 1974 work reported that in only one country in Latin America of seven studied was the figure of 80 percent still true. The larger countries, Mexico, Argentina, and Colombia imported between 10 percent and 39 percent of their programming. The figure is surely lower now. As in everything else, communication patterns are changing constantly.

Read (1976) also challenged the interpretation of gross export figures. Most of the television exports go where the television sets are, he says, citing a *TV Guide* estimate in 1972 that two-thirds of the total U.S. exports (based on sales not hours of programming) went to four countries: Canada, Australia, Japan, and the United Kingdom. The United States is also one of the largest importers of British programs, with the other Western, English-speaking nations of the Commonwealth also among the major customers of British exports. The principal stream of TV exports, Read concludes, is from the United States to seven huge markets, the four countries listed above, plus West Germany, France, and Brazil. These eight countries account for three-quarters of all TV sets in the world and most of the world traffic in television.

The United States, although it imports a tiny percentage of its total TV fare, is important because of the size of the market and the virtual total saturation of TV in the country. A single program, Read claims, on American television has the potential of reaching more people than exposure in all of the countries of the Third World.

Reversing the Flow. Television in the United States speaks with more international voices than is commonly assumed. Much of the foreign programming appears on public television, which imports or jointly produces 11 percent of its programming, excluding repeats, reruns, and programs sold directly to local stations. In the face of arguments of the dominance of U.S. television abroad, it is ironic that so much criticism of government-supported public broadcasting at home accuses the medium of speaking too often with a foreign —usually British—accent. For example, the BBC's production of the Shakespeare plays was originally set for partial funding from the Corporation for Public Broadcasting, until labor leaders complained about the lack of American actors. Alternative funding from private U.S. sources was found and the production went on—with the accents of the King's English preserved.

Noncommercial broadcasting is a major outlet for imported programming in both radio and television. A substantial number—no precise figures exist—of radio stations rebroadcast BBC programs. National Public Radio distributes about a dozen BBC programs to its member stations, many of which also use tapes of music, press summaries, and news from foreign embassies in Washington. A listener-supported station in Raleigh, N.C., monitors and rebroadcasts live world news from the BBC World Service almost every hour and regularly presents programs from Switzerland, Canada, Sweden, Australia, France, and the United Nations.

It is the second generation of television, however, that provides the largest and fastest-growing window for imported programming. This is the system of cable television, now operating in about one home in three in the United States and expected to double or triple by the end of the decade, that brings programming distributed by satellite to homes via local cable systems. Most new systems now offer 35 to 40 channels, and the standard may soon be 60 to 100.

What do these satellite-to-cable systems bring? More of the same, so far. But as the new specialty "narrowcast" services proliferate—first the movie and sports channels seeking a narrow slice of the audience, then news, and now culture—the opportunity for foreign nations to get their programming on American television is almost unlimited. This may be the easiest part of achieving a balanced communications flow. In fact, the invasion has already begun.

The most obviously "foreign" service in the United States is the Spanish International Network (SIN), owned largely by Mexican broadcast interests, which operates over-the-air in more than a dozen American cities and is distributed by satellite to cable in nearly 100 more. The fare of SIN is so far mostly dreary—soap operas and Spanish movies for the most part—but it is definitely Latin American and available to most Spanish-speaking U.S. residents.

Then, on the Satellite Programming Network (SPN) there is Tele-France USA, three hours a night, five nights a week of programs from France. The schedule includes language lessons, current events, and a heavy dose of movies. And on the competing USA Network there is Ovation, four programming hours a week (repeated three times) of material from Britain, Canada, and Australia, also with a potpourri of current events and culture. SPN also presents weekly programs from Japan, Scandinavia, the Netherlands, Israel, and Asia. The short-lived CBS Cable and the Entertainment Channel imported 40 percent of their material. The culture channels still on the air, ARTS and Bravo, continue to provide prime-time programming dominated by foreign productions of foreign culture (Tyler 1981).

The list of current and future foreign programs on American TV goes on and on: Canadian football and Australian rugby on the Entertainment and Sports Programming Network; children's programs on Nickelodeon and Calliope; and movie channels, which bring the best and worst of the world's cinema. For anyone tied into this noisy world, there is already a full Spanish-language network from Latin America, a prime-time network from France and the equivalent of about one and-one-half Anglophone networks. In central North Carolina (where SIN is not available), a crude calculation indicates something like 100 hours a week of foreign-produced television is available. A good argument can be made that there is more international television fare on American screens than anywhere else in the world.

It is not beyond the imagination—and certainly not beyond technical capabilities—to picture a near future with TV services broadcasting around the world directly from satellites or via satellite to cable. If the most likely future has a BBC channel distributed live to North America or a PBS or CBS beamed to Western Europe, a link between Africa and Latin America is certainly possible as well. And a Third World service, perhaps under United Nations auspices with global distribution, is also feasible. If the West is likely to continue its dominance in international communications, the future promises, nevertheless, to offer more diversity of sources, more two-way flow and, for those countries that allow it, greater freedom to choose from among this diversity. This is the essence of what the MacBride Commission defines as communications democracy.

REFERENCES

Boyd, Douglas A., and Ronald R. MacKay. 1978. *An analysis of ten international radio news broadcasts in English to Africa.* Medford, Mass.: Fletcher School of Law and Diplomacy.
Gerbner, George, and George Marvanyi. 1977. The many worlds of the world's press. *Journal of Communication* 27(1): 52–66.
Harris, Phil. 1977. *News dependence: the case for a new world information order.* Leicester: University of Leicester. Mimeo.
Horton, Philip C., ed. 1978. *The Third World and press freedom.* New York: Praeger.
International Commission for the Study of Communication Problems. 1980. *Many voices, one world.* New York: Unipub.
_____. n.d. *Origin and mandate.* Document No. 2. Paris: UNESCO. Mimeo.
Legum, Colin, and John Cornwell. 1978. *A free and balanced flow.* Lexington, Mass.: D. C. Heath.
Lerner, Daniel. 1958. *The passing of traditional society.* New York: Free Press.
Masmoudi, Mustapha. 1979. The new world information order. *Journal of Communication* 29(2): 172–85.
Massing, Michael. 1979. The wire services' banana republics. *Columbia Journalism Review,* Nov.–Dec., 45–49.
Nordenstreng, Kaarle, and Herbert I. Schiller, eds. 1979. *National sovereignty and international communication.* Norwood, N.J.: Ablex.
Read, William H. 1976. Global TV flow: another look. *Journal of Communication* 26(3): 69–73.
Righter, Rosemary. 1978. *Whose news?* New York: Times Books.
Schiller, Herbert I. 1973. *The mind managers.* Boston: Beacon.
Schramm, Wilbur. 1978. International news wires and Third World news in Asia. Medford, Mass.: Fletcher School of Law and Diplomacy.
Shaw, Donald L. 1967. News bias and the telegraph: a study of historical change. *Journalism Quarterly* 44(1): 3–12.
Stevenson, Robert L., and Mark T. Greene. 1977. Another look at bias in the news. Paper presented to the Association for Education in Journalism, Madison, Wis.
Tyler, Ralph. 1981. Culture comes to cable. *TV Guide* 29(18): 38–42.
Wells, Alan. 1972. *Picture-tube imperialism? The impact of U.S. television on Latin America.* New York: Orbis.

Research Methodology

Robert L. Stevenson

THIS project can be traced to the biennial UNESCO General Conference that took place in Nairobi in the autumn of 1976. It was the first general conference that debated the issues in what has become known as the new world information order. After extended and heated debate, the conference deadlocked over proposed resolutions on the role of mass media. In good parliamentary fashion, the conference settled for resolutions calling for more study, while substantive resolutions on the social responsibilities of mass media were withdrawn.

Out of this impasse came a resolution inviting the director general of UNESCO to undertake a broad study of communications problems in modern society. This was the basis for the UNESCO International Commission for the Study of Communication Problems—the famous MacBride Commission —whose report was published in 1980 as *Many voices, one world.*

Another resolution invited the director general to include in the UNESCO budget for 1977–78 "a study of the image of foreign countries representing different social systems and developmental stages as portrayed in the mass circulation press of respective countries." The resolution, which was introduced by the Scandinavian countries, India, and Yugoslavia, called for special emphasis "to the image given over the past twenty years by mass media in industrialized countries of the developing countries and of the changing economic and political relations in the international community."

The following summer, UNESCO assigned responsibility for the project to the International Association for Mass Communication Research, an organization of about 1,000 communication scholars in 60 countries, which has nongovernment organization (NGO) status at UNESCO. The president of IAMCR was Prof. James D. Halloran, director of the Centre for Mass Communication Research at the University of Leicester in the United Kingdom. At the meeting at UNESCO in July, 1977, Halloran, representing IAMCR, agreed to coordinate the project and subsequently wrote to IAMCR members inviting their participation.

In February, 1978, project coordinator Paul Hartmann, a research fellow at Leicester, developed a detailed set of instructions and invited the IAMCR members who had responded to Halloran's earlier invitation to test the design. At the IAMCR congress in Warsaw in September, 1978, members interested in the project discussed some pretest data and suggested study revisions. In February, 1979, the final instructions were sent to participants.

Richard R. Cole of the School of Journalism at the University of North Carolina at Chapel Hill accepted responsibility for the United States' contribution to the project. Cole, who shortly thereafter became dean of the School of Journalism, enlisted the cooperation of several colleagues at Chapel Hill and at the School of Journalism at Indiana University. These four associates, who have participated actively in the project, were Robert L. Stevenson and Donald L. Shaw at Chapel Hill and David H. Weaver and G. Cleveland Wilhoit at Bloomington.

Two decisions were made by this group that expanded the U.S. contribution to the total IAMCR project. One decision was for the Indiana team to study news agency coverage while the Chapel Hill team would emphasize news media coverage. The second decision produced a request to the United States International Communication Agency—now the U.S. Information Agency—for technical and financial assistance to expand the study to include countries not represented in the cooperative project.

From participation in the pretest and response to Halloran's original invitation, it was clear that Europe would be overrepresented in the final cooperative project and that important areas of the Third World—particularly Latin America, where no nations participated, and Africa, where only one nation was represented—would be excluded from what was becoming an important contribution to the growing debate over the new world information order.

USICA agreed to help fill in the gaps by requesting selected overseas posts to assemble the requisite samples of news media and by providing funds that allowed the team at UNC-CH to expand its analysis to include media of 13 additional countries. In addition, the project received support from two other sources. Several graduate students at UNC-CH volunteered to help in the coding, and colleagues at Indiana University and the University of Arkansas at Little Rock agreed to examine news media from countries with which they had close ties. As a result, it was possible to expand the study to three additional countries—Iceland, Turkey, and Greece—and to include regional services of the major Western news agencies. Altogether the U.S. teams gathered data from 17 countries while scholars elsewhere obtained data from an additional 12 countries.

Weaver and Wilhoit at Indiana sampled U.S. domestic news wire content from the offices of the student daily. For additional coverage, we contacted the four major Western news agencies (the Associated Press, United Press International, Reuters, and Agence France-Presse), TASS, and the new Non-Aligned News Agencies pool to enlist their cooperation.

TASS and the pool did not respond to our inquiries, but from the Western agencies we collected samples of international regional coverage that roughly coincided with national news media content. Because of the volume of material involved, we limited the study of news agencies to the four Western service files to Latin America and to two files to the Middle East and Africa.

The project called for analysis of foreign news content over the equivalent of a two-week period in 1979. One week was assembled by taking one day every two weeks, beginning with the first Monday of April and ending with the last Friday in June. The second week was a continuous week, from Monday, April 23, through Saturday, April 28.

Coding took place during the spring and summer of 1979. At Chapel Hill, where a great deal of the work was done in foreign languages, this task was carried out by foreign students living in the area and by American students with strong knowledge of languages and, in many cases, experience in the countries with whose media they were working.

In general, each national team in the joint project worked independently and interpreted the instructions on its own. A meeting of many of the participants at UNESCO headquarters in Paris in December, 1979, attempted to reconcile some of the data-gathering problems after the fact, and agreed on a common analysis of the results. The group agreed on a set of tables and supporting data that would be the basis of a composite report to be submitted to UNESCO and set a deadline of April 30, 1980, for submission of the material.

The Paris working group also selected a four-person committee to prepare the final report. That group consisted of Frank Ugboajah, Nigeria; Kaarle Nordenstreng, Finland; Annabelle Sreberny-Mohammadi, Iran; and Robert L. Stevenson, United States. The group met at Leicester for a week in July, 1980, and outlined the composite report. At that time, Sreberny-Mohammadi replaced Hartmann, who had become seriously ill. She wrote the composite report, which was discussed in draft form at the IAMCR congress in Caracas in September, 1980. The final report, containing data from 29 countries, was submitted to UNESCO in the spring of 1981. That report has yet to be published. This book for the most part is based upon data gathered by U.S. scholars for 17 nations around the world.

RESEARCH DESIGN. The design of this analysis of foreign news content produced a broad-brush picture of foreign news. It was largely descriptive rather than focused on specific (and complicated) issues that had emerged in the UNESCO debate. And it was, on the whole, a rather simple project conceptually and methodologically.

This design was necessary because many of the participating teams lacked financial and technical resources to carry out a more complex project and because any effort to deal directly with the political issues—such as operationalizing "cultural imperialism"—would inevitably have brought the participants to the same kind of impasse that delegates to the UNESCO General Conference reached. Such concepts have many meanings.

The project was appropriate because a reasonably comprehensive worldwide inventory of current foreign news content characteristics, though obviously pertinent to the international debate, was lacking. Consistent with the objectives of the project, we, the project participants, argue that this macrolevel study of foreign news is a necessary foundation upon which more sophisticated and more narrowly focused studies can be built. Further studies are very much needed.

The project was similar to all-inclusive, descriptive analyses of news content that had been done at least 25 years earlier. Its immediate inspiration, however, was two studies done in Britain by Golding and Elliott (1979) and McQuail (1977). The Golding and Elliott project was sponsored by the International Broadcast Institute and emphasized a descriptive analysis of broadcast news; the McQuail study dealt with newspaper content and was undertaken with the sponsorship of the Royal Commission on the Press.

All three projects, like the dozens of atheoretical, descriptive analyses that preceded them, defined a number of variables that collectively were intended to say something useful about the manifest content of the news. Sreberny-Mohammadi's report (1981, 14) summed up the guiding principles of the UNESCO study this way:

> The method here measures rough volume only and attempts to present the overall structure of international news reporting and the basic foci of attention. The major concern was with the following variables: where the news occurred: *Location*; where the news item originated: *Source*; who made the news: *Position and nationality of actor*; what the news was about: *Topic*; the news context: *Theme*.

To specify the details of the design, we quote extensively from the materials supplied to the scholar participants:

Media to be covered

(a) Three or four daily papers in each country, including wherever possible the largest circulation national daily. Papers should be selected so as to be broadly representative of the national press. Since conditions vary from country to country—there may not be a national press, for instance—choice of papers is left to the local investigators bearing in mind the overall objectives of the research.

(b) The main broadcast news, whether radio or television, or both. Only news bulletins as such are to be included, not documentaries or current affairs or sports programs. Only the *main* news bulletin of the day is to be analyzed for any one broadcasting channel, to avoid duplication of data. Broadcast news *must* be tape-recorded for analysis; if video equipment is not available for television, at least the sound must be recorded—notes can be made on the visuals as necessary.

Sampling

The study design calls for one continuous week and one com̨
(excluding Sundays) in 1979. Since the sample of days is so small it is
that all participants code the same days' output. In the interests of cc
the study within a reasonable time the composite week has been chosen ᴛᴗ ѕpan a
limited period only rather than the whole year. Sample day dates are as follows:

Continuous Week	Composite Week
Monday, April 23	Monday, April 2
Tuesday, April 24	Tuesday, April 17
Wednesday, April 25	Wednesday, May 2
Thursday, April 26	Thursday, May 17
Friday, April 27	Friday, June 1
Saturday, April 28	Saturday, June 16

Missing dates: Should a paper or bulletin not be available for a particular
sample day—e.g., because of a strike or public holiday—it should be replaced by
the nearest available issue before or after the missing day (and not already included in the sample). This will probably result in an imbalance in days of the
week in the sample (e.g., two Mondays), but it is felt that in such circumstances
the principle of maintaining maximum contiguity to original sample dates is
more important than that of balancing days.

Unit of analysis

The unit of analysis is the news item. In newspapers this means all the material printed under a single heading (or, occasionally, under a subheading in larger
items where material under other subheadings deals with different subject matter). For broadcast news, an item is all the material following an introductory
statement on one topic. The announcement of a new (though possibly related)
topic signals a new item that should be coded separately. The use of a linking
phrase between items, such as "Meanwhile in Tel Aviv..." does not of itself
mean that the two topics should be treated as one item. In practice there is little
difficulty in distinguishing one item from another.

Material to be included

Include only items dealing with events or situations outside the home country, or events in the home country in which foreign nationals take part or which
are presented as having substantive relevance to foreign situations. Stories at
home about private individuals whose foreign nationality is incidental to the
story, like "Mr. Rossini, an Italian living in Bonn, has won a lottery..." should
not be included. Include such material only where the foreign nationality is an
important element in the story; and here it is nationality not *ethnic* membership
that matters. Similarly passing references to foreign countries in material about
home events in phrases like "Russian-made" or "The minister, back from his
holiday in Spain..." do not qualify as an item for inclusion.

Some problems may arise where, for instance, there is a foreign immigrant
group present in the home country or where foreign troops form an integral part
of the home country's armed forces. The local investigator will be the best judge
in these circumstances, but generally speaking such groups would not automatically make an item "foreign news" unless their presence or activity is presented
as pertaining in a nonincidental way to a foreign country.

For broadcast bulletins, spot reports as such are to be ignored, for purposes of the "core" analysis.

The coding schedule

(Following are the 17 variables which were defined for the study. We will indicate the range of values possible.)

1. Institution code.
2. Item serial number.
3. Medium.
4. Sample day number.
5. Section of newspaper. For the "common core" of the study only material on general news pages is to be included. This coding is provided for anyone wishing to analyze material in specialized sections as well.
6. Type of item. News story; editorial; feature; reader's letter; picture only.
7. Source of item. Home country agency, Reuters, UPI, AP, AFP, TASS, other agency; own correspondent or staff correspondent; other domestic medium; other foreign medium; other; unidentifiable.
8. Length in column-centimeters or seconds. The length of a broadcast item is timed in seconds. The length of a newspaper item is the total column length occupied by the item (including the space taken by headline and picture, if any) measured in centimeters, based on the *standard column width for that paper*. Thus, a two-column-wide block of print ten centimeters high measures twenty column centimeters.
9. Presence and space of picture.
10. Story event or issue. (This was intended to permit the identification of specific events that occurred during the sample period for separate analysis. The study did not use this variable.)
11. Story type. Home news abroad; foreign news at home; foreign news abroad; other or uncertain.
12. Location. This concerns the first and main event in the story. The location is that of the immediate news event. Thus Geneva peace talks on Rhodesia take place in Switzerland. The only exception to this is meetings of the United Nations; these take place at "The U.N."
13. Relations between states. This concerns relations between states considered as political entities, not just between individuals and groups of different nationalities. Thus an Egyptian marrying an Israeli, or an international sporting contest should be coded "No," unless these events are presented as having implications for, or resulting from, political relations between the states concerned. Yes or no.
14. Topics. These concern the kind of event or situation that the item is mainly *about*. It will be possible to analyze this data at two levels: (a) the level of broad categories of the main headings—Political, economic, and so on; and (b) in more detail at the level of the subtopics within each broad category, e.g., military topics are subdivided into armed conflict, peace moves, and other.

The prime classification is the *main topic*—what the item is *mainly* about. Each item is to be allocated to one and only one main topic category. There will then be as many main topics as there are items. There will inevitably be some ambiguous cases and difficult decisions. This problem can be partly overcome by the classification of *subsidiary* topics. Thus if there is some doubt about whether a story is mainly about political or military matters, and it is decided to classify it as "military" as the main topic, the political aspect can still be retained in the data by coding "political" as a subsidiary topic.

There is provision for coding *up to* three subsidiary topics. Three are not obligatory; many stories will deal with only one topic, the Main Topic. The criterion for recording a subsidiary topic is whether it forms a substantive part of the item, that is, if it were absent, would the sense of the item be substantially changed? Thus a passing reference to a recent drought in an economic story would not make "natural disaster" a subsidiary topic. If the story were *about* the economic consequences of the drought then "disaster" probably would be a subsidiary topic. The list of topics:

TOPICS

Diplomatic/political activity *between* states;

Politics *within* states: internal conflict or crisis; elections, campaigns, appointments, government changes; other political, including legislation;

Military and defense: armed conflict or threat of; peace moves, negotiations, settlements; other, including arms deals, weapons, bases, exercises;

Economic matters: agreements on trade, tariffs; other international trade, imports, exports, trade balance; capital investment, stock issues, state investments (not aid); stock exchange, share prices, dividends, profits (not new stock issues); other economic performance, output, growth, sales (for economy as whole or particular enterprise); prices, cost of living, inflation; industrial projects, factories, dams, ports, roads; agricultural matters, projects, crops, harvest; industrial/labor relations, disputes, negotiations, wages; monetary questions, exchange rates, money supply; other economic;

International aid: disaster or famine relief; aid for economic purposes, e.g., industrial development; military aid, weapons, advisers, training; other aid, e.g., for education, family planning;

Social services: social problems generally, health, housing, illiteracy, etc.; educational provision; health provision (not family planning); family planning; other social services and social welfare matters;

Crime, police, judicial, legal and penal: nonpolitical crime, police, judicial and penal activity; political crime, as above; non-criminal legal and court proceedings, e.g., claims for damages; other crime/legal;

Culture, arts, archaeology;

Religion;

Scientific, technical, medical;

Sports: international; non-international;

Entertainment, show business (except personalities);

Personalities (not politicians): sports; entertainers; others;

Human interest, odd happenings, animals, sex;

Student matters;

Ecology: energy conservation; pollution; other;

Natural disasters (floods, earthquakes, drought);

Other.

15 and 16. <u>Main actor</u>. Actors are the subjects of the story; individuals, groups or other entities doing things or affected by events, in a way that is essential to the story or comment. Where a person or group could be omitted from the story without altering its substance, they should not be recorded as actors. "President Carter arrived in Paris today for discussions with the French Prime Minister"—here the President and the Prime Minister are both actors. "President Carter, accompanied by his wife, arrived in Paris for discussions. . ." Here "his wife" may not need to be recorded as an actor, particularly if she is not

mentioned again. If in doubt in such cases, include them as actors. The object is not to fill the data with marginal "actors" that are only mentioned in passing.

Actors may be individuals, plural or institutional. Thus each of the following groups could be an actor: "the president," "the crowd," "troops," "the committee," "the party," "Britain." The main actor is the main subject of the story, usually the first mentioned. "Other" actors are others essential to the story. There may be no human actor, e.g., "A hurricane has caused extensive damage..." or no *main* human actor, e.g., "A hurricane has caused extensive damage and killed five people..." Here the five people would probably only be "other" actors unless the story is mainly about their deaths, rather than about the hurricane. Unless they are further differentiated they would be entered only once as a group under "other actors."

(a) Nationality.

(b) Position/sphere—Record here the position of the actor, the capacity in which they appear, or their sphere of activity as presented in the story. Sports people will normally be coded "sports." A sportsman who is also a politician will be recorded as such if that is the main capacity in which he appears in the story. The ruling party in a country would be recorded as such; an individual representative of the party (e.g., a leader or official) acting in that capacity would similarly be recorded as "ruling party."

"Legitimate political opposition" means opposition political parties or their representatives operating within the normal constitutional arrangements of the country in question, as officially understood in that country.

"Non-legitimate political opposition" means political parties, or groups contending for power, that are outlawed or denied constitutional means of political activity in their country, e.g., certain black parties and movements in South Africa. [There is no evaluation implied here. "Legitimate/illegitimate" is as officially regarded *within* the country concerned.] A similar distinction applies between regular and irregular military. Sometimes guerrillas and non-legitimate political opposition groups may be the same people and they should be classified as political or military according to whether they are presented in the news item mainly in their political or in their military roles.

A pressure group is a group pursuing some limited objective or interest short of winning political power itself, e.g., pressing for changes in the law or the recognition of the rights of minorities by means other than gaining office.

There is a certain unsatisfactoriness about the "Position/sphere" classification in that two principles of classification are involved—that of position or role as such, and that of sphere of activity—and that these overlap in some cases and not in others. Thus an "actor" classified as "chief executive, or president" is always unambiguously an individual in a political role. In other cases, "actors" classified as "ruling party," "industry," or "sports," for instance, may be individuals, collectivities, or even near-abstractions, e.g., "The chairman of General Motors has said...," "General Motors has announced a new range of products ...," "The industrial sector has performed well..." would all be coded "industry." It seems that this part of the coding works well enough in practice.

(c) Quoted? Where any actor is quoted directly or indirectly, code "yes."

The codes: Position/sphere: symbolic/nominal head of state; chief executive, prime minister, president; other executive, government minister, cabinet, the government as a whole; legislature, parliament, congress, or committee thereof; ruling party; legitimate political opposition; non-legitimate political opposition; other politician (national); local government official or politician; ambassador or diplomat; military—regular forces of state; military—irregular, guerrillas, terrorists; industry; trade unions, workers or equivalent, as distinct from management; pressure group; religious; sports; media—"this paper," the one being coded; other medium, or media in general; academic, educational, scientific; police; judiciary, lawyers; criminals, prisoners; celebrities, show business; aristocracy, royalty (in non-political capacity); nation(s); United Nations; other inter-governmental bodies, OAU, NATO, OPEC, EEC; other international bodies, e.g., Red Cross; ordinary people, citizens; other; no human actor.

THEMES

17. <u>Themes and references</u>. Each of these is simply coded as present or absent. The idea is to pick up news-angles, conceptual frameworks and the like that are present in the content but which may not emerge clearly from the classification of Topics and other coding. The "themes" and "references" suggested vary somewhat in their levels of generality, and in some cases overlap with some of the Topics. Mostly, however, they are conceived as aspects of news coverage that cut across the topic classification. The overall rule is that the theme or reference in question should be quite clearly present in the news item in a way that would be recognized by almost anyone. In the case of the asterisked items, only the actual words in the list (or forms of them) are to be taken as indicating the presence of the theme. Otherwise, the practical rule is that if the theme is clearly there (in the text, and not just in the mind of the analyst) code it as present, even if it is only a marginal aspect of the coverage; and if in doubt, don't.

The list of themes: Nuclear arms proliferation/limitation; espionage; racism, racial discrimination, apartheid; religious or ethnic antagonisms; political independence (of any nation); economic self-sufficiency (of any nation); home country as benefactor to foreign country; home country as beneficiary of foreign country; aid to developing country(ies); development of Third World countries; population explosion/control; energy shortage/oil supply; ecology, environment, pollution (not energy); human rights; religious freedom; freedom of speech, opinion; individual freedom (other than speech or religion); torture; subversion; terrorism; East-West detente, coexistence; East-West division (political), Iron Curtain, etc.; U.S.S.R.-China division; rich-poor, developed-developing, North-South division; social equality/inequality; corruption in public life; *imperialism, colonialism, neo-colonialism (on the part of any power); *socialism; *communism; *fascism; *democracy; *capitalism; *totalitarianism.

U.S. coders made minor changes in the larger study instructions received from Leicester.

Two variables were added. The first variable added an evaluation of the affective treatment of each country coded under *nationality of actor.* The coding options were "positive," "negative," and "neutral or mixed." Coders were instructed to look for specific evaluative references to actors and not to make inferences from the events themselves. So, for example, even a negative event like political disruption would be coded as "neutral or mixed" if the report did not contain explicit evaluative references. The category of "neutral or mixed" was also used if the affective evaluation could be seen as positive from the cultural perspective of one country but negative from the perspective of another.

The second variable coded a direction for *each theme*. Many themes, of course, were directional by definition, but others—particularly the ideological themes identified by the asterisks—could be positive or negative. And we wanted to look for differences in the presentation of ideological references.

COUNTRIES AND MEDIA. As noted earlier, we went to USICA with a request for support in filling in some of the geographic and political gaps in the joint project and left to the agency the decision on what countries to include. A cable was sent to a number of foreign USICA posts inquiring about their ability to collect the necessary materials and willingness to do so. At the same time, the criteria for selection of media were forwarded, and the decision about specific media was left to individual posts.

From the posts' replies, 13 countries were eligible for inclusion in the project. From other quarters, we were able to extend the analysis to three other countries. A graduate student from Iceland volunteered to code media from his country, and professional colleagues at other universities agreed to add Turkey and Greece to the list of countries. For the latter two countries, however, the sample was limited to a single newspaper. Our final sample consisted, then, of data from 17 countries. The countries and specific media were

North America

United States: *New York Times, Washington Post, Los Angeles Times, New York Daily News*, Minneapolis *Tribune,* Charlotte *Observer*, and CBS Evening News

Latin America

Argentina: *Clarin, La Opinion, Cronica*, Radio Rivadavid, Television 11 and Tele Noche

Brazil: *O Estado de Sao Paulo, Jornal do Brasil*

Mexico: *El Universal, Excelsior, TV Horas*

Africa

Algeria: *El Moudjahid*, Al Sha'ab, national television

Ivory Coast: *Fraternite Matin*, national television

Kenya: *Nairobi Standard, Daily Nation*, national radio

Tunisia: *La Presse, L'Action*, Al'Amal national television

Zambia: *Zambia Times, Zambia Daily Mail*, national radio and television

Zaire: *Elima, Salonga*, national radio

Middle East

Egypt: *Al Ahram, Al Akhbar, Al Gumhuriyah*, national radio

Asia

Indonesia: *Kompas, Sinar Harapan, Merdeka*, national radio and television

Thailand: *Siam-Rath, Thai-Rath, Dao-Sham*, national radio and television

Eastern Europe
Soviet Union: *Pravda, Izvestia, Komsomolskaya Pravda*, national television
Western Europe
Greece: *Ta Nea*
Iceland: *Morganbladid, Thjodviljinn, Dagbladid*, national radio and television
Turkey: *Milliyet*

CODING PROCEDURES. In the summer of 1979, we assembled a team of coders, supervisors, and others who handled various technical aspects of the project. In most cases, the coders were foreign students living in the area or American students with good knowledge of the language and culture of the countries whose media they examined.

We began by practicing on samples of the U.S. media with the coders working in groups and discussing nuances of the coding instructions and problems not covered by the instructions. We tested all coders on a small sample of news stories, deliberately selected because of their complexity, before allowing them to begin work in earnest. When coders had mastered the coding schedule, they began to work. Most coding was done in groups under the supervision of a project director so that questions immediately could be answered and coders periodically checked.

In one sense, reliability can be manipulated by selection of the items tested. For example, reliability would approach 1.0 for mechanically coded variables like day and medium and should be close to 1.0 for variables like length and type of news story. Beyond that, a separate level of reliability would obtain for each type of analysis. If we analyzed data according to the 18 main topic classifications rather than the 41 specific subcategories, for instance, reliability would be higher. And likewise, if we looked for agreement among coders in all four topic categories rather than the single main topic, the coefficient of reliability would improve.

Most of the national teams reported a pi (Scott's coefficient) of 0.7 to 0.8 for the major topic classification across a sample of news stories with a representative range of length and complexity. Our figures for this coefficient ranged from 0.6 to 0.9.

In addition, we approached the problem of reliability in a different way by looking at the overall results different coders produced from roughly equivalent material. As a second stage in the training, coders worked for several days on the U.S. newspapers before moving to the media from their own countries. We did not randomly assign the newspapers or news stories to coders, but most coders worked with several papers and coded a wide variety of content. From the several hundred stories each coder handled, we compared overall frequency distributions of several key variables like topic, nationality, themes, and affective treatment.

The correlations (Pearson r) of overall results between pairs of coders were high and in most cases reached 0.9 or higher. From this, we concluded that most disagreements among coders that reduced reliability could be attributed to random errors resulting from the lack of theoretical or exhaustive descriptive definitions of the variables.

Additional evidence of overall reliability came from an examination of other comparable projects reported over the last ten years. These studies, reported in the next section, covered a wide range of samples of time and media and an equally wide range of complexity and sophistication. When they are compared with our project on the basis of key descriptive elements like geographic and topic emphasis, the similarity is remarkable. Samples as distant in time as a decade and as dissimilar as one paper per country for one day and a half dozen papers for two weeks produce results that in most cases are indistinguishable. Judging from their foreign news content, newspapers are stable institutions, regardless of the nation in which they are published.

METHOD OF ANALYSIS. As we have seen, many key elements of a descriptive study like this are necessarily arbitrary. What sample of time should be used? How should media be selected? What aspects of content should be coded? And, of course, on what basis should data be analyzed?

This latter issue, a crucial one, was represented in this study by two problems (1) the base on which percentages and other statistics would be calculated and (2) the use of single or multiple classifications in describing the news stories.

The news story was the unit of coding, but the analysis could be based on the total number of stories or the total length or space rather than the total number of stories. The argument against using the total number of stories is that a front page story running several columns is given the same weight as a one-paragraph filler on the back page if all stories are given equal weight. On the other hand, basing the analysis on the total amount of space can give undue emphasis to one or two unusually long stories. In general, computer programs are better equipped to analyze *cases* (each story being a case) than *sums of variables* (such as length). Here, the length variable was a hybrid because it measured length of print stories in standardized column-centimeters but length of electronic media stories in seconds.

The second problem can be illustrated by the example of one event that occurred during the sample period—the signing of SALT II by Presidents Carter and Brezhnev in Vienna. That was an important part of détente. What is the geographic reference for the story? Is it North America or Eastern Europe? Or is it Western Europe because the event took place there?

The same problem arises with topic. If one counts all of the topics in a story—main topic and three subordinate topics—and bases the analysis on all mentions of topics, then the complex story gets counted four times while a simple story with only a single topic gets counted once. The base then becomes some undefined concept of "total topics represented" rather than a measure of space or number of stories.

Another practical problem is that totals of percentages based on multiple coding will vary widely. This makes comparison across categories difficult. And explaining why columns of percentages do not add up to 100 percent can be challenging as well.

But what difference does it make if the SALT story is classified "Western Europe" because it took place there even if neither of the major actors was a Western European? And what about analyzing only the main topic of a story even though one, two, or three subordinate topics were part of the story?

For the December, 1979, meeting in Paris, we analyzed several key elements of the Mexican data to see how the results would be influenced by the necessary—and necessarily arbitrary—decision whether to analyze stories or total length, all topics or main topic, and geographic location or all geographic areas mentioned. The results of this test are in Tables 2.1 and 2.2.

In Table 2.1, we compare the range of topics—here the 18 original major categories are reduced to 12—in the foreign news of Mexican media four ways: first all topics mentioned, and then main topic only, based upon *total column-centimeters* and also all topics and then main topic based on *total number of stories*. Table 2.2 presents the same breakdowns for geographic reference, comparing the physical location of the story with the geographic location of the actors by total space and total number of stories. To make the comparisons easier, we have also transformed the frequency distributions to standardized z-scores and ranks.

One can compare the different approaches in a number of ways. We computed a series of correlations (Pearson r and Spearman rank-order coefficients) to see how much the results would be altered by different methods of analysis.

Results of these analyses were reassuring. (See Table 2.3.) In every comparison—all topics with main topic and geographic location with all geographic mentions by space and number of stories—the results were nearly identical. All correlation coefficients were 0.9 or higher. Our colleagues in Paris decided in favor of simplicity and agreed to use the total number of stories as the base of analysis and to analyze only the main topic and geographic location of the story. We adopted the same principle for our own analysis.

Table 2.1. Topics in foreign coverage of the Mexican media

	All mentions			Main topic only		
	%	Z	rank	%	Z	rank
Total column-centimeters ($n = 136,070$)						
Int'l politics	21	0.60	5.5	10	0.24	5.5
Domestic politics	25	0.98	3	12	0.52	4
Military, defense	11	−0.34	7	3	−0.73	8
Economics	30	1.45	1	17	1.22	2
Int'l aid	2	−1.18	10.5	2	−1.20	9.5
Social problems	1	−1.28	12	1	−1.30	11.5
Crime, justice	7	−0.71	8	4	−0.59	7
Education, science, culture	28	1.26	2	22	1.91	1
Sports	23	0.79	4	17	1.22	2.5
Human interest	21	0.60	5.5	10	0.24	5.5
Accident, disaster	2	−1.18	10	2	−0.87	9.5
Other	4	−0.99	9	1	−1.00	11.5
Total number of stories ($n = 2,436$)						
Int'l politics	22	0.84	4	11	0.39	6
Domestic politics	23	0.95	3	12	0.53	4.5
Military, defense	10	−0.38	7	3	−0.77	8
Economics	30	1.66	1	21	1.83	1
Int'l aid	2	−1.20	11	1	−1.06	10
Social problems	1	−1.30	12	0	−1.20	12
Crime, justice	9	−0.49	8	5	−0.48	7
Education, science, culture	24	1.05	2	14	0.82	3
Sports	19	0.54	5.5	18	1.39	2
Human interest	19	0.54	5.5	12	0.53	4.5
Accident, disaster	3	−1.10	9.5	2	−0.91	9
Other	3	−1.10	9.5	1	−1.06	10.5

Table 2.2. Geographic emphasis in foreign coverage of Mexican media

	All mentions			Location		
	%	Z	rank	%	Z	rank
Total column-centimeters ($n = 136,070$)						
North America	36	1.06	2	20	0.66	2.5
Latin America	41	1.44	1	46	1.91	1
Africa	12	-0.76	5	3	-0.87	7
Middle East/Egypt	10	-0.91	6	6	-0.60	5
Asia	7	-1.13	8	4	-0.77	6
Western Europe	28	0.45	4	20	0.66	2.5
Eastern Europe/USSR	8	-1.06	7	9	-0.83	6
World in general	34	0.91	3	10	0.24	4
Total number of stories ($n = 2,436$)						
North America	22	0.13	4	23	1.00	2
Latin America	46	1.91	1	32	1.87	1
Africa	6	-1.05	8	3	-0.93	7.5
Middle East/Egypt	9	-0.83	6	6	-0.63	5
Asia	9	-0.83	6	5	-0.73	6
Western Europe	30	0.11	3	21	0.81	3
Eastern Europe/USSR	9	-0.83	6	3	-0.93	7.5
World in general	31	0.80	2	8	-0.45	4

Table 2.3. Correlations among techniques of analysis of Mexican media.

Number of stories and column-centimeters	
Geographic origin	$r = +.94$
All geographic references	$+.91$
Main topic	$+.92$
All topics	$+.99$
Single coding and multiple coding	
Geographic location, stories	$+.63$
Geographic location, column-centimeters	$+.78$
Topic, stories	$+.94$
Topic, column-centimeters	$+.93$

SUMMARY. Details of these instructions to coders show that cross-cultural research is challenging, even if the specific research problem is relatively "simple" in concept and design. Few people really are familiar with cultures beyond their own, although they may know several languages. In coding, language nuances may be missed. Grouping many individual subject topics into larger analysis "categories" is risky, although necessary. Judging *common* themes across *different* language, political, and social systems is trying. Such cross-cultural projects are the content analyst's nightmare.

Yet, to conduct such research—which is very much needed—judgments have to be made. The IAMCR group attempted to account for a wide variety of differences, to make compromises where necessary (after discussion), and to gather data as relevant as possible to the issue of how nations treat each other in their news.

Within the context of the new world information order debate, however, these data demonstrate that studies of how nations talk to each other is far more complicated than those on how individuals talk to each other. Individuals can be friends with individuals from other nations, and often are. By contrast, nations share similar or dissimilar national interests. National relationships are not a reification of personal friendships. It is far more complicated.

Still, the conceptual questions, and suspicions, raised by the notion of a need for a new world information order must ultimately be based upon some knowledge of information exchanges—upon the concept of newspapers, radio, television, and perhaps even travelers. This study attempted to devise a reasonable approach to gathering baseline data upon which to extend the current new world information order dialogue.

REFERENCES

Golding, Peter, and Philip Elliott. 1979. *Making the news*. London: Longman.
International Commission for the Study of Communication Problems. 1980. *Many voices, one world*. New York: Unipub.
McQuail, Denis. 1977. Analysis of newspaper content. Research Series 4, Royal Commission on the Press. London: HMSO.
Sreberny-Mohammadi, Annabelle. 1981. *The world of the news: the news of the world*. Final report of the "foreign images" study undertaken by the International Association for Mass Communication Research for UNESCO. Mimeo.

CHAPTER 3

Patterns of Foreign News

Robert L. Stevenson and Richard R. Cole

IN the pages that follow are the results of a relatively limited analysis of the data from the 17 countries we have studied. To comment·on each of those pages would require at least as much paper as the tables themselves and would surround the reader with so many numbers that any sense of their meaning would be lost. Our detailed analysis is presented in other parts of this book; here we examine in general terms what the data tell us about some of the charges and complaints we have discussed previously. We will examine each of the tables in turn, then consider how data from various tables relate to the five specific charges discussed earlier.

CONSISTENCY OF CHARGES. In Table 3.1, the many worlds of the world's media are represented. We have included the data from our analysis of the 17 countries and a number of comparable studies that expand the coverage to more than 40 nations. The results are striking in their consistency, especially when one considers that they cover research carried out over almost a decade, samples as short as a day and as long as two weeks, from a single paper in each country to as many as six newspapers and at least a half dozen separate projects.

In every one of the countries in our analysis and in every additional study except one (a study of one Venezuelan newspaper), more attention is given to the local region than to any other part of the world. The Mexican media give more attention to Latin America than to anywhere else; the Zambian media give more time and space to Africa, the Thai media to Asia, the Icelandic to Western Europe, and so on. The proportion of regional news ranges from about one-third of all foreign coverage to about two-thirds. On the average, about half of the foreign news in Third World media originates in the local geographic region.

Behind the local region in visibility in most media systems are the First

World regions of Western Europe and North America. In most countries of the study, Western Europe gets more attention than North America. In Africa and Asia, about 10 percent of the total foreign news originates in North America, which is about half the proportion of news coming from Western Europe. The visibility of North America is greater than that of Western Europe in the Mexican media sample, but in the other Latin American countries—where U.S. influence is also highly visible—the media give more attention to news from Western Europe than their powerful northern neighbor.

The two areas that are largely invisible in these media-made world maps are Eastern Europe (outside of the press of the Soviet Union) and other Third World regions. Very little news appears in the media of Latin America from Africa or Asia, very little news from Latin America appears in African or Asian media, and so on. And across the globe—Western Europe, the Middle East, Africa, Asia, and the Western Hemisphere—the nations of Eastern Europe and the Soviet Union are the least visible. On the average, only about five percent of the foreign news comes from this important part of the world.

How much coverage is enough? Some of the proponents of the new world information order argue a kind of one-person-one-column-centimeter standard, suggesting that the three-fourths of the world's population in the Third World deserve about that proportion in the total news flow. As we will see below, in parts of the Third World, that proportion is reached.

But one can ask whether other criteria of newsworthiness are not also important. For example, it could be argued that regional coverage is important to promote understanding and cooperation at that level. And as we have seen, in every part of the world, foreign news reflects that consideration. What about cultural and historical ties, some positive, like the traditional link between Western Europe and North America, and others negative or bittersweet, like the ties between parts of the Third World and its former colonial occupiers? Do these justify consideration in news selection?

The problem of foreign news coverage is that of journalism in general: the problem is less what to put in the news than what to leave out. Who gets too much coverage in the media of the world? Who should be left out?

Table 3.1. Geographic origin of foreign news stories

	Source	Sample	No.	N Am	L Am	Africa	Mid E	Asia	E Eur	W Eur	General
North America											
United States 6 papers, TV	UNESCO	14 days, '79	1,487	26%	7%	10%	16%	14%	6%	16%	5%
UPI A wire	Rimmer	6 days, '77	214	25	14	9	10	12	6	22	2
Wash. Post	Pinch	5 days, '77	186	...	7	11	17	25	11	29	...
Network TV	Hester	1 newscast/mo. 72-76	610	...	3	7	19	32	5	29	5
Latin America											
Argentina 3 papers, TV	UNESCO	12 days, '79	1,017	13	32	5	20	3	3	18	6
Brazil 2 papers, TV	UNESCO	12 days, '79	630	12	29	5	14	7	6	23	4
Mexico 2 papers, TV	UNESCO	12 days, '79	1,188	23	30	5	10	7	3	16	6
Peru 1 paper	Pinch	5 days, '77	195	12	33	4	9	6	5	31	...
Venezuela 1 paper	Pinch	5 days, '77	134	17	30	0	10	6	1	36	...
Africa											
Algeria 2 papers, TV	UNESCO	12 days, '79	935	3	3	50	21	3	5	13	3
1 paper	Dajani-Donohue	3 weeks, '71	...	11	8	9	22	3	7	7	34
Ghana 1 paper	Pinch	5 days, '77	79	4	1	58	14	10	5	8	...
Guinea 1 paper	Skurnik	1976	171	5	1	58	9	2	3	14	6
Ivory Coast 1 paper, TV	UNESCO	12 days, '79	390	3	2	56	11	5	5	11	7
1 paper	Skurnik	1976	247	1	4	49	19	2	0	14	0
Kenya 2 papers, TV	UNESCO	12 days, '79	501	8	1	46	13	7	4	11	11
1 paper	Skurnik	1976	264	7	5	41	18	6	3	17	2
1 paper	Pinch	5 days, '77	212	13	5	32	18	6	3	26	...
Madagascar 1 paper	Pinch	5 days, '77	78	14	1	26	24	5	15	14	...
Mali 1 paper	Pinch	5 days, '77	56	4	2	54	16	2	2	21	...

Table 3.1 (*continued*)

		Source	Sample	No.	N Am	L Am	Africa	Mid E	Asia	E Eur	W Eur	General
Nigeria	1 paper	Pinch	5 days, '77	58	7	2	53	10	5	0	22	...
	28 TV programs	Golding-Elliott	1971-72	...	8	3	30	8	17	6	14	14
Senegal	1 paper	Skurnik	1976	160	7	5	51	13	2	1	16	5
	1 paper	Pinch	5 days, '77	156	2	3	67	7	5	3	13	...
Tanzania	1 paper	Skurnik	1976	159	5	3	43	14	5	4	20	...
	1 paper	Pinch	5 days, '77	129	3	2	73	12	4	1	6	...
Tunisia	3 papers, TV	UNESCO	12 days, '79	1,303	7	2	36	24	6	4	16	5
	1 paper	Pinch	5 days, '77	91	8	0	8	46	4	2	32	...
Zaire	2 papers, radio	UNESCO	12 days, '79	419	5	2	53	16	4	3	12	6
Zambia	2 papers, radio, TV	UNESCO	12 days, '79	516	8	1	46	17	6	3	14	6
Middle East												
Egypt	3 papers, radio	UNESCO	12 days, '79	1,322	13	2	12	48	8	2	13	3
	1 paper	Pinch	5 days, '77	201	14	2	7	38	3	6	29	...
	1 paper	Dajani-Donohue	3 weeks, '71	...	14	2	5	35	4	12	6	23
Kuwait	1 paper	Pinch	5 days, '77	211	8	0	4	54	7	6	21	...
	1 paper	Dajani-Donohue	3 weeks, '71	...	9	1	2	55	3	5	8	17
Lebanon	1 paper	Dajani-Donohue	3 weeks, '71	...	10	1	1	54	6	9	7	12
Saudi Arabia	1 paper	Dajani-Donohue	3 weeks, '71	...	15	1	2	36	1	4	7	35
Syria	1 paper	Danjani-Donohue	3 weeks, '71	...	12	3	3	35	3	16	7	20

40

Region / Country	Sample	Source	Period	N								
Asia												
Composite paper	(15 papers)	Schramm	5 days, '77	1,977	19	1	5	6	48	2	19	...
India	1 paper	Pinch	5 days, '77	79	6	0	5	15	59	5	9	...
Indonesia	4 papers, radio, TV	UNESCO	12 days, '79	811	9	3	7	15	46	3	13	4
Malaysia	1 paper	Pinch	5 days, '77	125	8	2	1	10	59	5	16	...
Singapore	1 paper	Pinch	5 days, '77	220	16	2	5	9	42	3	23	...
Thailand	1 paper	Pinch	5 days, '77	267	9	1	4	13	51	3	19	...
Thailand	3 papers, radio, TV	UNESCO	12 days, '79	500	8	2	7	11	51	4	13	4
Western Europe												
Eurovision		Golding-Elliott	28 days, '71-72	345	9	2	4	4	21	14	41	5
Greece	1 paper	UNESCO	12 days, '79	205	22	2	3	8	4	9	50	3
Iceland	3 papers	UNESCO	12 days, '79	689	18	3	9	10	6	4	41	9
Ireland	28 TV programs	Golding-Elliott	'71-72	...	3	1	3	2	8	3	75	5
Sweden	28 TV programs	Golding-Elliott	'71-72	...	7	3	5	5	20	8	40	12
Turkey	1 paper	UNESCO	12 days, '79	327	13	3	3	16	6	5	52	3
United Kingdom	11 papers	McQuail	12 days, '75	2,483	19	3	12	10	13	6	35	2
Visnews		Golding-Elliott	28 days, '71-72	371	9	4	16	11	23	3	27	7
Eastern Europe												
Hungary, Czechoslovakia	10 papers	Gerbner-Marvanyi	1 week, '70	...	8	14	2	5	10	34	25	...
USSR	3 papers, TV	UNESCO	12 days, '79	997	7	3	4	6	15	34	14	18

Sources for Table 3.1:

UNESCO: current study.
Dajani, Nabil, and John Donohue. 1973. A content analysis of six Arab dailies. *Gazette* 19:155–70.
Gerbner, George, and George Marvanyi. 1977. The many worlds of the world's press. *Journal of Communication* 27:52–66.
Golding, Peter, and Philip Elliott. 1979. *Making the News*. London and New York: Longman.
Hester, Al. 1978. Five years of foreign news on U.S. television evening newscasts. *Gazette* 24:86–95.
McQuail, Denis. 1977. Analysis of newspaper content. Research Series 4, Royal Commission on the Press. London: HMSO.
Pinch, Edward. 1978. A brief study of news patterns in sixteen Third World countries. Medford, Mass.: Tufts University (Murrow Reports).
Rimmer, Tony. 1980. Foreign news in UPI's "A" wire in the USA: a descriptive analysis of content for February 13–18, 1977. Paper presented to the International Communication Association, Acapulco, Mexico.
Schramm, Wilbur, et al. 1978. International news wires and Third World news in Asia. Medford, Mass.: Tufts University (Murrow Reports).
Skurnik, W.A.E. 1979. Foreign news coverage compared: six African newspapers. Paper presented to the African Studies Association, Los Angeles, Calif.

Note: In this study, Western Europe includes only Britain and France; only China is included in Asia; Turkey, Pakistan, and Cyprus are coded under General.

EVENNESS OF COVERAGE. As a measure of the evenness of coverage of different parts of the world, we have calculated the sample variance for each percentage distribution in Table 3.1. Although the eight areas are not equal in total population, they do form the major geographic and cultural regional groupings of the globe. And it could be argued that equitable distribution among such regions would be an improvement over the imbalanced coverage that now exists.

If the media gave equal attention to each of the areas—12.5 percent of the total foreign news to each, including the category marked general or multi-area—the variance from the mean would be zero. As media move away from this theoretically "evenhanded" coverage of the world, giving more attention to some areas and less to others, the variance increases. If the media of a particular country gave all of their coverage to just one area and none to any of the seven others, the variance would be at a maximum. As the variances in Table 3.2 show, no one media system or world region has a monopoly on "evenhandedness," as defined in this study.

The division of the nations of the planet into three distinct "worlds" provides a shorthand that is useful on occasion, but ignores critical distinctions among countries. The term "Third World" is particularly troublesome because the category includes several countries with the highest per capita incomes in the world as well as the nations with the lowest income. Because so many of the issues in the world information order debate are framed in these terms, however, we have used the term in discussing the debate and have grouped the data accordingly. In the tables, we have used labels like "market economies," "planned economies," and "developing countries" as a more accurate description of the groups than the usual ideological distinctions.

Table 3.2. Equality of distribution of foreign news stories

Country	Variance*	
Nigeria (TV)	61	(Most even
Madagascar	71	coverage of
United States	86	the world)
Tunisia	88	
Mexico	118	
United Kingdom	118	
Indonesia	128	
Peru	132	
Sweden (TV)	133	
Brazil	133	
Iceland	135	
Kenya	141	
Soviet Union	156	
Venezuela	170	
Argentina	171	
Algeria	173	
Malaysia	177	
Zambia	180	
Turkey	205	
India	253	
Egypt	255	
Thailand	257	
Singapore	258	
Zaire	269	
Nigeria	296	
Kuwait	299	
Mali	312	
Ivory Coast	318	
Ghana	334	
Senegal	476	(Least even
Ireland (TV)	526	coverage of
Tanzania	583	the world)

*Sample variance calculated from distribution of percentages in Table 3.1.

INVISIBLE SOCIALISTS. As shown in Table 3.3, it is the Third World, not the First World, that dominates the news of the Third World. As we saw in Table 3.1, it is the Second World of the planned economies of Eastern Europe and the Soviet Union that are nearly invisible in the foreign news of most countries.

Table 3.3. Distribution of foreign news stories by world group

	Market economies	Planned economies	Developing countries
United States	61%	6%	34%
Mexico	49	4	48
Argentina	34	3	63
Brazil	35	5	59
Tunisia	33	4	63
Algeria	24	4	72
Zaire	22	5	74
Ivory Coast	17	6	77
Kenya	33	4	63
Zambia	29	2	69
Egypt	29	2	68
Indonesia	35	3	62
Thailand	27	4	69
Iceland	71	4	25
Turkey	49	5	46
Soviet Union	28	41	31

Note: Columns may not total 100% because of rounding.

Except for Mexico, where news from the First and Third Worlds is about even, Third World news in Third World media is greater than First World media by a ratio of about two to one. The three countries of the industrialized West in the sample all give most attention to that part of the world, but even there, Third World outnumbers news from Eastern Europe and the Soviet Union by a ratio of about six to one. In the West as well as in the Third World, it is the countries of Eastern Europe and the Soviet Union that are almost "invisible" in the map drawn by the media.

"BAD" NEWS. The complaint that international news emphasizes "bad" news, such as social disruption and natural calamity, is addressed in Table 3.4. And it is clear from this table that accidents and disasters are not big news in any part of the world. Across all nations, regions, political, and economic systems, one pattern emerges: news is politics. Between one-quarter

Table 3.4. Distribution of main topic of foreign news stories

	United States	Mexico	Argentina	Brazil	Tunisia	Algeria	Zaire	Ivory Coast
Int'l politics	13%	11%	16%	11%	31%	36%	39%	25%
Domestic politics	15	12	16	23	16	15	17	19
Military, defense	11	3	5	6	11	12	8	9
Economic matters	14	20	9	18	8	5	7	11
Int'l aid	1	1	0	1	1	1	3	1
Social services	2	0	1	1	1	2	2	3
Crime, legal	9	5	6	7	5	3	4	4
Culture	7	9	5	10	3	5	2	1
Religion	2	2	1	2	1	0	1	1
Science	1	3	3	2	3	5	1	2
Sports	10	16	20	12	11	8	8	11
Entertainment	1	5	7	1	1	1	1	1
Personalities	4	5	4	1	1	1	1	1
Human interest	3	4	2	4	2	2	2	1
Student matters	0	0	0	0	0	1	1	0
Ecology	2	0	0	0	1	1	0	0
Natural disaster	3	2	4	1	1	2	1	2
Other	2	1	2	1	2	1	3	6

Note: Columns may not total 100% because of rounding.

Table 3.4 (continued)

	Kenya	Zambia	Egypt	Indonesia	Thailand	Iceland	Turkey	Greece	Soviet Union
Int'l politics	18	23	20	13	13	15	31	15	41
Domestic politics	18	21	17	13	10	17	19	19	18
Military, defense	8	9	16	9	9	5	3	8	8
Economic matters	12	11	10	17	10	8	13	3	6
Int'l aid	4	3	3	5	2	1	9	2	1
Social services	1	2	2	1	4	1	1	4	2
Crime, legal	11	12	5	5	6	4	4	8	1
Culture	2	1	4	3	1	5	1	1	5
Religion	1	1	2	1	0	1	1	2	0
Science	3	1	5	3	3	2	1	8	5
Sports	12	9	6	19	15	16	5	8	7
Entertainment	3	1	2	1	6	5	1	1	0
Personalities	2	2	3	5	2	4	2	3	0
Human interest	1	1	1	0	4	9	2	6	0
Student matters	1	0	1	1	0	0	0	1	1
Ecology	1	0	1	1	3	3	5	2	0
Natural disaster	2	3	2	4	3	5	3	3	1
Other	1	2	0	1	10	1	0	7	0

Note: Columns may not total 100% because of rounding.

and one-half of all foreign news in all of the countries dealt with domestic affairs in other countries or with international relations. A second cluster of three topics, each averaging about 10 percent of the total, concerns economics, defense matters (including war), and the less serious topic of sports. Beyond these five general categories, there is no category of main topic averaging anything like 10 percent of the total consistently across all countries.

The patterns just noted are consistent both across media of all of the countries and, within each country, across all areas of the world and world groups. Here we must shift to summary statistics to express these relationships. If we reported all of the data, we would have a separate large cross-tabulation for each country. And if we wanted to look both at main topic by geographic origin and main topic by world group in each country, we would have to present 34 separate tabulations.

Instead, we have correlated the frequency distributions of main topics in First World and Third World coverage in each country. The correlation coefficients in Table 3.5 are the zero-order Pearson correlations calculated from the number of stories in each of the 12 main topic categories. We interpret the generally high correlations in Table 3.5 as evidence that all nations' media treat the two sometimes hostile world groups in about the same way. Countries that score a relatively low correlation generally have some special emphasis on one part of the world that reduces the overall relationship. In Iceland, for example, an important part of coverage of Western Europe deals with sports, a topic almost entirely lacking in its coverage of the Third World. In the U.S.

Table 3.5. Correlations between main topics in First and Third World coverage

United States	$r = .54$
Mexico	.83
Argentina	.82
Brazil	.89
Tunisia	.72
Ivory Coast	.86
Kenya	.66
Zambia	.82
Algeria	.72
Zaire	.81
Egypt	.76
Indonesia	.71
Thailand	.47
Iceland	.26
Turkey	.86
Soviet Union	.90

media, one difference is the emphasis on domestic politics in coverage of the Third World, while economics is heavily linked with news from the First World.

NEWS BIAS. A different way of addressing the question of how different countries and political systems are treated is shown in Table 3.6. As we pointed out in the discussion of the information order debate, an argument can be made that what most people see as "news bias" is often information that is inconsistent with the idea they have about what the news should be. Most of what people get out of the news depends on what expectations they bring to it.

This is shown in Table 3.6, which demonstrates that most of the news does not have an openly identifiable direction or affect (emotional feeling) to it. Most news is essentially neutral until it is interpreted by readers, listeners, or viewers. In all countries in the study, at least half of the news was judged neutral or mixed by coders working with strict guidelines of what constituted "positive" and "negative" evaluation. In many of the countries, the proportion of neutral or mixed news reached 80 percent and occasionally even 90 percent. When we look at patterns within each country, some patterns emerge, but these are not strong or consistent. What is surprising is how little of the news is clearly evaluative, even in countries where Western standards of "objectivity" or nonpartisanship are rejected.

The question of cultural values is tied up in the use of positive and negative evaluations in the news, but it is also addressed directly in Table 3.7, which deals with the presence and absence of a set of 33 themes and references. What is surprising here, as with the previous tables, is what is not in the table. In all countries, at least half of the news does not contain any of these political, ideological, and cultural themes. In the wire service files, which we include in this table, the proportion is higher, consistent with the AP's dictum: no adjectives.

An important consideration in the flow of news from news agency—largely, but not exclusively Western—to media system is the degree to which the agency material influences the local editor. To use the popular term, it is often argued that the wire services set the media agenda by telling local editors (and their readers, in turn) what parts of the world and what issues they should think about, even if the big news agencies do not influence directly how the news is presented.

We find some evidence of that when we compare the "menu" of news provided by the news agencies with the "diet" of news selected by the media. The similarities are shown in Table 3.8, which correlates the distributions of main topics and themes and references in the three Latin American media samples with the four Western news services available to them. The correlations are stronger for topics than for the set of themes and references that we have used as a major measure of cultural values.

Table 3.6. Affect or direction of foreign news stories

	United States	Mexico	Argentina	Brazil	Tunisia	Algeria	Zaire	Ivory Coast
Positive	10%	8%	20%	29%	7%	7%	2%	0%
Negative	7	8	10	11	5	10	1	1
Neutral, mixed	84	81	70	60	88	83	97	99

	Kenya	Zambia	Egypt	Indonesia	Thailand	Iceland	Turkey	Greece	Soviet Union
Positive	7	1	21	3	4	9	9	23	8
Negative	8	3	13	3	6	13	3	18	8
Neutral, mixed	85	96	66	94	90	78	88	58	84

Note: Columns may not total 100% because of rounding.

Table 3.7. Themes and references in foreign news stories

	United States	Mexico	Argentina	Brazil	Tunisia	Algeria	Zaire	Ivory Coast
No themes	48%	67%	72%	62%	64%	65%	57%	52%
Nuclear arms control, proliferation	6	2	3	4	3	1	3	3
Espionage	2	0	1	1	0	0	1	1
Racism, apartheid	5	1	2	2	2	5	4	4
Religious, ethnic antagonism	7	3	2	2	4	2	3	4
Political independence	8	3	4	3	9	11	6	9
Economic self-sufficiency	4	2	3	2	2	2	4	4
Home country as benefactor	3	0	0	1	0	0	0	1
Home country as beneficiary	1	0	0	2	0	0	4	1
Aid to developing countries	2	1	1	1	4	3	8	4
Third World development	2	4	4	1	3	3	6	11
Population control, growth	1	0	0	0	0	0	0	0
Energy shortage, supply	6	7	3	4	4	2	2	4
Ecology, pollution	2	0	1	1	1	1	0	1
Human rights	9	3	4	5	3	3	2	3
Religious freedom	2	1	0	1	0	0	0	0
Freedom of speech	3	2	0	3	2	3	3	4
Other individual freedoms	3	2	2	0	2	3	3	4
Torture	2	1	0	0	1	1	1	1
Subversion	1	1	1	1	1	1	0	1
Terrorism	8	3	5	9	4	3	3	4
East-West detente	4	2	1	3	2	1	2	3
East-West division	2	0	0	0	1	0	1	1

	Kenya	Zambia	Egypt	Indonesia	Thailand	Iceland	Turkey	Greece	Soviet Union
USSR-China division	1	1	1	1	1	1	0	0	1
North-South division	2	1	4	1	1	1	1	2	3
Social equality, inequality	1	1	3	1	2	0	1	1	1
Public corruption	3	2	1	1	3	2	2	2	1
Imperialism, colonialism	1	1	1	1	1	1	7	3	4
Socialism	1	1	1	2	3	1	1	1	1
Communism	4	1	1	2	5	1	1	1	1
Fascism	0	0	1	0	1	0	1	0	1
Democracy	1	1	1	2	4	0	1	1	1
Capitalism	1	1	1	0	1	0	1	0	0
Totalitarianism	0	0	0	0	1	0	0	0	0
	Kenya	Zambia	Egypt	Indonesia	Thailand	Iceland	Turkey	Greece	Soviet Union
No themes	47%	46%	65%	69%	59%	71%	91%	33%	49%
Nuclear arms control, proliferation	1	1	2	3	1	2	0	3	13
Espionage	1	1	1	1	2	0	0	3	2
Racism, apartheid	7	7	1	1	0	1	0	3	5
Religious, ethnic antagonism	7	5	2	2	16	3	1	17	1
Political independence	6	8	4	4	3	12	1	8	7
Economic self-sufficiency	3	4	2	1	4	1	1	3	1
Home country as benefactor	2	0	1	0	0	1	0	1	3
Home country as beneficiary	1	2	1	2	2	1	2	2	0
Aid to developing countries	4	4	8	2	2	1	1	2	0
Third World development	5	3	1	5	3	1	1	1	0
Population control, growth	0	0	0	1	4	0	0	4	0
Energy shortage, supply	5	4	2	4	3	2	2	1	1

Table 3.7 (continued)

	Kenya	Zambia	Egypt	Indonesia	Thailand	Iceland	Turkey	Greece	Soviet Union
Ecology, pollution	2	1	1	1	1	4	0	10	0
Human rights	9	7	3	3	8	3	0	3	2
Religious freedom	1	0	2	0	0	0	0	1	0
Freedom of speech	3	4	2	1	1	1	0	3	0
Other individual freedoms	3	4	2	0	1	1	0	2	0
Torture	2	1	1	1	0	0	0	4	0
Subversion	2	2	0	1	0	0	1	2	0
Terrorism	7	7	8	4	1	2	0	8	2
East-West detente	1	1	2	1	1	2	1	3	13
East-West division	2	1	0	0	2	2	0	1	2
USSR-China division	0	0	0	2	1	0	0	0	1
North-South division	2	1	0	3	0	1	0	1	1
Social equality, inequality	1	1	1	1	2	0	0	1	0
Public corruption	3	4	2	1	4	0	0	1	0
Imperialism, colonialism	2	4	0	1	0	1	0	0	14
Socialism	1	0	0	1	0	1	0	0	9
Communism	1	1	2	1	1	1	0	0	7
Fascism	1	2	0	0	0	0	0	0	8
Democracy	1	2	0	1	0	0	0	0	3
Capitalism	1	1	0	1	0	1	0	0	1
Totalitarianism	0	0	0	0	0	0	0	0	0

Note: Multiple coding, totals may exceed 100%.

Table 3.8. Correlation between media and news agency coverage in Latin America

	AP	UPI	AFP	Reuters
Main topic				
Mexico	$r = .83$	.87	.85	.74
Argentina	.87	.86	.90	.87
Brazil	.75	.78	.83	.70
Themes and references				
Mexico	$r = .68$	.53	.54	.65
Argentina	.67	.57	.59	.65
Brazil	.49	.34	.59	.31

To rephrase the agenda-setting hypothesis slightly, we can see evidence that the Western news agencies do influence what parts of the world national media pay attention to and what kinds of news they deal with. But when the question of cultural values is raised—represented in this study by the themes and references—the linkage is weakened. There are close similarities in the Latin American data at least (the only part of the world where we can make relatively close comparisons) in terms of the parts of the world that get attention and in the news topics that get reported but considerably less in the crucial transfer of cultural values. They, to a larger extent, are added to the news at the national level.

Identifying the influence of the Western news agencies is difficult because of the wide variance of identifying and crediting sources. The media in some countries do not credit their foreign news at all, or they rewrite it with credit to a national news agency or simply to "agencies."

WHERE NEWS COMES FROM. The problem of sorting out where foreign news comes from makes it difficult to compare the data in Table 3.9. The generally low proportion of foreign news attributed to the Big Four Western agencies certainly underestimates their influence because a great deal of the uncredited news or that credited to the national agencies originates with these Western services. Based on the evidence, however, it can be said that the four Western agencies serve as a major source of international news but surely not the only one and not necessarily even the dominant source.

Two other points can be noted in these tables. One is the lack of visibility of news agencies such as TASS, which appears in only one country outside of the Soviet Union, and the Non-Aligned News Agencies pool, which appears not at all. In Latin America, however, we noted significant use of several of the medium-sized Western European agencies. In general, the new regional

Table 3.9. Sources of foreign news stories

	USA	Mexico	Argentina	Brazil	Tunisia	Algeria	Zaire	Ivory Coast
	4%	0%	0%	0%	1%	21%	1%	0%
Home country agency	4	0	0	0	1	21	1	0
Reuters	4	0	0	0	0	2	0	1
UPI	7	10	6	1	0	0	0	0
AP	19	11	5	0	0	0	0	0
AFP	0	15	9	0	2	5	0	2
TASS	0	0	0	0	0	0	0	0
Other agency	1	0	17	0	0	0	1	1
Own correspondent	35	28	1	10	6	6	13	17
Other medium, home	1	12	0	0	0	0	0	0
Other medium, foreign	1	1	1	3	0	0	1	0
Other	10	5	8	18	0	1	0	65
No source	15	23	53	67	91	65	86	30
Multiple sources	5	4	4	2	0	0	0	0

	Kenya	Zambia	Egypt	Indonesia	Thailand	Iceland	Turkey	Greece	Soviet Union
Home country agency	1%	38%	3%	26%	2%	0%	43%	3%	0%
Reuters	6	0	2	4	0	25	3	7	0
UPI	5	0	2	2	0	0	0	7	0
AP	4	7	3	9	12	16	14	27	0
AFP	0	1	5	25	2	0	14	5	0
TASS	0	1	0	0	0	0	0	0	49
Other agency	0	1	2	3	0	5	3	3	1
Own correspondent	15	18	24	21	16	24	36	11	22
Other medium, home	0	0	0	0	0	0	0	0	0
Other medium, foreign	1	1	1	1	1	4	5	6	1
Other	30	14	2	8	11	2	4	15	14
No source	31	33	44	26	57	32	4	22	18
Multiple sources	0	0	12	1	1	2	0	0	0

Note: Multiple coding, totals may exceed 100%.

and alternative agencies, which have emerged in recent years in response to the information order debate, have not yet become visible in the world's press.

In contrast to the continuing importance of the big agencies and the lack of visibility of some of the new agencies are the media's own correspondents, who provide some 15 to 25 percent of all foreign news, even in some of the smallest and poorest countries. National news agencies, as well, in many countries, supply a significant share of foreign news, even though in some cases that may mean merely choosing among a variety of news sources and editing a composite file from several sources. Of course, these gatekeepers are important because they have the opportunity to intervene at the national level in news flowing into the country from all parts of the world.

There is in the foreign news of these 17 countries a wide diversity of sources in use and, as we have seen earlier, an even wider diversity available for use.

COMPLAINTS CONSIDERED. We now consider the five complaints raised in the debate over the new world information order in light of the results of our study.

1. World news is defined by the West, distorting or excluding authentic but non-Western values of the Third World.

The striking lack of differences of foreign news in very different countries argues in favor of an almost universal redefinition of news: news is politics and foreign affairs, and newsmakers are government officials. The activities of ordinary citizens—particularly those who do not act in exceptional ways— are not news in any part of the world.

Proximity and timeliness seem to be nearly universal news values. In every country, more attention was given to news from the immediate geographic region than to any other part of the world and, other factors being equal, what happened today was more likely to appear in the newspapers and broadcast news than events that happened before today.

Is this evidence of Western dominance? It is hard to find definitions of news other than the traditional Western definition of news as the exceptional event. Lenin argued that news was the unfolding of history according to Marxist predictions, and some Third World leaders have advocated a definition of news that puts more emphasis on the positive aspects of nationbuilding. We found evidence of the use of these alternative definitions of news, although most of it was concentrated in domestic coverage rather than in foreign news. On the whole, however, we were impressed with the amount and variety of information available to editors in various parts of the world but with the narrow and limited use made of it.

The remarkable similarity between the profile of foreign news—in terms of geographic distribution and topics—in the Western news services and media of most countries suggests that the prominence of the Western agencies is at least partly a function of their ability to provide information that can be used almost universally with a minimum of editorial attention. In most cases —including the United States—the media profile is almost a random sample of the news agency profile, indicating that reliance on it is the path of least resistance to editors. Given the constraints of space and time that editors around the world work under, the path of least resistance is a reasonable (if not professionally defensible) explanation of many editorial actions.

2. This cultural filter excludes much of the world, especially that part not of immediate interest to the West.

A point we have made often in this report is the amount and variety of information available to crucial gatekeepers like editors and national news agency officials in all parts of the world. A single Western news agency regional file provides more information than almost any Third World newspaper or news agency can use, and most of these media subscribe to two or three Western agencies plus up to a half dozen or more other services. The two parts of the world that are largely invisible in the media world are (1) the nations of Eastern Europe and the Soviet Union and (2) the Third World in other parts of the Third World.

How can we increase the flow of information among these areas? Is it appropriate for the Western agencies to do most of the reporting from the socialist countries? After all, TASS operates around the world now, and most of the Eastern European countries also have news agencies operating in many parts of the world. The invisibility of the socialist Second World seems to be a function of its inability to provide timely, unembellished information to a world that is suspicious of the information now available in abundance.

The question of whether Third World editors would print more information about other Third World areas if it were available must also be raised. Are African readers really interested in events in Latin America? Do Asian readers want more information from Africa? The emphasis on regional affairs we saw earlier in all parts of the world can be interpreted as media ethnocentrism or as a reflection of legitimate special interests in the immediate region. But that emphasis, plus the information from international hot spots, leaves little time or space for reporting from the rest of the Third World or from socialist countries. The question that confronts all editors rises again: what must be left out?

A second point that is threaded throughout this report is the similarity between media systems in very different parts of the world. And a criticism that can be leveled at all media systems relates to this complaint against Western journalism: no media system seems to be capable of sustained coverage of any part of the world. Lippmann's (1922) characterization of the press as a restless searchlight, illuminating one part of the society briefly, then moving on to another, is pertinent here. News coverage is sporadic, moving from one exceptional event to another, seldom providing adequate warning of major social changes or sustained coverage once the attention of reporters and readers has moved on to another event. In fairness, though, we should acknowledge that this study has focused on precisely the fast, daily media that are the least capable of sustained, thoughtful coverage. As originally developed, the study included only the main news pages of daily newspaper editions, precisely the sources most likely to have timely, event-oriented coverage of disruptive events, while it excluded even the Sunday editions and feature sections as well as weekly and monthly magazines and current events programming on TV.

Is more information the answer? We have observed the flood of information now available and the difficulties of reporters and editors who must decide less what to put in the newspapers and broadcast reports than what to leave out. And the capacity of the public for more information, particularly information that gets away from the pervasive emphasis on timeliness and drama, seems to be limited. In the United States, it is possible to surround oneself with news, quite literally 24 hours a day. And the American public is not known either for its interest in world affairs or for its knowledge of them. Increasing the amount of information available does not seem likely to bring about an increase in knowledge or understanding of other parts of the world.

3. What little information from the Third World that does get into the world news system emphasizes negative aspects of the fragile Third World.

We have noted the curious phenomenon that just about everyone is convinced that the news is biased against what he or she believes in. And we have also cited studies that challenge this assertion. The professional criterion of objectivity—of treating different sides of an issue more or less the same—is, on the whole, met by Western journalists. Very few examples can be found of journalists who deliberately skew their reporting to the benefit or disadvantage of any point of view. What seems to happen is that the terse, unembellished style of Western reporting invites the reader or viewer to fill in the gaps with his or her own interpretation. When information that is incompatible with the reader's or viewer's own conceptions—and any "balanced" report will almost inevitably include this kind of information—the individual responds psychologically to the discordant information, not to that which supports his or her views.

The same phenomenon seems to apply to international news. When the manifest content of news is examined—and this is the only aspect of news that can be measured reliably—when explicit rules are laid out and followed, when the coder is required to point to specific words or phrases as evidence of favorable or negative coverage, then most of it disappears. Even in the Soviet media, there is amazingly little positive or negative emphasis in manifest content.

Two specific elements can be addressed directly in our study. One is the alleged emphasis on natural disasters and accidents in the news from the Third World. The response to this charge is simple: it is not true. The highest proportion of material in this category was six percent, and in most media systems in the world, it was about half of that level. We could find no evidence that more attention was paid to this category of news in the Third World than in any other part of the globe.

The second point is that a significant part of Third World coverage does deal directly or indirectly with war, political disruption, and social instability. This varies from country to country, but a large—and perhaps inordinate— part of news from the Third World does deal with disruption. But two comments can be made about this emphasis in foreign news.

The first is that we reject the random model of news that argues that coverage of every part of the world ought to be identical because, in fact, social disruption is greater in the Third World now than in other areas. Without arguing the justification for this state of affairs or attempting to fix the blame, it can be argued that the reporting from the Third World reflects the political situation in that part of the world.

The second point is that when similar events erupt in the West, they, too, get heavy coverage both in the Western media and in the Third World. Terrorism in Italy and Germany, religious antagonism in Northern Ireland, and racial violence in the United States, all get at least as much coverage as comparable events in the Third World.

The irony is that Third World complaints about Western media emphasis on violence and social disruption could be mirrored by complaints about coverage of the West in Third World media. It may be of some comfort that such events in both parts of the world are generally still exceptional enough to be considered newsworthy. The real tragedy would be if war and other forms of violence and hostility became so commonplace that they were no longer newsworthy.

4. Distorted, negative treatment of the Third World in the Western media is transferred to the Third World itself because of the latter's dependence on the Western news agencies.

The "dependence" of the Third World on the Western news agencies turns out to be far less pervasive than is asserted by many critics. In most cases, about one-fourth of all foreign news is credited to one of the four Western agencies, although the practice of attribution varies from country to country and much of the news credited to the home country agency or printed without attribution originates with the world agencies. In countries that use national news agencies, roughly 20 percent to almost half of all foreign news is credited to that source. And in all of these countries, even the poorest and smallest, between 10 percent and 40 percent of all foreign news is credited to the media's own correspondents.

There is no question about the role of the Western news agencies. They are important to the Third World, surely more important than the numbers in our report indicate. But that importance, we believe, is a function of their ability to deliver timely accounts of events around the world rather than some intentional or unintentional effort to dominate the flow of news.

Even if a large part of the news credited to a national news agency or the media's own correspondents is, in fact, derived from the four Western agencies, an important point should not be overlooked: they can select the information they want from a vast amount, from a wide variety of sources. They can edit the information they select to reflect whatever social values they want included or excluded. The local gatekeepers—typically national news agency officials or editors of a handful of national newspapers or broadcast organizations—are of crucial importance in deciding what picture of the world is made available to audiences in the Third World. Their power often has been ignored or, at best, understated by critics of the existing information order.

5. Development news is lacking.

The one part of the current debate that the study did not address directly was the question of development news. Part of the problem is the lack of a clear definition of what development news is. On one hand, it is usually considered to be information about the slow but important progress of the Third World toward social, political, and economic maturity. It is the kind of news, not related to specific, fast-moving events, that too often gets left out of the news in the crush of more pressing events. Too often this kind of information, even when it is available, gets held over day after day while editors hope for a slow enough news day to squeeze it in but eventually discard it when the slow news day fails to materialize.

These problems are not unique to the West, of course. Third World editors operate under the same restrictions and the same hopes, and they also find that such material gets held over until it is finally discarded.

Defined this way, development news has the same difficulty competing for scarce time and space as other information not tied to today's events. And Third World editors seem no better than their Western counterparts at finding room for it. Development news, like all news not tied to today's exceptional events, is usually what gets left out.

But development news sometimes refers to the specialized information needed by countries to promote their own development. Here the definition refers less to technical information than to the shared experience in the Third World of struggling to overcome the legacy of poverty, illiteracy, and colonial domination. Our coders were surprised to find how much of this kind of positive information—the good news from the Third World—was in the news media we examined. Most of it dealt with domestic news, the 50 percent to 60 percent of the media content not included in the study, so we captured very little of it in our analysis. But a recurrent question as the project developed was why this information could not be made available to other countries if they wanted it and why this transfer needed to depend on the Western wire services.

If development news is considered a special kind of news with interest limited largely to the immediate geographic region, then it seems an appropriate content for some of the new regional agencies and exchanges to specialize in. In fact, since so much of the domestic news of most Third World countries consists of this kind of information, an enterprising editor could get access to it simply by subscribing to the media of the neighboring country. To the question of why the people of Zambia must learn about Botswana only through the Western news agencies, it can be pointed out that the Zambian editor can find out directly what is happening in Botswana by subscribing to the Botswana newspaper. And if he wants to pass that information along to readers, that paper could serve as a ready-made source. Most of the information is not related to daily events so that the time delay is not significant. And the news complements or supplements that supplied by the Western agencies so that the editor is not competing directly with the world agencies, which are much richer in reportorial and technical resources.

Something of this spirit of exchange is contained in the Non-Aligned News Agencies pool and in proposals for other regional or supplementary agencies. The problem may be less one of the supply of information than of the interest of Third World editors in printing it. The failure of the Non-Aligned News Agencies pool to gain acceptance to date is partly due to the content, which consists largely of self-serving statements from national agencies. But it also reflects a lack of interest on the part of Third World editors in other parts of their own geographic region and even less interest in other parts of the Third World. The lack of development news in the media of most of the world seems to reflect more an absence of interest in that kind of information than a lack of access to it.

SUMMARY. What can we say to summarize this study of diverse media systems in countries of widely differing political and economic conditions? Gerbner's study in the mid-1970s described the "many worlds of the world's press." We, too, found great diversity in content and sources. But we also found similarities, more than we expected, and we conclude that many of the issues raised in the world information order debate are less problems of Third World journalism than problems of journalism that all practitioners of the craft need to address. All media systems define news narrowly, all reporters quote a narrow range of newsmakers, all editors put a heavy emphasis on what happened today in the world's hot spots.

Are the media as bad as critics claim? These data indicate that they are not. Are they as good as they could be? Certainly not. The common efforts of journalists around the world, sensitized by Third World complaints and demands for more equitable treatment in the world of the world's news, could have a significant impact on the way all people around the world see each other. This study suggests, we believe, that efforts ought to be continued to achieve a free and balanced flow of news to improve the vital world of international news.

REFERENCES

Lippmann, Walter. [1922] 1965. *Public opinion*. Reprint. New York: Free Press.
Gerbner, George and George Marvanyi. 1977. The many worlds of the world's press. *Journal of Communication* 27(1): 52–66.

National News Systems

IN the first section of this book, we defined the issues that comprise the debate over a new world information order and addressed them with data from the foreign news content of news media of 17 countries and about two dozen other comparable studies that have been carried out in the last decade.

On the whole, we did not find evidence to support most of the claims about the dominance of Western media in the world and their treatment of the Third World. What we did find was a remarkable similarity of handling of foreign news in media systems as different in social purpose as those of the United States and the Soviet Union and those that function in countries as different as Iceland and Indonesia, Mexico and Zambia.

Of course, our perspective was necessarily broad in that first look at the data; we were looking at the world of foreign news through a wide-angle lens. Now we want to examine this large data set in more detail, and we want to address some of the questions raised in the first section in greater detail. In this section, we move from a wide-angle lens to a close-up lens.

The seven chapters in this section—all but one based on the 17-nation data set—represent studies of national news media systems. All are comparative in that they incorporate data from several nations. And all add depth or additional perspectives to the analysis and discussion in the first section.

These seven chapters address three general areas of the new world information order debate. This section is a closer look at the assertion that the Third World is subjected to special negative treatment in the world's press.

In " 'Contingencies' in the Structure of Foreign News," Chapter 4, we pursue the surprising and disturbing finding that foreign news is handled about the same in press systems in all of what Hachten (1981) defines as five concepts of the press: authoritarian, Western, Communist, revolutionary, and development.

By using contingency analysis, the authors are able to get beyond the summary figures in each national press sample and into the linkages *among* the categories. As they put it, this approach examines "the mix of the ingredients in the recipe, not just the amount of any single ingredient." In this case, they focus on three key variables: topics in foreign news, geographic location, and social role of the newsmaker. They examine the foreign news in five countries, chosen to represent diversity in press theory, to see how topics, geography, and newsmakers are associated or disassociated. Many of the linkages are obvious: politicians are quoted in political stories, and businessmen are featured in economic news; military and defense topics are linked to parts of the world threatened by war.

The chapter concludes with a reinforcement of a point made in the first section: "The data reported here suggest a narrow definition of news and a limited journalistic sense of who ought to be given access to the media. . . . In the whole range of human activities, all sorts of important activities get forced out of the news in order to report politics and international affairs."

The question of whether news from and about the Third World is especially (and unfairly) negative is approached directly in Chapter 5, " 'Bad News' and the Third World." The authors find some evidence to support that complaint but argue that the issue is more complex than some of the rhetoric suggests.

By isolating "bad news" topics like "armed conflict," "internal conflict," "natural disasters," and "nonpolitical crime," the authors find that news from the Third World does indeed contain more conflict than news from the West but that the reverse is true for other kinds of bad news. It was mainly the West and to a lesser extent the socialist Second World that were overrepresented in news of accidents-disasters and nonpolitical crime.

Two factors add insight into this political question. For one thing, the authors find that Third World editors often overselect a diet of bad news from the large and diverse menu of news available to them. To some degree, the heavy diet of bad news *about* the Third World (and rest of the world as well) *in* the Third World is the result of editorial decisions made there, not in New York, London, or Paris.

The second factor concerns more what the news *should be*, rather than what it *is*. Should the news be *balanced* so that every part of the world is represented about the same, or should the news reflect some generally agreed-on version of reality? Should it be *accurate*? The authors present evidence that political disruption does indeed occur more frequently in the volatile Third World than in the West, and on that basis, they argue that the imbalance in coverage of conflict is a reasonable reflection of events.

Are critics of Western news values likely to be persuaded by this evidence? Probably not, but the following chapter deals with the same issue from a different perspective. Here, in the second general area of this section, we look for explanations of the *perception* of negative Third World coverage. In Chapter 6, the authors examine "The cultural meaning of Foreign News" by measuring coverage of two Third World countries in two American newsmagazines. They incorporate Charles Osgood's famous "semantic differential" technique and data Osgood and his colleagues gathered in a massive multi-national study of the connotative or subjective meanings of a standard "dictionary" of common words.

The authors, in a figurative sense, use cultural mirrors to reflect newsmagazine coverage of these two developing countries. They find, first of all, that words linked to both countries carry a strongly positive cultural meaning, a somewhat less strong but still positive image of power, and essentially a neutral connotation of activity, the three dimensions measured by the semantic differential.

Beyond that, there are some differences between the two countries, but the greatest source of difference is the cultural differences assigned to the words by people in Lebanon and Mexico. The authors conclude that "most of the difference [in coverage of these two countries by the newsmagazines] is in the eye of the beholder, or more accurately in this case, in the eye of the reader."

One of the problems of foreign news coverage, as these chapters show, is that people and countries differ in what they get from the news. And, of course, they differ as well on what they believe the purpose of the press ought to be.

The declaration on mass media, approved by UNESCO in 1978 after debate and compromise, talks about the contributions of the news media to strengthen peace and international understanding, to promote human rights, and to counter racism and incitement to war. These are noble ideals, of course, but are they proper objectives for the press, and can they work?

Chapter 7, "A Comparative Study of Third World Elite Newspapers," anticipates these questions by examining the dual-tiered press of three Arab nations. In many new nations that were once ruled by European imperial powers, the language of the former ruler is still the language of elites. And the press in that language is assumed to serve the bilingual, cosmopolitan interests of an elite readership. In contrast, the Arabic press is assumed to reflect the interests of a nonelite mass readership. In this case, the comparison is between the French-language press and the Arabic press in Algeria and Tunisia.

As is true of many of the analyses reported in this book, the research expectations were not supported. The author found that "readers within a country receive a diet of similarly colored news, language notwithstanding... If we had to affix labels, we might regard all four Algerian and Tunisian dailies as elite-appeal newspapers, considering their uniform emphasis on international politics, domestic politics, and economics."

The author cautions against assuming that the characteristics and functions of the elite press in the West can be transported to the Third World. And increasingly at UNESCO and other forums in which the new world information order is debated, the argument is heard that Western models of news media are inappropriate to the Third World and can be detrimental to Third World development.

We return to the UNESCO declaration to see whether the press can operate to promote peace and international understanding. The last three chapters in this section can be considered tests of alternative concepts of the social role of news media, the third general area this section addresses.

The first of these, "Friend or Foe? Egypt and Israel in the Arab Press," is a case study of media treatment of political crisis. In this case, the "event" is the dramatic rapprochement between Israel and Egypt, which was greeted with strong opposition by most other Arab countries. How would the press of three Arab countries—Egypt, Algeria, and Tunisia—deal with this event in the months after the peace treaty between Egypt and Israel?

The test of any commitment to an ideal comes when it must be applied to an extreme case. If justice is measured by justice given to the worst criminal and freedom of speech by the freedom for the hated idea, then the commitment to the use of mass media to promote peace and understanding must be tested when adversaries are involved.

The author finds that the press of Tunisia and Algeria reflected their governments' policies toward Egypt and Israel, which were not favorable to peace and understanding. In contrast, the Egyptian press did seem to shift its views of a former enemy, although press treatment became largely neutral rather than positive. Can the mass media transcend traditional hostilities and policies of their government? This chapter does not give much support to those who would argue that the ideals of the new world information order can be realized only if the news media are made a part of their government.

The second case study involves a similar circumstance: how the media of two countries, traditionally and recently hostile, mirrored each other. In "Greece and Turkey Mirrored," the author finds that the two countries and Cyprus, a third country of mutual interest, get a great deal of attention. But the analysis raises the issue of fairness of coverage and what the author calls "shortsightedness in...handling of news from the 'other' country." He concludes that the major papers in these two countries do not contribute to a reduction of tensions between Greece and Turkey.

The same theme is raised in the last chapter in this section, "Leaders and Conflict in the News in 'Stable' vs. 'Pluralistic' Political Systems." The point of departure of this analysis, however, is not the new world information order but the much older and essentially Western perspective of "free" versus "controlled" press systems.

Although careful to recognize that "freedom" means different things in different societies, the authors raise the question of whether the degree of independence available to mass media will influence the kind of foreign news selected for the mass media. The answer is a strong "yes."

Using Freedom House classifications, this chapter finds that news media in "free" (or "diverse") nations give less attention to national leaders as newsmakers than do media in "not free" (or "stable") countries and that they are more selective in their use of conflict news. Foreign news in "not free" or "partly free" media systems was also found to emphasize official relations among nations more than it did in the press of "free countries." The authors conclude that whatever the labels, the traditional way of separating countries does permit us to identify useful differences in the way their media cover foreign news and that the news media do seem to perform as their underlying philosophies direct.

In a sense, this last chapter brings us full circle. We began with an examination of the patterning of foreign news in diverse press systems and a lack of clear and predictable patterns. But as these varied analyses were introduced, structure began to emerge, and differences became clearer. The important question, what the news media *ought* to do and what social role they *ought* to fulfill, of course, is still with us. But these seven separate studies of the actual performance of diverse national press systems can help answer that question.

REFERENCE

Hachten, William A. 1981. *The world news prism: Changing media, clashing ideologies.* Ames, Iowa: Iowa State University Press.

"Contingencies" in the Structure of Foreign News

Robert L. Stevenson and Kirstin D. Thompson

THE analysis to date has been largely at the aggregate or macro level, presenting totals for each country. This is not surprising. With a data set as large as the one generated in this project, any simple cross-tabulation of two variables generates 29 tables when the analysis is extended to all of the participating countries. While the report to UNESCO does contain some examination of differences within countries, most of these crucial comparisons remain to be done. And if we are to uncover some of the subtle but vital differences in the complex world of foreign news, we need to look for patterns within countries as well as differences across countries.

CONTINGENCY ANALYSIS: LOOKING FOR LINKAGES. National aggregate figures cannot examine the way news is put together: which areas are linked to what topics, which newsmakers are linked to what topics, or which newsmakers are linked to what areas. These within-country differences deal directly with some of the major Third World charges.

Contingency analysis—looking at the way aspects of foreign news content are linked together—has several advantages. The biggest is that contingencies are free of most of the problems caused by the arbitrary definitions used in any descriptive content analysis and free of the influences of other arbitrary methodological considerations as well. Although it is not really true—as some critics argue—that the results of a descriptive content analysis can be predetermined by the way the categories are defined, content analysis is particularly susceptible to the influence of a whole range of arbitrary decisions that must be made in any content analysis project, such as the sample of time and content, the attributes of the news that are coded, and the boundaries that are defined to distinguish among categories.

Contingency analysis, however, examines the linkages between categories rather than frequencies of occurrence within categories. It is the mix of ingredients in the recipe, not just the amount of any single ingredient. This allows the researcher to get closer to the matter of why readers, listeners, or viewers may perceive the content differently. Pool (1959, 196), summarizing the theory and method of the "representational model" in content analysis, describes it this way:

> Contingency analysis is a quantitative procedure. It involves counting. But the form of the hypothesis and of the critical observations is different from that in a simple frequency analysis. Contingency analysis asks not how often a given symbolic form appears in each of several bodies of text, but how often it appears in conjunction with other symbolic units.

The UNESCO/IAMCR data are appropriate for contingency analysis for several reasons. The study has most of the strengths and weaknesses of descriptive general news content analyses. The categories defining topic, geography, and newsmaker were all-inclusive but not mutually exclusive. No conceptual basis was provided for distinguishing between, for example, international politics and economics. Anyone who has attempted a similar project can appreciate the difficulty of deciding how to categorize a news account of a congressional debate on, say, international trade.

Boundaries between the essentially descriptive categories in this project were established by committee decision, tradition, and common sense. Coder reliability tests in each country established evidence of adequate reliability *within* countries. Reliability *between* countries was not formally measured, but the consistency of results across the entire 29-nation data set can be taken as evidence that all national teams were proceeding in essentially the same direction. All the data used in this chapter were coded by the American team for which we have evidence of acceptable coder reliability.

Coder reliability was tested at various times and in various ways during the project and ranged generally from .75 to .90. For the categories and level of analysis reported here, reliability is in the range of .80 and higher.

The study allowed multiple coding. While a main topic was coded, the schedule allowed coding of up to three additional subsidiary topics. Similar rules governed the coding of nations mentioned in the news and status of newsmakers. Coders identified up to four topics in each story and four news figures or "actors" categorized by social role and nationality. The result is a data set that minimizes the problems inherent in descriptive content analysis and maximizes the potential for contingency analysis. Therefore, we have data on foreign news in a variety of countries that capture most of the subtle intricacies of interest to us and a technique that allows us to shake out the linkages among pertinent categories.

SPECIAL DATA COLLECTION NOTES. In this chapter, we included data from five countries. We picked the United States and the Soviet Union as leaders of the two most dissimilar media systems and three Third World countries. Brazil was included because it is a Western-oriented media system of the Third World and has one of the most developed press and broadcast systems. Algeria and Zambia were selected to provide a good contrast in the Third World and because both countries have undergone media revolutions of a sort (Barton 1979) that included the mobilization of the media in support of the government. They present good examples of the alternative media systems that some Third World representatives have argued are appropriate for the Third World. The specific media analyzed in each country are:

United States: *New York Times*, *Washington Post*, *New York Daily News* (to meet the IAMCR criterion of including the largest-circulation daily paper), *Minneapolis Tribune*, *Charlotte Observer*, *Los Angeles Times*, and CBS Evening News

Soviet Union: *Pravda*, *Izvestia*, *Komsomolskaya Pravda*, *and "Vremya,"* *the prime-time, half-hour, TV newscast*

Brazil: *O Estado de Sao Paulo* and *Jornal do Brasil*

Algeria: *El Moudjahid*, *Al Sha'ab*, and Algerian television

Zambia: *Times of Zambia*, *Zambia Daily Mail*, Radio Zambia, and national television

We can identify the linkages in each table simply. Osgood (Pool 1959, 61) outlines the procedure:

> The message is first divided into units, according to some relevant criterion. The coder then notes for each unit the presence or absence of each content category for which he is coding. The contingencies or co-occurrences of categories in the same units are then computed and tested for significance against the null (chance) hypothesis. And finally, patterns of such greater-than- or less-than-chance contingencies may be analyzed.

With these data, we can calculate the estimated joint occurrence of each combination of categories based on the overall frequency of occurrence of each category separately. For example, if "North America" is included in 30 percent of all foreign news stories in the Brazilian media and "international relations" also occurs in 30 percent of the stories, we would expect by chance to find that 9 percent of all stories (.30 x .30 = .09) deal with both North America and international relations. We can compare the actual frequency of joint occurrence with the expected frequency and, with a simple chi-square test, isolate those cells that occur significantly more or less frequently than chance would predict.

The result of this simple analysis is an indication of the clustering of categories or patterning of the news. We can identify which topics are linked to which parts of the world, which kinds of actors are linked to what topics, and so on. And we can isolate both positive and negative linkages: combinations of categories that occur more frequently than we would expect by chance and those that occur less often than we would expect by chance as well.

We can address the charge that some parts of the world are singled out for negative coverage in the Western media. And we can also compare the amount and kind of structuring of the news that occurs in the press of the United States to see if it carries over to other parts of the world.

We proposed no specific hypotheses for this analysis, but the thrust of the UNESCO debate would argue that patterns in the U.S. press, which allegedly treats the Third World differentially and negatively, would carry over into the press of a country like Brazil, which presumably is influenced by the United States, but not into the press of countries like Algeria, Zambia, and the Soviet Union, which claim to be free of the dominance of the West. Finally, by comparing this rather wide range of press systems—East, West and semi-radical Third World—we can examine in more detail than have previous studies some of the differences in the way these five national media systems construct the social reality they present to their readers, listeners, and viewers.

Because so many comparisons are involved (276 separate tests for the data from each country) we can reduce the probability of Type II error by adopting an alpha level of .01 rather than the usual .05.

RESULTS. The statistically significant linkages in the samples of media content of these five countries are presented in Tables 4.1 through 4.5.

Most of the contingencies that get "shaken out" of the data with this analysis are perhaps obvious and expected: politicians are cited in political news but not in sports; industrial leaders are quoted in economics stories; sports and entertainment figures are featured in "soft news" stories but not quoted in stories about foreign relations or politics. There are no surprises here. Nor are there unusual linkages among topics and regions or regions and actors.

What does stand out in these patterns of linkages is the *absence* of any consistency in foreign news coverage. Do U.S. media link the West with favorable topics and the Third World with negative topics? Do patterns in the American press carry over to Third World media? Is there any pattern beyond the obvious linkages (political figures with political topics, for example) and what appear to be random patterns?

On the whole, we would argue that the answer is "no," but with some qualifications.

UNITED STATES. More linkages are present in news of the immediate area than in other areas. In the U.S. press, positive linkages are found with North America and international politics, economics, and sports. The latter is largely a function of the Canadian participation in professional sports.

Coverage of Africa and the Middle East is heavily the "hard news" of foreign and domestic politics and military-defense actions. These linkages are generally not found in coverage of Western Europe, which is the one area where science, education, culture, and human interest material is heavy. National political leaders are overrepresented in news from Africa and the Middle East and generally cited in political, diplomatic, and military stories. Ordinary "people" (rather than public figures) are cited above chance only in Asia and the Pacific and usually in the small segment of foreign news not given to politics and diplomacy.

SOVIET UNION. In the Soviet press, there are positive linkages between Eastern Europe and topics like sports and the catchall of education, science, and culture. Negative links are detected between the region and both domestic politics and military-defense. Most of the "hard news" linkages are in news from Asia, although domestic politics coverage is heavy from Latin America and Africa. Coverage of North America underrepresents domestic politics but overrepresents military-defense. The Soviet media give rather heavy emphasis to "the people" as a news source although our coders report that this is frequently a vague reference to the Soviet people (as in, "The Soviet people support...") rather than the use of private citizens as sources directly.

BRAZIL. In the Brazilian media, we find a heavy concentration of "hard news" in coverage of the Middle East and Africa but linkages with sports, human interest, and disasters in coverage of North America. Economics is positively linked with both sectors of the hemisphere. Both domestic politics and military-defense activities are significantly underrepresented in Latin American coverage. There are some similarities in the patterning of Brazilian and United States foreign news coverage in that they both emphasize hemispheric coverage of economics but generally give low attention to domestic politics. Coverage of the Middle East and Africa focuses heavily on politics and defense.

ZAMBIA AND ALGERIA. The foreign coverage in the Zambian and Algerian media does have some common themes: an emphasis on international politics in news from Africa and the Middle East, negative linkages with some of the "soft news" topics like education, science, and culture in those areas.

Table 4.1. Linkages in foreign news stories—United States media

	Above average associations	Below average associations
Topic by Region		
North America	International politics; economics; sports	Domestic politics
Latin America	Crime, police	Military, defense
Africa	International politics; domestic politics; international aid	Education, science, culture
Middle East	International politics; domestic politics; military, defense	Sports; human interest
Asia Pacific	International aid	Domestic politics
Western Europe	Education, science, culture; human interest	International politics; domestic politics; military, defense; international aid
Eastern Europe	International politics	Domestic politics; economics
Global	Economics; international aid	Human interest
Actor by region		
North America	Industry; entertainment, sports	Military; populace
Africa	National politicians; military	Industry; culture
Middle East	National politicians; military	
Asia Pacific	Industry; legal; populace	
Western Europe	Culture; entertainment; sports	National politicians; military
Eastern Europe		Industry
Global	International politicians; populace	Military; entertainment; sports
Topic by actor		
National politicians	International politics; domestic politics; military, defense; economics; international aid; crime, police	Sports; human interest

International politicians	International politics; military, defense	International aid; social services; sports
Military	International politics; domestic politics; military, defense; crime, police	Economics; education, science, culture; sports
Industry	Economics	International politics; domestic politics; military, defense
Culture	Social services; education, science, culture; human interest; other	International politics; military, defense; economics; sports
Legal	Crime, police	Economics; education, science, culture; sports
Entertainment, sports	Crime, police; sports; human interest	International politics; domestic politics; military, defense; economics; international aid; social services; education, science, culture
Populace	Social services; education, science, culture; human interest; accidents, disaster	Sports
Other sources	Education, science, culture; human interest; accidents, disaster; other	Domestic politics; military, defense

Table 4.2. Linkages in foreign news stories—Soviet media

	Above average associations	Below average associations
Topic by Region		
North America	Military, defense	Domestic politics; education, science, culture; sports
Latin America	Domestic politics	Military, defense
Africa	Domestic politics	
Middle East	International politics; military, defense	Sports
Asia Pacific	International politics; domestic politics; military, defense; international aid	Sports
Western Europe	Other	Military, defense; international aid; sports
Eastern Europe	International politics; education, science, culture; sports	Domestic politics; military, defense; social services
Global		Education, science, culture
Actor by region		
Africa	Populace	
North America		Entertainment, sports
Middle East	National politicians; military; populace	Entertainment, sports
Asia Pacific	National politicians; military; populace	Entertainment, sports
Western Europe	Entertainment, sports	Military; populace
Eastern Europe	Culture; entertainment, sports	Military; legal; populace
Global		Culture
Topic by actor		
National politicians	International politics; domestic politics; military, defense	Social services; education, science, culture; sports; other

International politicians	International politics	Domestic politics; sports; human interest; other
Military	Military, defense	Crime, police
Industry	Economics	International politics; military, defense
Culture	Education, science, culture; human interest	Domestic politics; sports
Legal	Domestic politics; crime, police	International politics
Entertainment, sports	Sports	International politics; domestic politics; military, defense; education, science, culture
Populace	Domestic politics; military, defense; international aid; social services; human interest; accidents, disaster; other	Education, science, culture
Other	Education, science, culture	International politics; accidents, disaster

Table 4.3. Linkages in foreign news stories—Brazilian media

	Above average associations	Below average associations
Topic by Region		
North America	Economics; sports; human interest; accidents, disaster	Domestic politics
Latin America	Economics; sports	Domestic politics; military, defense; crime, police
Africa	International politics; domestic politics; education, science, culture	
Middle East	International politics; domestic politics; military, defense; crime, police; education, science, culture	Sports
Asia Pacific	International politics; military, defense	
Western Europe	Education, science, culture; human interest	Military, defense; international aid
Eastern Europe	International politics; military, defense	Economics
Global	Economics	
Actor by region		
North America	Industry; entertainment, sports	National politicians; military; populace
Latin America	Industry; entertainment, sports	National politicians; military
Africa	National politicians	Military; entertainment, sports
Middle East	National politicians; military; populace	Industry; entertainment, sports
Western Europe	Culture	
Eastern Europe	National politicians	Industry
Global	International politicians; populace	

Topic by actor

National politicians	International politics; domestic politics; military, defense; economics; international aid	Education, science, culture; sports; human interest
International politicians	International politics	International aid; sports
Military	Domestic politics; military, defense; crime, police	Economics; education, science, culture; sports
Industry	Economics	International politics; domestic politics; sports
Culture	Education, science, culture; other	International politics; economics; crime, police; sports
Legal	Domestic politics; crime, police	Military, defense; economics; education, science, culture; sports
Entertainment, sports	Sports; human interest	International politics; domestic politics; military, defense; economics; crime, police
Populace	Domestic politics; military, defense; social services; human interest; accidents, disaster	Education, science, culture; sports

Table 4.4. Linkages in foreign news stories—Algerian media

	Above average associations	Below average associations
Topic by Region		
North America	Military, defense; international aid; accidents, disaster	
Africa	International politics; accidents, disaster; other	Military, defense; crime, police; education, science, culture; human interest; accidents, disaster
Middle East	International politics; domestic politics; military, defense	Social services; education, science, culture; sports; accidents, disaster
Asia Pacific		Military, defense
Western Europe	Sports; human interest	International politics; military, defense
Eastern Europe	Sports	Domestic politics; military, defense
Actor by region		
North America	Other	National politicians
Africa	National politicians; international politicians; culture	Military; industry; legal; entertainment, sports; other
Middle East	National politicians; military; populace	
Asia Pacific		Military
Western Europe	Industry; entertainment, sports	National politicians; military; populace
Eastern Europe	Entertainment, sports	Military; populace
Global	International politicians; industry; populace; other	National politicians

Topic by actor

National politicians	International politics; domestic politics; military, defense; international aid	Education, science, culture; human interest
International politicians	International politics; military, defense; economics	Education, science, culture; sports
Military	Domestic politics; military, defense; crime, police	International politics; economics; education, science, culture; sports
Industry	Economics; social services; education, science, culture; sports	International politics; military, defense
Culture	Social services; education, science, culture; human interest	International politics; military, defense; sports
Legal	Social services; education, science, culture	International politics
Entertainment, sports	Sports; human interest	International politics; domestic politics; military, defense; economics; crime, police
Populace	Military, defense; human interest	Sports
Other	Education, science, culture; human interest; accidents, disaster	International politics

Table 4.5. Linkages in foreign news stories—Zambian media

	Above average associations	Below average associations
Topic by Region		
North America	Education, science, culture	
Africa	International politics; economics	Education, science, culture; accidents, disaster
Middle East	International politics; military, defense	
Asia Pacific	Education, science, culture	Sports
Western Europe	Sports	Domestic politics; military, defense
Eastern Europe	International politics	Accidents, disaster
Global	Accidents, disaster	Domestic politics
Actor by region		
North America		Military
Middle East	National politicians; military, defense	Entertainment, sports
Western Europe	Industry; entertainment, sports	National politicians; military
Eastern Europe		National politicians; military; other
Global	International politicians; populace; other	
Topic by actor		
National politicians	International politics; domestic politics; military, defense; economics; international aid	Sports

International politicians	International politics; economics; international aid	Sports
Military	Domestic politics; military, defense; crime, police	Economics; education, science, culture; sports
Industry	Economics	International politics; military, defense
Culture	Social services; crime, police; education, science, culture	International politics
Legal	Crime, police	International politics
Entertainment, sports	Sports	International politics; domestic politics; military, defense; economics; crime, police
Populace	Human interest; accidents, disaster	Sports
Other		Accidents, disaster

On the whole, there are few linkages in coverage of North America or Western Europe, and both media underrepresent domestic political coverage of Eastern Europe. In the Algerian press, political figures are overrepresented as sources in coverage of politics and nonpoliticians generally are underrepresented. The Zambian media, in contrast, are closer to distributing the sources across geographic regions in a random pattern.

On the whole, as noted earlier, what is striking is an absence of consistent patterns within the foreign coverage of any one press system or among the five systems. The linkages that do emerge seem to be explainable in terms of logical connections between categories (as in political figures cited in stories about international affairs) or the set of news events we encountered in our sample (like the social and political upheaval in the Middle East and the lack of that kind of event in Western Europe and North America).

A SHARING OF VALUES. The data reported here suggest a narrow definition of news and a limited journalistic sense of who ought to be given access to the media. For example, we have found in every country little attention in coverage of international affairs to unofficial sources—"people" in various capacities outside of government. And in the whole range of human activities, all sorts of important activities get forced out of the news in order to report politics and international affairs.

Are these weaknesses of foreign news coverage a reflection of Western news values? Perhaps, but what is striking in our current analysis is the similarity of coverage in media systems as diverse as those of the United States and the Soviet Union and as deliberately non-Western as those of Zambia and Algeria. The problems this analysis shows, including the narrow definition of news and newsmaker, seem to be more problems of journalism than evidence of Western dominance. We apparently share more than we admit.

REFERENCES

Barton, Frank. 1979. *The press of Africa: Persecution and perseverance*. London: Macmillan.
International Commission for the Study of Communication Problems. 1980. *Many voices, one world*. New York: Unipub.
Masmoudi, Mustapha. 1979. The new world information order. *Journal of Communication*, 29(2):172–85.
Pool, Ithiel de Sola, ed. 1959. *Trends in content analysis*. Urbana: University of Illinois Press.
Stevenson, Robert L. 1980. Other research and the world of the news. Appendix to Annabelle Sreberny-Mohammadi et al. 1981. *The world of the news; the news of the world*. Report to UNESCO from IAMCR.

Stevenson, Robert L., Richard R. Cole, and Donald Lewis Shaw. 1980. Patterns of world news coverage: A look at the UNESCO debate on the "new world–information order." Paper presented to the Association for Education in Journalism meeting, Boston, Mass.

CHAPTER 5

"Bad News" and the Third World

Robert L. Stevenson and Gary D. Gaddy

IN recent years one can detect a subtle but important shift in the kind of questions about news coverage being raised in the new world information order debate. The new questions have less to do with issues of balance or fairness in coverage of the Third World than with definitions of news. Events, it is argued, are not news; positive accomplishments rather than conflict should be reported so that news can play a positive role in political and social development.

Of all the complaints against Western news media that have been made in the debate over a restructuring of the world information system, none has been made with more passion than the charge that the Western media single out the developing world for inaccurate, unfair coverage. The issue of Third World coverage by Western media raises the question of what coverage of the Third World *is*. A more basic issue, however, is what media coverage *ought* to be. Should news coverage of any part of the world (or issue or organization) be fair, or should be it be accurate?

TWO STANDARDS OF BIAS. By this distinction, we want to point out that two different standards for evaluating news coverage can be invoked, and that departure from either can be considered "bias." On one hand, we can argue that coverage should be *balanced*; that is, major parts of the world, all political parties, and relevant sides of issues should be given equivalent coverage. Both or all should be given equal space or time; the coverage should be similar in content and tone. That is one argument.

On the other hand, we can also argue that coverage should accurately reflect some objective reality. This reality could be defined as technical accuracy —a reporter should get his or her quotes right—or it could be some broader definition of newsworthiness. Mustapha Masmoudi (1979: 173) adopts the criterion that all people are equally newsworthy when he argues that the Western agencies "devote only 20 to 30 percent of news coverage to the developing countries, despite the fact that the latter account for almost three-quarters of mankind." And, of course, reality can be defined in a much more complex way so that, like beauty, it rests mostly in the eye of the beholder.

The challenge with having these two measuring sticks for assertions in the new world information order debate is that they can produce conflicting results. If coverage is carefully "balanced" so that each side of an issue or each part of the world gets the same amount and type of coverage, we could argue that such coverage is inaccurate because it makes unequals equal. But at the same time, coverage that takes into account differences can be considered unfair because it is not balanced. Coverage could be considered "imbalanced" if nearby countries get more attention than distant ones, major parties get more attention than minor ones, or political leaders get more attention than ordinary citizens. But a good case could be made that such discrepancies reflect reasonable criteria of accuracy. Journalists can be damned if they do (report accurately) and damned if they don't. They can also be damned if they do (report fairly) and damned if they don't.

METHOD. Do Western media single out the Third World for negative coverage? We want to expand that question in three directions. One is to consider the question in terms of both "imbalanced" coverage and "inaccurate" coverage. For the first part, we will consider whether the Third World is treated differently in the news than the advanced industrial nations of the Western "First World"; for the second part, we will look for some independent standard of what goes on in different areas of the world to use as a criterion.

And we will expand the question as well by looking at coverage not only of the Western media but coverage in the media of other social systems as well. In this way, we can test whether problems of coverage of the Third World are problems of Western journalism or, as we argue elsewhere in this book, problems of journalism in general.

Finally, we will consider, with sketchy data from several parts of the world, what local editors select from the information made available to them by the major Western news agencies. This comparison of foreign news "diet" in local media and foreign news "menu" available from the news agencies is an important part of the question of coverage of the Third World. As we have noted previously, the volume and diversity of information available at the local level are less problems than the inability or unwillingness of local editors to make use of that diversity to present a broad spectrum of events and perspectives to their readers and viewers.

RESULTS. In this analysis, we divided the countries of the world into the three broad and inexact groups that are used in the international debate: Western industrialized nations of the "First World"; the industrialized socialist countries of the "Second World"; and the remaining nations, which form the "Third World." This latter group, of course, includes some of the countries with the highest per capita income in the world as well as the poorest. And it also includes several that politically are "tilted" toward East or West like Cuba and South Korea.

While we acknowledge the problems of dealing with a diverse entity like the Third World, it is relatively easy to define this "world" from membership in the Non-Aligned Movement and United Nations nonaligned group of members. And it is useful to address our research to the political issue as it is defined.

For each country and news agency regional file in our sample, we compared the distribution of news topics from the Western First World and the Third World. In each case, we represented the level of similarity with a simple Pearson correlation coefficient (r) calculated by treating each of the 18 main topic categories as a case and the number of stories on that topic from the two sections of the world as values. The correlation coefficients for the national media and news agency files are shown in Table 5.1.

On the whole, there is a remarkable similarity in the way the news media of diverse countries treat these two parts of the world. Where the correlation is relatively low, it is usually related to some special characteristics of news in one area. For example, in Icelandic media, a great deal of coverage of Western Europe is sports, while very little of Third World coverage is coded in that topic. That one discrepancy accounts for a large part of the relatively low correlation. In the distribution of other categories—particularly heavy coverage of politics and economics, light coverage of science and education—the distributions of First and Third World are similar. Of course a summary statistic like a correlation coefficient can mask important differences within each data set.

We can look at some more detailed aspects of "bad news" by isolating certain main topics and comparing the frequency with which they occur in the media of various countries and in the news agency files. In some cases in a conventional descriptive content analysis like ours, we cannot distinguish "bad news" from "good news." For example, the coding category "diplomatic/political activity between states" could be either positive or negative depending on the nature of the activity. But some categories are clearly negative. To look at differences in coverage of the three worlds, we isolated the main topic coding categories that were clearly negative:

1. internal conflict or crisis, armed conflict or threat of armed conflict

Table 5.1. Correlations between coverage of First and Third Worlds in selected national and news agency files

United States	$r = .54$
Mexico	.83
Argentina	.82
Brazil	.89
Tunisia	.72
Ivory Coast	.86
Kenya	.66
Zambia	.82
Algeria	.72
Zaire	.81
Egypt	.76
Indonesia	.71
Thailand	.47
Iceland	.26
Turkey	.86
Soviet Union	.90
AP to Latin America	.85
UPI to Latin America	.83
Reuters to Latin America	.88
AFP to Latin America	.87
Reuters to Middle East	.81
AFP to Francophone Africa	.65

2. political crime
3. non-political crime, accidents, and natural disasters

In Table 5.2, we compare the proportions of news stories in the media of selected countries that are coded with any of these "bad news" topics as the main topic.

For this analysis, we selected part of our full data set for illustration. We were interested in representing as many parts of the world and types of media systems as possible. We also wanted to compare, where possible, the "diet" of bad news selected by national gatekeepers with the "menu" of bad news available to them through the news agencies.

We also wanted to provide some breakdown of these overall trends, although size prevents us from reproducing all of the possible charts that could be derived from these summary figures. As examples, Table 5.3 provides the same breakdowns for news stories coded as internal conflict, armed conflict, natural disaster, and nonpolitical crime.

Table 5.2. "Bad news" in selected news agencies and national media

News agencies and media	First World	Second World	Third World
Agencies to Latin America	17%	20%	26%
Argentina	20	26	25
Brazil	29	32	26
Mexico	13	27	25
AFP to Africa	24	43	39
Zambia	39	50	49
Zaire	27	13	25
Kenya	25	28	46
Algeria	18	7	25
Tunisia	23	16	24
Ivory Coast	12	16	31
Soviet Union	21	18	51
United States	23	26	58
Iceland	16	24	58
Greece	16	0	67

Table 5.3. Coverage of armed conflict, internal conflict, natural disasters, and nonpolitical crime in selected news agencies and national media

News agencies and media	First World	Second World	Third World
Armed conflict			
Agencies to Latin America	2%	5%	11%
Argentina	3	20	10
Brazil	6	22	11
Mexico	1	22	12
AFP to Africa	2	17	20
Zambia	7	14	23
Zaire	4	13	13
Kenya	3	16	17
Algeria	2	5	15
Tunisia	3	13	12
Ivory Coast	2	16	13
Soviet Union	6	11	30
United States	6	5	28
Iceland	1	3	38
Greece	2	0	29
Internal conflict			
Agencies to Latin America	3	1	8
Argentina	5	4	14

Table 5.3 *(continued)*

News agencies and media	First World	Second World	Third World
Brazil	13	11	14
Mexico	3	4	15
AFP to Africa	9	17	15
Zambia	16	36	29
Zaire	11	0	12
Kenya	7	3	29
Algeria	9	0	12
Tunisia	6	3	14
Ivory Coast	4	4	17
Soviet Union	9	5	26
United States	6	1	29
Iceland	2	0	29
Greece	4	0	50
Natural disasters			
Agencies to Latin America	7	4	6
Argentina	6	0	3
Brazil	4	2	2
Mexico	5	1	2
AFP to Africa	4	9	3
Zambia	9	7	2
Zaire	3	0	1
Kenya	4	10	1
Algeria	6	2	1
Tunisia	4	2	2
Ivory Coast	4	0	3
Soviet Union	3	2	1
United States	4	4	4
Iceland	7	6	3
Greece	5	0	4

PATTERNS THAT EMERGE. On the whole, these tables do provide some support for the arguments that the Third World gets heavier coverage of bad news. Except for the AFP regional wire to Africa, a higher proportion of news from that part of the world contains bad news than from the Northern Hemisphere countries of East and West. And when the two categories of internal and external conflict are examined, the difference tends to be greater. A lot—on the average about 25 percent, although the figures vary widely—of Third World news reported in all parts of the world contains some element of domestic or international conflict.

However, when we look at nonpolitical bad news, such as natural disasters and nonpolitical crime, we find a different pattern. First of all, a relatively small proportion of news stories deal with these topics, and in general, they are reported more from the First and Second Worlds than from the Third World. It is important to distinguish between political bad news that is concentrated in the Third World and nonpolitical bad news that is not.

"BAD NEWS" SELECTION. And what about the selection of bad news by national gatekeepers? Here we can compare news agency menus and national media diets as well as national media diets among different countries.

There is considerable support for the argument that national media editors often overselect bad news, although the pattern varies widely. In general, editors use a higher proportion of political bad news than the agencies supply, and the overselection is often greatest in Third World coverage. On the whole, nonpolitical bad news is underselected in countries outside of the West where by tradition accidents and crime are newsworthy.

Two comparisons are especially interesting for the lack of differences between widely different media systems. In most of the tables, the media of the Soviet Union and the United States look similar. Both report a great deal of bad news from the Third World; both emphasize political bad news in Third World reporting. The difference between them is in nonpolitical bad news, which gets more attention in the U.S. media. Their coverage of bad news in the First and Second Worlds is quite similar.

The other interesting similarity in the data is the media of Zambia and Kenya. Both countries share the heritage of British colonialism, but their media are quite different. The Kenyan media, mostly independently owned although under government control, are much closer to the British tradition and even resemble the British popular press. The Zambian media, in contrast, are fully mobilized to support the government and are highly political. Yet in almost all of the comparisons shown in the charts, including the overselection of bad news from the wire service menu, they are striking in their similarity.

At this point, we can emphasize the importance of distinguishing between political bad news, which does get widely covered around the world and especially in coverage of the Third World, and nonpolitical bad news, which on the whole does not get much attention and, in fact, is more frequent in the coverage of East and West than in coverage of the Third World.

UNFAIR EMPHASIS? Do we then conclude that the kind and degree of imbalances can be taken as evidence supporting Third World charges of unfairness? Perhaps, but two caveats are in order. One is that many Third World editors themselves contribute to that imbalance by overselecting political bad news. The other, more important, caveat is that the difference might be explainable by the other criterion of journalistic performance: accuracy.

One of the problems of dealing with accuracy as a criterion of journalistic performance is that it requires some standard against which the journalistic output can be measured. In this case—unless we adopt a random model that everyone, every place, and everything are equally newsworthy—we need some independent criterion of what happens in various parts of the world to see if the discrepancies noted here are inaccurate reflections of events.

BIAS AS INACCURACY. One of the ironies of trying to use such a criterion of journalistic performance is that journalism itself is usually the standard by which reality is defined. Events are something like the tree falling unobserved in the forest: does an event take place if a journalist is not there to record it? How do we know what happens in the world if we cannot read about it?

The problem of defining reality independently of news accounts is difficult but not insoluble. We can at least get an approximation of reality.

One such solution is in the Conflict and Peace Data Bank (COPDAB), an inventory of domestic and internal events around the world, developed by Prof. Edward E. Azar, formerly of the University of North Carolina and now at the University of Maryland. COPDAB contains records on more than 500,000 events occurring from 1948 on, as reported in more than 70 sources. Many of the sources are journalistic, but they cover a broad spectrum of geographic origin, language and scope, and they are supplemented by official documents and reference sources like *Facts on File.*

In one sense, we are still forced to define the world by what is reported about it, but COPDAB represents the most comprehensive compilation of events that we are aware of and is probably as complete an inventory of world affairs as can be compiled from public sources.

To see what *really* happened in the world, we selected events occurring in 1978 (the latest part of the data set available and not too far removed from the time period of our study) for comparison with news coverage. Each event in COPDAB is coded by the country or countries involved so we can isolate domestic and international events. And each event is coded on a 15-point scale that ranges from conflict on one (high) end to cooperation on the other (low) end. As our measure of conflict, we used events coded 13, 14, or 15. At the international level, these include (15) extensive war acts causing death, dislocation, and high strategic cost; (14) limited war acts; and (13) small-scale military acts. Nonmilitary hostility (border skirmishes, blockades, or assassinations) was excluded so that "conflict" would approximate our category "armed conflict."

On the domestic scale, we used the same three categories: (15) highest level of structural violence and acts of internal war; (14) abolition of civil rights;

and (13) physical violence and military unrest. This group was considered to approximate the "internal conflict or crisis" category of our study.

Our purpose in using the COPDAB was to establish an independent criterion of conflict events occurring in the world to see if the kinds of discrepancies between coverage of the Third World and the developed nations could be explained as a reasonably accurate reflection of reality in those parts of the world. Of course, this does not deal with the issue of whether news *ought* to emphasize conflict rather than cooperation or whether events by themselves should be the basis of news reporting.

In Table 5.4, we show the proportions of events occurring in the three worlds that can be considered internal or external conflict. The results are striking. First of all, it will be noted that a relatively small proportion of all international events (less than 2 percent of the more than 14,000 events in the 1978 file of Azar's data bank) are extreme enough to get coded as "conflict." If we compare this datum with the proportion of news coverage in almost all parts of the world that deals with a comparable degree of conflict, we see how little of the world gets into the news.

News, as has been argued and acknowledged by all sides in the UNESCO debate, is largely conflict. Or more accurately, that tiny part of the total relations among nations that represents serious violent conflict is newsworthy, while most of what else happens among nations is not. It may be of some comfort to note that international conflict is still rare enough to make the news; when it gets so routine and expected that it no longer makes the news, we will have more reason to worry than we have now.

What about the charge or explanation for the heavy concentration of bad news from the Third World? The data here bear out the hint in the chapter on news agency coverage by Weaver and Wilhoit that there is more conflict in the Third World. It is more than just a matter of perception. In the COPDAB for 1978, four times as many events in the socialist Second World involve international conflict as in the Western world; and the proportion of Third World events involving international conflict is about 30 times as high as it is in the West. Conflict is not evenly distributed. If news orients on conflict (and it does all over the world), then conflict news is not evenly distributed.

When we look at domestic events occurring over the same time period in the three worlds, we see that there is a much greater proportion of events in all parts of the world that involve domestic conflict (although the scales of in-

Table 5.4. **Conflict in external and internal events in three worlds in 1978 file of Conflict and Peace Data Bank (COPDAB)**

	First World	Second World	Third World
External events	0.08%	0.62%	2.45%
Internal events	17.97	26.25	33.88

ternational and domestic events are somewhat different). And we see the same pattern among the three worlds, although the differences are much smaller. The proportion of Second World events with domestic conflict is about 1.5 times as great as in the West; in the Third World, about twice as great a percentage of domestic events contain high levels of conflict.

We present the comparisons between COPDAB and the results of our study not to assert that COPDAB represents some kind of universal "reality" but to provide some basis for evaluating the kind of coverage that different parts of the world get in the world's press. There is no data bank of the world's "reality," of course, but other references could be used for a comparison with the media version of the world. We could count the coups and earthquakes around the world—to use the title of Rosenblum's book (1979)—and see whether they are all reported or reported in about the same way.

We could also use data of terrorism and military actions that are recorded in a fairly complete and authoritative way by a number of international bodies for comparisons with media coverage. On the whole, we suspect we would find results comparable to the data we have presented here: violence and conflict get reported in pretty much the same way wherever they occur. Certainly conflict in the West—such as violence in Northern Ireland, terrorism in West Germany and Italy, and racial conflict in the United States—gets the same kind of heavy media coverage in the West as do coups and earthquakes.

REFERENCES

Masmoudi, Mustapha. 1979. The new world–information order. *Journal of Communication* 29(2):172–85.
Rosenblum, Mort. 1979. *Coups and earthquakes.* New York: Harper & Row.
Tatarian, Roger. 1977. *News flow in the Third World.* Paper presented at a conference on the Third World and Press Freedom at the Edward R. Murrow Center for Public Diplomacy, Fletcher School of Law and Diplomacy, Tufts University, Medford, Mass.

CHAPTER 6

Cultural Meaning of Foreign News

Robert L. Stevenson and J. Walker Smith

AMONG the complaints against the dominance of the West in international communication, one that has received relatively little attention from researchers is the charge that Western news coverage of the Third World is filtered through a narrow cultural filter that, at best, is insensitive to non-Western cultural values and, at worst, is a distortion of those values.

In this chapter, we address the question of whether complaints about treatment of the Third World in the Western media could be explained on another basis. We examine the *subjective* or *cultural* meanings that are attached to words used in coverage of two diverse countries of the Third World. Using data collected by Charles Osgood (Osgood, May, and Miron 1975) in a large-scale international test of the familiar semantic differential, we can examine differences in coverage of Lebanon and Mexico in two American newsmagazines and relate those differences to differences in subjective meanings attached to that coverage in the two cultures. We ask whether *coverage* of these two countries differs *or* whether the *perception* of differences lies in the cultural meanings attached to the coverage.

WESTERN VALUES IN WORLD NEWS? Complaints against Western news coverage of the Third World cover two distinct grievances. On one hand, it is charged that Western news interest in the three-quarters of humanity who inhabit the less-developed countries is limited mostly to coverage of coups and earthquakes, which is the subject of a witty and perceptive book by Mort Rosenblum (1979).

Gerald Long, managing director of Reuters (1977), acknowledges that

> It is pointless to try to separate, in any society, what are called its news values and its general values, national or international. The values which are called

news values will have been formed by the various processes in the society that form values. It is the same process that molds all values.

But do these general cultural values lead to a distortion of Third World coverage or impose an alien system? In earlier chapters of this book, we argue that one of the reasons for the special importance, and de facto dominance, of Western news agencies around the world is that their coverage is mostly free of such cultural and political labels. We have also found evidence that most of the political shadings were added at the level of Third World national news agency or media. Harris (1977) describes the process in Ghana:

> While the use of political adjectives (in Western agency coverage) annoyed the foreign staff the problem was not insurmountable—all that was really involved was changing the adjective. One of the most common examples cited in this context was the substitution in stories about Rhodesia, South Africa, Angola, etc., of "nationalists" or "freedom fighters" for "guerrillas" or "terrorists." Another example was that stories about Ian Smith would generally be rephrased to describe him as the "racist Ian Smith." One minor reservation was made about such substitution by a few foreign editors, particularly with reference to changing "terrorist" to "nationalist" or to "freedom fighter"—this substitution would only be made if the editor believed that the "cause for which they are fighting is just"—that is, in the African interest. This, in practice, meant that most stories would be amended.

If Ian Smith fared badly at the hands of the Ghana News Agency in 1976, his press image has not improved since then. In our study, for example, we found constant references in the Zambia media to the "racist puppet Ian Smith" and his "sham, bogus election" in the spring of 1979. It is not likely that these adjectives were in the original AP or Reuters copy. It is easy to dismiss these complaints of Western bias as a function of national pride or lack of familiarity with the methods of skeptical and sometimes cynical Western reporters. And indeed we suspect that cross-cultural bias, like political bias (Stevenson and Greene 1980), is more in the eye of the beholder than in the media themselves.

LANGUAGE AND CULTURE. In dealing with these complaints of bias, another factor must be taken into consideration—cultural differences in the meanings of words. By this phrase, we do not mean problems of translation or finding the equivalents in different languages but rather the subjective meaning in words that makes, as George Steiner (1977) put it, "house" different from *Haus* or *casa* or *dom*. Steiner argues:

> Each and every human tongue is a distinct window onto the world. Looking through it, the native speaker enters an emotional and spiritual space, a frame-

work of memory, a promontory on tomorrow, which no other window in the great house at Babel quite matches. Thus every language mirrors and generates a possible world, an alternative reality.

Osgood's method of specifying cross-cultural differences of subjective meaning was his familiar semantic differential (Osgood, Suci, and Tannenbaum 1957), which isolated and measured three dimensions of connotative or subjective meaning. He argued that each person defined the personal or subjective meaning of words on the basis of three universal dimensions: evaluative (whether the object was judged "good" or "bad"); activity (whether it was "active" or "passive"); and potency (whether it was "strong" or "weak"). This conception of subjective meaning (and the measurement technique which derived from it) is surely one of the most popular and important contributions ever made to social measurement. The semantic differential has traveled around the world and been borrowed by users with interests as diverse as political campaigns and psychotherapy.

The original formulation of the semantic differential emphasized individual differences, but in the cross-cultural studies, the emphasis was on isolating differences among different language and cultural groups. Osgood argued (Osgood, May, and Miron 1975) that while differences in subjective meaning were found in individuals, cultural or linguistic differences existed as well; that is, each language group defined words differently, beyond individual differences. One of the major outcomes of the project was the development of "linguistic atlases" that specified the cultural values assigned to a common vocabulary list of 620 words by each of the 23 language groups in the project.

These linguistic atlases can be used to test how (and whether) news coverage of Third World countries likely is perceived differently in different countries. If, in fact, subjective meanings of words used in news reporting vary from country to country, these differences could account for at least part of the difference between rigorous quantitative analysis that finds little difference between First and Third World news coverage in the Western media, and Third World perceptions of unfairly negative coverage. Part of the difference could be in the eye of the beholder.

SUBJECTIVE MEANING: TEST CASES. To examine subjective meanings of words in international news coverage, we focused on two very different Third World countries, Lebanon and Mexico. We collected stories about these two countries from 1979 issues of *Time* and *Newsweek*. This analysis used data other than newspaper data collected for the Unesco project. These magazines were chosen for two reasons: (1) although the two magazines circulate widely throughout most of the world, they appear only in English; (2) unlike the news agencies and newsfilm services from which "alien" values can be expunged by national gatekeepers, newsmagazines exist only in the form in which they are originally edited. Of all the Western media that circulate in the Third World, the newsmagazines are the most "foreign," both in language and editorial control.

From the first two paragraphs of each story about Lebanon and Mexico, we identified words that were included in the list of 620 in Osgood's atlas. We excluded explicit references to other countries, but did not limit ourselves to specific references to the two countries on the assumption that meanings attached to countries can come from the broader context in which information about those countries is presented as well as from explicit assertions about them. Of course, the list of words did not include all of the references to the two countries. And the list, on the whole, emphasizes mundane, commonplace words more than emotion-laden words. But while we cannot capture all of the references to Lebanon and Mexico in the two magazines with this technique, the "scoop," as it were, is the same for both so that the samples are equivalent.

IN THE EYE OF THE BEHOLDER. For each word in the sample, we recorded the cultural values associated with each culture. These ranged from + 3 (good, strong, active) to –3 (bad, weak, passive). With the data set, we can answer these questions:

1. Are the two countries treated differently on each of the three dimensions of subjective meaning?

2. Are there differences in the subjective meanings attached to the coverage by the two different language/cultural groups?

We can expand the analysis by holding up a kind of cultural mirror to see how Mexican readers of *Time* and *Newsweek* would see coverage of Mexico differently from the way Lebanese readers would and, in a similar fashion, how readers in these two countries would differ in their perceptions of the way Lebanon was covered. The words are the same; the cultural meanings attached, however, are not.

The analysis takes the form of three 2 x 2 analyses of variance in which the factors are (1) the country referred to in the newsmagazines (Mexico or Lebanon), and (2) the country from which the subjective meaning is taken (also Mexico or Lebanon). The dependent variables are the three dimensions of the semantic differential—evaluation, activity, potency. While it is possible to combine the data into a single 2 x 2 x 3 design, the size of the data set becomes unwieldy, and higher order interactions (which are the only additional source of variance) are likely to be uninterpretable.

RESULTS. Table 6.1 summarizes statistics from the two independent variables

Table 6.1. Mean values and correlations of three dimensions of subjective meaning in newsmagazine coverage of Mexico and Lebanon

	Evaluation	Potency	Activity
Total	0.98	.67	−.01
Coverage of:			
Mexico	1.08	.65	.02
Lebanon	0.86	.70	−.05
Eta	0.12	.03	.06
Perceived by:			
Mexico	0.91	.61	.35
Lebanon	1.05	.74	−.39
Eta	0.08	.10	.61
R	0.14	.10	.61

and three dependent variables. Correlation coefficients (eta) between the pairs of independent variables are included.

The news about these two countries, on the whole, is more "good" than "bad" (+0.98 on a scale from −3 to +3), somewhat more "strong" than "weak" (+0.67 on the same scale) but neither "active" nor "passive" (−0.01). Mexico and Lebanon were, according to our criteria of subjective meaning, given rather strong positive coverage.

But we do see some evidence of differences between Lebanon and Mexico. Coverage of Mexico is somewhat more positive than that of Lebanon, while the subjective meanings of the words used are more positive to Lebanese than Mexican readers.

To see how these two independent variables operate together, we turn to a set of three simple 2 x 2 analyses of variance in which the cultural meanings assigned to the words drawn from the newsmagazines as measured by Osgood are the dependent variables and the independent variables are the countries being described (Mexico or Lebanon) as perceived by natives of the same countries. The results of this analysis are shown in Tables 6.2, 6.3, and 6.4.

In the evaluative dimension, which is the strongest of the three dimensions and generally accounts for the most variance in the measurement of subjective meaning, differences in both country described and country perceived are significant; the former is significant at the <.01 level, while the latter is significant at <.05. This means that Mexico was described by words that are seen as more favorable by both Mexicans and Lebanese. Evaluative meanings also differ significantly between the two cultures. From the etas in Table 6.1, we see that the difference in coverage of the two countries accounts for somewhat more variance than differences in cultural meanings—.12 vs. .08. The multiple correlation (R) indicates that the two variables together produce a correlation of .14, not dramatic, but generally in the range that one finds in social science research.

Table 6.2. ANOVA summary table of evaluative dimension (as perceived by country)

Source of variation	Sum of squares	df	Mean square	F	Significance of F
Main effects	15.135	2	7.567	9.594	0.000
Country	10.568	1	10.568	13.398	0.000
Perceive	4.493	1	4.493	5.697	0.017
2-way interactions	0.708	1	0.708	0.898	0.344
Country perceive	0.708	1	0.708	0.898	0.344
Explained	15.843	3	5.281	6.695	0.000
Residual	741.435	940	0.789		
Total	757.278	943	0.803		

Table 6.3. ANOVA summary table of potency dimension (as perceived by country)

Source of variation	Sum of squares	df	Mean square	F	Significance of F
Main effects	4.548	2	2.274	5.399	0.005
Country	0.473	1	0.473	1.122	0.290
Perceive	4.090	1	4.090	9.710	0.002
2-way interactions	0.754	1	0.754	1.790	0.181
Country perceive	0.754	1	0.754	1.790	0.181
Explained	5.302	3	1.767	4.196	0.006
Residual	395.907	940	0.421		
Total	401.209	943	0.425		

Table 6.4. ANOVA summary table of activity dimension (as perceived by country)

Source of variation	Sum of squares	df	Mean square	F	Significance of F
Main effects	129.734	2	64.867	278.515	0.000
Country	1.327	1	1.327	5.699	0.017
Perceive	128.542	1	128.542	551.912	0.000
2-way interactions	0.169	1	0.169	0.724	0.395
Country perceive	0.169	1	0.169	0.724	0.395
Explained	129.903	3	43.301	185.918	0.000
Residual	218.929	940	0.233		
Total	348.832	943	0.370		

956 cases were processed.

For the potency dimension (strong-weak) and activity dimension (active-passive), the results are somewhat different. There is no difference in coverage of the two countries in potency but some difference (significant at $<.05$) in activity. However, in both cases, there are strong differences (significant at $<.01$) in the cultural meanings of the words. The Lebanese, as we saw in Table 6.1, perceive these words as more potent than the Mexicans, while the Mexicans attach a cultural meaning of much greater activity to them than do the Lebanese. In both dimensions, the variance explained by the differences in cultural meanings is much greater than that explained by differences in coverage itself. Together, the two independent variables produce a multiple correlation of only .11 on the potency dimension but a multiple correlation of .61 on the activity dimension.

WHAT RESULTS REVEAL. What do these results tell us about the nature of newsmagazine coverage of these two very different Third World cultures? First, as other studies have shown, we find no evidence to support the argument that these two countries of the Third World are covered in mostly negative ways. In this case, using subjective meanings of words associated with the two countries, we find a strong positive cultural meaning, a somewhat less strong but still positive image of power and essentially a neutral coverage of activity.

There are differences in coverage between the two countries. Mexico is linked to words that generally carry a more favorable connotation than is Lebanon and also words that are seen in both cultures as more active. The difference on the first dimension is strong; the latter difference is weaker. We would have to examine the actual words to see if they could be linked to differences in specific events, but it is likely that coverage of Lebanon included the civil war, which would be perceived as negative in any culture. In contrast, in 1979, Mexico was in the news in the United States because of its increasing economic power and associated wealth; we would expect coverage of that type to contain positive subjective evaluations.

The important differences, however, are in the cultural differences in the meanings of the words associated with the two countries. Lebanese and Mexican readers would, in fact, see quite different meanings in the same words: Lebanese would see the coverage of both countries as more positive and powerful than would Mexicans. Mexican readers would perceive the coverage of both Mexico and Lebanon as more active than would Lebanese readers. The words remained the same but the readers did not.

REFERENCES

Harris, Phil. 1977. *News dependence: The case for a new world information order.* Leicester: University of Leicester. Mimeo.

Long, Gerald. 1977. News values are social values. *Issues in Communication*, no. 1:10

Masmoudi, Mustapha. 1977. The new world information order. *Journal of Communication* 29(2):172-85.

Osgood, Charles E., William H. May, and Murray S. Miron. 1975. *Cross-cultural universals of affective meaning.* Urbana: University of Illinois Press.

Osgood, Charles E., George J. Suci, and Percy Tannenbaum. 1957. *The measurement of meaning.* Urbana: University of Illinois Press.

Rosenblum, Mort. 1979. *Coups and earthquakes.* New York: Harper & Row.

Steiner, George. 1977. The coming universal language. *Atlas World Press Review* 24 (Oct.):24-26.

Stevenson, Robert L., and Mark T. Greene. 1980. A reconsideration of bias in the news. *Journalism Quarterly* 57(1):115-21.

CHAPTER 7

Comparative Study of Third World Elite Newspapers

Anne M. Cooper

IN every major country, one newspaper, and often two or three, stands out as a journal of elite opinion that caters to the intelligentsia and the opinion leaders, however variously defined (Merrill 1968, 12; Merrill and Fisher 1980, 10). Elite newspapers are taken seriously. They are the kind "which libraries and universities in all countries feel must be made available to their students" (Merrill, Bryan, and Alisky 1970, 14). Because of their importance, they are indexed, microfilmed, content analyzed, and otherwise dissected by researchers in various disciplines.

The Elite Press and *The World's Great Dailies* outline certain hallmarks of "elite" and "mass" newspapers (Merrill 1968, chaps. 1–3; Merrill and Fisher 1980, 3–43). The "mass" press offers scattershot items—short, disorganized snippets of this and that—rather than a synthesized look at the world. At its most extreme, it is trivial, entertaining, splashy, superficial, alarmist, voyeuristic, sensationalistic, and gossipy. It emphasizes personalities over ideas, atypical incidents of conflict over long-range trends. It tends to create envy, suspicion, and nationalistic feeling rather than emphasizing similarities between nations. It is a "bad" press, if popular.

The "elite" press, on the other hand, is reliable, responsible, serious, carefully edited, influential, well printed, and dignified in makeup. It goes beyond reporting facts to include background, point out trends, and indicate future implications. While analytical, it evidences concern for humanity and social progress. Its strong, lively editorials are rooted in a continuing policy. Its outlook is international. It is a "good" press, if boring.

This chapter contrasts the content of a sample of elite and mass newspapers in Tunisia and Algeria.

We may define the elites who read these newspapers as people who affect policies and public opinion in political, economic, or cultural matters. These influentials—"public officials, scholars, journalists, theologians, lawyers and judges and business leaders" (Merrill 1968, 12; Merrill and Fisher 1980, 10)—are "better educated and have a greater interest in public affairs than the average readers of the mass (or popular) press" (Merrill 1968, 11; Merrill and Fisher 1980, 9).

Identifying the world's topflight elite newspapers—the *New York Times*, the *Times* of London, *Pravda*, *Le Monde*, and a handful of others—has presented few problems. The "recurrence of certain names in the lists and surveys" (Merrill 1968, 43; Merrill and Fisher 1980) of elite journalism shows clear agreement as to which papers belong, which do not. The constraint of government control does not automatically eliminate a newspaper; however, most of Merrill's "50 best" dailies are "free." For this and other reasons, newspapers in Third World countries are largely excluded.

But exclusion from the charmed circle does not make Third World newspapers unworthy of study. They may still "have many features of the elite" (Merrill 1968, 43). The press exhibiting those features will hereafter be called "elite-appeal journalism."

If the West's elite press merits extensive study, then the Third World's elite-appeal press deserves at least some attention. Even more so than in the developed world, "most developing countries are ruled directly or indirectly by small and powerful elites." (Todaro 1977, 24) This group has a disproportionately large share of land, capital, education, and income. Since income in most Third World nations is much less equally distributed than in developed nations, the "rich individual can dictate the overall pattern of production, since his demand preferences carry more weight in the consumer goods market than those of the poor person" (Todaro 1977, 97–98). Furthermore, in many countries, the distribution in recent years has gotten more unequal, not less (Todaro 1977, 109).

Thus Third World elites and their sources of information "matter." And within the Third World, the Arab world clearly is of interest. As columnist Meg Greenfield writes of the Islamic nations in general, "No part of the world is more important to our [U.S.] well-being at the moment," and "no part of the world is more hopelessly and systematically and stubbornly misunderstood by us." (Greenfield 1979, 116).

Our lack of understanding extends to the Arab world's mass media. William Rugh's book, *The Arab Press*, the first in English to treat systematically mass media in the 18 nations of the Arab world, was published in 1979. The only previous book by a Westerner appeared in 1952, discussing the media in just five states (Lebanon, Syria, Jordan, Iraq, and Egypt) (McFadden 1953).

We may define any elite-appeal newspapers in terms of their content. They should, according to Merrill (1968, 24–25), emphasize four types of news:

1. politics/international relations

2. business/economics
3. education/science/culture
4. humanities, especially the fine arts, literature, philosophy, and religion

Moreover, when studying Arab world elite-appeal newspapers, we need to consider also the special role of language. The coexistence of foreign and native languages, a legacy of colonialism, remains especially strong in the Arab world.

There, elites' fluency in two or more languages contrasts with high illiteracy among the masses: it was 73 percent among adults (aged 15 and over) in the Arab world in 1975 (Todaro 1977, 239). Patai notes that the political elites of the Arab world, except those of the Saudi Arabian peninsula, are usually bilingual and bicultural to such an extent that one can speak of their split personality (*izdiwaj*). The elites' Western orientation creates a gulf between them and the Arab masses (Patai 1973, chap. 12).

In addition to Arabic, most elites of the eastern Arab world speak English (or both French and English), while those in Morocco, Algeria, and Tunisia (the Maghreb) typically speak French. The press of nine Arab nations reflects this linguistic diversity. In Egypt and Lebanon, Arabic newspapers account for the bulk of total newspaper circulation. (See Table 7.1.)

But in all three Maghreb nations, French-language circulation tops that of Arabic. (This does not mean, of course, that more people speak French than Arabic; Arabic newspapers are passed around more and are often read aloud in villages, coffeehouses, or factories [Merrill, Bryan, and Alisky 1970, 302; Schramm 1959, 81].) Thus the Maghreb represents a ready-made laboratory to test the differences between an elite (French) and mass (Arabic) press.

HYPOTHESES. If Patai is right, the elite newspapers—those read by the bilingual, well-educated, internationally minded intelligentsia of the Maghreb—will be those in French; the mass newspapers, those in Arabic. If Merrill is right, this elite press will pay more attention to certain types of serious coverage, exhibiting a diet of news quite different from that of the Arabic press.

Furthermore, Merrill implies that distinguishing traits of elite and mass newspapers hold across national borders, especially in similar cultures. For example, the *National Enquirer* of the United States has a diet similar to that of the British tabloid the *Daily Mirror*, while the *Times* of London resembles neither of these as much as it resembles the *New York Times*. By analogy, the foreign-language newspapers, if elite, should exhibit more similarities to each other than to the indigenous, mass-appeal Arabic press.

We can restate the above ideas in terms of the following hypotheses:

1. *Topics.* The foreign-language press should give relatively greater emphasis to politics, economics, and culture/science, while the Arabic press

Table 7.1. Arabic, French, and English daily newspapers in the Arab world

Country	Arabic		French		English	
	Number of papers	Circulation	Number of papers	Circulation	Number of papers	Circulation
Egypt (1976)	4	1,285,000	2	13,000	1	35,000
Lebanon (1979)	9	83,900	2	35,000	2	9,500
Morocco (1979)	6	107,000	4	135,000	—	
Algeria (1976)	2	75,000	2	190,000	—	
Tunisia (1976)	2	62,000	3	77,000	—	
Iraq (1976)	4	82,000	—		1	3,500
Jordan (1976)	3	39,000	—		1	1,000
Saudi Arabia (1976)	7	95,000	—		2	11,200
Kuwait (1979)	5	107,000	—		2	17,000

Source: Rugh, William A., 1979. *The Arab press.* Syracuse, N.Y.: Syracuse University Press. Tables 2, 4, 5, 6, 7, and 8.

should emphasize sports/entertainment, police/crime, and human interest content.

2. *Themes.* The foreign-language press should give relatively greater emphasis to news relating to aid/development, energy/ecology, and the superpowers, while the Arabic papers should emphasize national pride, atrocities, corruption, and ideologies.

3. *Correlations.* The match of topic and theme rankings should be higher across languages than within countries.

4. *Themes vs. Topics.* The strongest correlations showing cross-language rather than in-country agreement should appear in themes rather than topics; themes represent interpretations of the news, whereas topics are given properties of the news.

METHOD. This study compares a Tunisian French-language daily, *La Presse* (circulation 30,000), with an Arabic daily, *Al'Amal*, or "Action" (27,000), and an Algerian French-language daily, *El Moudjahid*, or "The Warrior" (150,000), with an Arabic daily, *Al Sha'ab*, or "The People" (40,000).

Of those nations in the Arab world with a foreign-language daily press, Tunisia and Algeria lend themselves well to comparison. They share a similar culture, geography, ethnic composition, religion, and colonial experience with France. While it controlled the Maghreb, France allowed European-owned newspapers, but suppressed indigenous ones because of their nationalist sentiments.

Today both Algeria and Tunisia have a small, controlled national press system. Algeria has four newspapers; Tunisia has five. In a study of 117 press systems, Algeria ranked 6 and Tunisia 5 on a 9-point scale, where 1 equalled "most free" (Nixon 1965, 11–12). Controlled newspapers may still rank among the elite, according to Merrill. He calls those in open societies "quality" newspapers and those in closed societies "prestige" newspapers. Papers in free societies promote dialogue; those in closed societies give guidance (Merrill 1968, 11; Merrill and Fisher 1980, 9).

This paper draws on three types of information collected in the UNESCO study of international news. Each of the 2,295 foreign news articles collected in the Algerian and Tunisian samples could be coded for the presence of up to four topics, four types of actors, and four themes. The 47 detailed topics were collapsed into 12 general categories; the 34 types of actors, into 9; and the 33 themes, into 10. Stories were converted to a standard width to make lengths comparable.

Two rankings were drawn up for each newspaper, listing the percent of stories that included particular themes and topics. Spearman rank-order correlations were computed to assess the strength of association for the four topic and four theme rankings—in each case, for within-country and also for within-language (cross-national) comparisons.

RESULTS AND DISCUSSION

Topics. The left-hand column of Table 7.2 lists topics according to their prominence in the largest-circulation paper in the sample, *El Moudjahid* of Algeria, along with rankings of them in the other three papers. This French newspaper does match the expected pattern for an elite paper, with "serious" topics being more often mentioned than "lighter" topics.

However, these findings do not support Hypothesis 1. The French-language paper from Algeria most closely matches the Arabic-language paper from Tunisia, not the French one from Tunisia. Indeed, no paper in the sample shows a mass-appeal pattern. The highest any mass-appeal topic ranked was fifth, the position held by sports/entertainment in the Arabic *Al Sha'ab* and the French *La Presse*. If anything stands out, it is the similarity of diet that all four serve up to their readers, language notwithstanding.

Themes. Table 7.3 lists rankings of themes for each newspaper. This category, according to the coding instructions, was included to pick up "news angles" and "conceptual frameworks" that "may not emerge from the classification of topics and other coding." It is a subjective category. Clearly, the French-language coder saw more themes than did the Arabic-language coder.

The findings do not support Hypothesis 2. Indeed, the superpowers theme, which should rank high for the French papers, shows up in last place in the French-language *El Moudjahid*. Similarly, ideologies should rank high for the Arabic dailies; however, it stands high only for both Algerian papers, while coming in at rank 8 for both Tunisian papers.

Again, the most striking characteristic to emerge is a similarity across all four papers, in this case, the high salience of pride among all four.

Correlations. Table 7.4 lists Spearman rank-order correlations for the mentions of topics and themes as presented in Tables 7.2 and 7.3. Spearman's rho (r) assesses the similarity between two sets of rankings; it can tell us, as in this study, whether two apparently similar rankings of cases are in fact similar, and how similar they are.

Topics. The data partially support the idea that agendas associated with the French language are more strongly related than internal national agendas, since the correlation of topics in French papers across borders is higher than that of the Algerian papers. Support also exists for the idea that the Arabic language influences content; the correlation of topics in Arabic-language papers across borders is a strong +.93

The .92 figure suggesting strong internal ties within Tunisian newspapers is difficult to explain in light of these correlations, but it makes sense when set against the correlations that follow.

Table 7.2. Main topics in foreign news in Algerian and Tunisian press.

| | Algeria | | | | Tunisia | | | |
| | El Moudjahid (French) | | Al Sha'ab (Arabic) | | La Presse (French) | | Al 'Amal (Arabic) | |
Topic	Rank	%	Rank	%	Rank	%	Rank	%
Int'l politics	1	58.1	1	37.4	1	42.7	1	42.9
Domestic politics	2	31.6	2	28.0	2	23.6	2	35.9
Economics	3	23.3	6	9.5	3	19.9	3	18.6
Military/ defense	4	23.1	4	19.4	6	16.5	4	18.1
Culture/science/ religion	5	17.6	3	24.4	4	17.2	5	17.8
Police/crime	6	9.3	8	5.1	8	9.3	7	6.1
Sports/ entertainment	7	6.8	5	11.2	5	16.7	6	11.1
Social services	8	6.0	9	3.3	11	2.2	10	2.3
Int'l aid	9	5.6	10	2.0	10	3.0	9	2.8
Human interest	10	4.8	7	6.8	7	10.5	8	5.9
Disaster	11	3.3	11	1.9	9	3.9	10	2.3
Other		11.0		0.0		5.2		0.2
	n = 484		n = 644		n = 593		n = 574	

Note: % refers to the percentage of articles that mention each topic.

Table 7.3. Themes and references in foreign news in Algerian and Tunisian press.

	Algeria				Tunisia			
	El Moudjahid (French)		*Al Sha'ab* (Arabic)		*La Presse* (French)		*Al 'Amal* (Arabic)	
Theme	Rank	%	Rank	%	Rank	%	Rank	%
Pride	1	23.9	2	4.3	1	15.7	1	8.7
Ideologies	2	19.0	3	3.6	8	4.9	8	0.5
Rights	3	11.8	1	4.7	2	8.6	3	6.3
Race/ethnicity	4	11.6	4	3.4	3	7.9	5	3.8
Aid/ development	5	11.0	6	2.0	6	5.7	2	7.3
Atrocities	6	7.9	8	1.9	4	7.8	5	3.8
Energy/ecology	7	3.7	5	2.3	7	5.4	6	2.8
Social divisions	8	3.1	10	0.5	10	1.2	9	0.3
Corruption	9	2.5	7	1.7	9	1.9	7	1.7
Superpowers	10	2.1	9	1.4	5	6.4	4	4.5
	n = 484		n = 644		n = 593		n = 574	

Note: % refers to the percentage of articles that mention each topic.

Table 7.4. Spearman rank-order correlations of topics and themes within and between Algerian and Tunisian press

	Topics		Themes	
	r	sig.	r	sig.
Within Algeria				
French	.73	.003	.89	.001
Arabic				
Within Tunisia				
French	.92	.001	.83	.002
Arabic				
French: cross-national				
Tunisia	.81	.001	.56	.045
Algeria				
Arabic: cross-national				
Tunisia	.93	.001	.45	.096
Algeria				

Themes. These findings exactly reverse what was discovered for topics. Here, within-country factors affect newspaper content much more strongly than the power of language to operate across national borders. The split is unambiguous within countries, .89 and .83; across languages, only .56 and .45.

Themes vs. Topics. The findings regarding "themes" probably have more meaning for the topic at hand than those for "topics," since the themes tell us more about gatekeepers' biases or world views than do the topics. Beyond the initial decision to accept or reject a news item, gatekeepers do not have as much control over its intrinsic properties, such as who was involved and what type of event it was, as over what the event meant. The news of Algerian President Boumedienne's death in 1979 contained a given actor and topic, but a theme like national pride could be included or not at a gatekeeper's discretion, especially in a controlled newspaper with a government position to reflect.

Thus we can look most closely for insights at the themes findings, which do not support the idea of language affecting content. Rather, they tell us that factors within a country influence content more.

In sum, the findings in Table 7.4 using Spearman's rho can be seen as agreeing with those in Tables 7.2 and 7.3; none of them supports the original hypotheses.

However, we are left with some intriguing results apart from our interest in French newspapers as an elite press. While we cannot call Arabic a language of mass-appeal journalism on the basis of this study, we can say that gatekeepers working for Arabic-language papers seem to be choosing a highly similar diet of news items, at least in terms of news topics. It is a diet rich in international and domestic politics, military and defense news, and news of national political leaders and the populace.

SUMMARY AND CONCLUSIONS. Most Westerners would probably expect French-language newspapers published in the Arab world to have more elite characteristics than those in Arabic. The results of this study suggest otherwise: readers within a country receive a diet of similarly colored news, language notwithstanding. Furthermore, none of the newspapers studied exhibited a distinctly mass-appeal diet dominated by human interest, disaster, sports/entertainment, and police/crime news. If we had to affix labels, we might regard *all four* Algerian and Tunisian dailies as elite-appeal newspapers, considering their uniform emphasis on international politics, domestic politics, and economics.

Westerners should not assume that media systems and practices that work in the West will survive a transfer to the less-developed countries (LDCs). Furthermore, by learning from social scientists who have preceded them, mass media experts can avoid the trial-and-error method of finding out what works the way it *should* in the LDCs and what does not. As Gunnar Myrdal stated in *Asian Drama*, "When theories and concepts designed to fit the special conditions of the Western world. . .are used in the study of underdeveloped countries, where they do *not* fit, the consequences are serious" (1968, 16–17).

What concepts about elite-appeal journalism might not transfer well from the First to the Third World? What may distinguish elite-appeal journalism in LDCs? What special role does elite journalism play in LDCs? The present study suggests a reassessment of current ideas about elite journalism along the following lines:

1. Because illiteracy is as high as 95 percent in some LDCs, the "shape" of journalism may be an inverted pyramid (a preponderance of elite-appeal newspapers, few mass-appeal papers), rather than the upright pyramid that Merrill posits.

2. A larger percentage of newshole devoted to international affairs may characterize all newspapers, not just the elite, because LDCs' substantial "dependence on foreign economic, social and political forces. . .touches almost every facet of life" (Todaro 1977, 23).

3. LDC newspapers may appeal to elites, yet still be nationalistic, contrary to what Merrill says, because of the developmental goals shared by masses and elites alike. Here one can note the high position of the "pride" theme for all newspapers on Table 7.3.

4. All journalists, not just those on elite newspapers, may have an international outlook because of the " 'outward-looking' orientation of many LDC

professionals'' (Todaro 1977, 262), even to the extent of finding problems of underdevelopment and rural poverty not intellectually compelling.

5. The elite audience in LDCs, while clearly distinct from the rural, poor majority, may be more fragmented than in developed countries and thus not rally around one newspaper as Merrill suggests. The elite consists of a wealthy group, an overeducated but unemployed group, and a reformist student group.

6. An LDC newspaper may be elite while not looking elite; due to a small private sector (except in Latin America) and a lack of ads, budgets may not permit the equipment and newsprint that make for a dignified appearance, whether the paper is privately owned or government sponsored.

7. The role of female elite readers will vary more from country to country in LDCs than in the West, and so affect elite content aimed at them.

8. Newspapers in a foreign language are not necessarily more elite than those in a country's native language, as this study seems to show. Indeed, the concentration on foreign languages, beginning in primary schools in LDCs, has been roundly criticized (Todaro 1977, 241). This writer discovered while living in Tunisia that most people could speak French fluently, no matter what their age, education, or status.

REFERENCES

Abu-Laban, Baha. 1966. Factors in social control of the press in Lebanon. *Journalism Quarterly* 43(3): 510–18.
Almaney, Adnan. 1972. Government control of the press in the United Arab Republic, 1952–1970. *Journalism Quarterly* 49(2): 340–48.
Boyd, Douglas A. 1978. A Q-analysis of mass media usage by Egyptian elite groups. *Journalism Quarterly* 55(3): 501–7.
Greenfield, Meg. 1979. Islam and us. *Newsweek*, March 26, 116.
McFadden, Tom J. 1953. *Daily journalism in the Arab states*. Columbus: Ohio State University Press.
Merrill, John C. 1968. *The elite press: Great newspapers of the world*. New York: Pitman.
Merrill, John C., Carter R. Bryan, and Marvin Alisky. 1970. *The foreign press: A survey of the world's journalism*. Baton Rouge: Louisiana State University Press.
Merrill, John C., and Harold A. Fisher. 1980. *The world's great dailies: Profiles of fifty newpapers*. New York: Hastings House.
Myrdal, Gunnar. 1968. *Asian drama: An inquiry into the poverty of nations*. New York: Pantheon.
Nixon, Raymond B. 1965. Freedom in the world's press: A fresh approach with new data. *Journalism Quarterly* 42(1): 3–14, 118–119.
Patai, Raphael. 1973. *The Arab mind*. New York: Scribner's.
Rugh, William A. 1979. *The Arab press*. Syracuse, N.Y.: Syracuse University Press.
Schramm, Wilbur. 1959. *One day in the world's press*. Stanford, Calif.: Stanford University Press.
Todaro, Michael P. 1977. *Economic development in the third world*. New York: Longman.
Wynn, C. Wilton. 1948. Western techniques influence party newspaper in Egypt. *Journalism Quarterly* 25(4): 391–94.

CHAPTER 8

Friend or Foe?
Egypt and Israel
in the Arab Press

Anne M. Cooper

IN the declaration on the role of mass media approved by the UNESCO General Assembly in 1978, mass media were given a positive responsibility to contribute to peace and international understanding. The declaration was couched in such general terms that it was acceptable to Western nations, which generally believe that mass media ought to stand aloof from government, even in such noble issues as peace and human rights.

The UNESCO document (The Declaration of Fundamental Principles. . . 1978) weaves the positive obligation into nearly all of the 11 articles of the resolutions, but article III presents this new responsibility in greatest detail:

> 1. The mass media have an important contribution to make to the strengthening of peace and international understanding and in countering racialism, apartheid and incitement to war.
>
> 2. In countering aggressive war, racialism, apartheid and other violations of human rights which are *inter alia* spawned by prejudice and ignorance, the mass media, by disseminating information on the aims, aspirations, cultures and needs of all peoples, to make nationals of a country sensitive to the needs and desires of others, to ensure the respect of the rights and dignity of all nations, all peoples and all individuals without distinction of race, sex, language, religion or nationality and to draw attention to the great evils which afflict humanity, such as poverty, malnutrition and diseases, thereby promoting the formulation by States of policies best able to promote the reduction of international tension and the peaceful and equitable settlement of international disputes.

The challenge arises when nations disagree on what constitutes "violations of human rights" or "equitable settlement of international disputes." One nation's just war can be its neighbor's aggression just as one politician's news bias can be his or her opponent's fair coverage. As an earlier chapter on the cultural meaning of foreign news concludes, many of the differences in Western news coverage of various nations are in the eye of the reader or viewer.

It is precisely when relations between two nations are at their worst that the commitment to a new world information order, as explicated by the UNESCO declaration, is put to the test. Do mass media reflect the principles of the new world information order when reporting about events and nations that are contrary to the foreign policy interests of those countries?

News media coverage of events in the Middle East captured by the UNESCO/IAMCR study provides an opportunity to address this question.

ARAB COVERAGE OF ISRAEL AND EGYPT. This chapter will look at the mass media of three Arab countries involved in important events of 1979 to see how their media reflected the changes that occurred.

It was Egypt's change of policy toward Israel that set off shock waves in the Middle East and seemed to spell the end of her leadership of the Arab world. Tunisia, a moderate Arab country, and Algeria, generally considered to be a radical state, could be expected to reflect in their media two extremes in the range of reactions to Egypt's rapprochement with Israel.

Egypt had risen to assume leadership of the Arab world in the 1950s, after a military junta overthrew King Farouk in July, 1952, and a reformist, socialist republic was established. With anti-Zionism a pillar of her foreign policy, she fought against Israel in 1948, 1956, 1967, and 1973.

In the mid-1970s President Anwar Sadat began to change Egypt's position toward Israel, starting with the Sinai disengagement agreement signed by Egyptian and Israeli officials in 1974. Then in 1977 Sadat became the first Arab leader to visit the Jewish state. The Camp David accords were reached in September, 1978, followed by the signing of the Egyptian-Israeli peace treaty on March 26, 1979, in Washington, D.C.

The next day, 19 Arab League members met in Baghdad, and agreed to expel Egypt from league membership and move the league's headquarters from Cairo to Tunis. Only two league members, Oman and Sudan, did not break diplomatic relations with Cairo.

Although 1979 stands out because of a number of important events compressed into a short span of time, events in the Arab world have had ramifications for the United States since World War II. After the Arab oil embargo of October, 1973, to March, 1974, its impact has been impossible to ignore. Nevertheless, relatively little research on and analysis of Arab mass media have appeared in the West (Wynn 1948; Abu-Laban 1966). William Rugh's book *The Arab Press*, the first in any language to systematically treat mass media in the 18 nations of the Arab world, was published in 1979. The only previous book by a Westerner came out in 1952, treating just five states: Lebanon, Syria, Jordan, Iraq, and Egypt (McFadden 1953).

A few journal articles surveying Arab media have appeared in English (Wynn 1948; Abu-Lughod 1962; Adams 1964; Abu-Laban 1966; Mowlana 1976; Boyd 1978). Of single Arab countries, Egypt has been the most studied (Almaney 1972; Viorst 1974; Boyd 1975), while the three nations in the Maghreb—Morocco, Algeria, and Tunisia—have been virtually ignored. Within this limited literature, no content analyses have appeared recently.

This study attempts to partly fill that void by looking at the question of how official policy in three Arab countries is translated into media content. Given her controlled press system, we would expect Egypt, having just signed a treaty with Israel, to portray her new friend positively. Conversely, we would expect Algeria and Tunisia, having just broken diplomatic relations with Egypt, to portray that nation negatively.

In all three countries in question, the state owns and operates all radio and television stations, and influences newspapers both directly and indirectly. Constraints on media freedom are numerous (Gastil 1980). Two surveys of press freedom—defined in the Western sense as independence from government control—rank Egypt, Algeria, and Tunisia as "not free" (Merrill, Bryan, and Alisky 1970; Nixon 1965).

RESEARCH QUESTIONS

Problem Formulation. In his book on content analysis, Ole Holsti lists three uses of that method: describing message characteristics, inferring information about causes, and inferring information about effects. He warns against making assumptions about a source's reasons, values, motives, or intentions from content alone, however "it is hazardous indeed to assume, without corroborating evidence from independent, noncontent data, that inferences about the author may be drawn directly from content data" (Holsti 1969, 32).

Thus we do not seek to show that Arab media gatekeepers *want* to turn their audiences for or against Israel or Egypt, or that they approve or disapprove of Israel or Egypt. We hope rather to discern whether (1) the press in Egypt, Algeria, and Tunisia exhibit bias (non-neutrality) of news content in a patterned way; (2) the three countries, if biased, show similar patterns; and (3) these three controlled media systems differ from free media systems.

Does Egypt portray Israel in a completely positive way in the wake of the treaty? Do Algeria and Tunisia portray Israel negatively? Egypt negatively? Is there discrepancy or matching in the picture of Israel and Egypt in the press of each country? Are non-Arab media unbiased toward Israel? Toward Egypt?

Variables. An attitude, according to "most contemporary usages, involves... dispositions to evaluate objects favorably or unfavorably" (Insko and Schopler 1972, 1). Osgood, May, and Miron (1975) have confirmed that the evaluative response to stimuli, which they term *affect*, holds across language and culture. The positive and negative word lists developed by this research provide examples of the coloring that Arab gatekeepers might use and content analyzers might see as positive or negative.

We define the independent variables in this study as the formal or informal information policies or views held by Arab (Algerian, Egyptian, and Tunisian) gatekeepers toward Egypt and Israel. The dependent variable is affect or *coloring* of news stories about Egypt and Israel (positive, negative, or neutral/mixed).

In carrying out this study, we used the following conceptual definitions:

Affect: wording that creates in the mind of the average reader shadings of feeling

Positive affect: words presumed to create feelings of favor toward an object, event, or person, such as *good, true, kind, harmonious, optimistic*, or *reputable*

Negative affect: words presumed to create feelings of disfavor toward an object, event, or person, such as *bad, false, cruel, dissonant, pessimistic*, or *disreputable*

Mixed/neutral affect: words that are presumed to have neither a positive nor negative effect on a reader's feelings toward an event, object, or person

Bias: a significant proportion of positive or negative affect in news story content, as opposed to a preponderance of neutral/mixed affect.

Hypotheses (Verbal Model). Relations among variables may be stated as follows:

1. A difference exists in the affect used by Arab gatekeepers in their treatment of Egypt and Israel.

2. Bias (non-neutrality) exists in the Arab gatekeepers' treatment of both Egypt and Israel.

3. Compared to gatekeepers in controlled Arab mass media, those in free non-Arab media will show (a) less difference in treatment of Egypt and Israel and (b) less bias toward those two countries.

METHOD

A total of 952 news stories were coded from the Algerian media, 1,605 from the Tunisian media, and 2,135 from the Egyptian media. This analysis draws on two types of information in this three-country data set: nationality of the main actors in each story and affect toward these actors. Affect, not part of the original design was added at the request of the U.S. International Communication Agency (ICA) which supported the University of North Carolina part of the project.

Coders had to make more subjective decisions than the Holsti ideal of coding as a simple, clerical task (1969, 99). A graduate student from Egypt analyzed all the Arabic-language materials for Egypt, Algeria, and Tunisia; another coder dealt with the remaining media, which were in French. Intercoder reliability in a four-article test for these two was 63 percent for actors' nationalities and 63 percent for affect.

Units of Analysis and Sample. The population of this study is all news stories in all electronic and print media in the Arab world since March 26, 1979, the date of the signing of the Egyptian-Israeli Peace Treaty. Sampling among countries in the Arab world was done by the ICA on the basis of importance to the United States and existence of a variety of established daily media. Egypt, Algeria, and Tunisia were all judged to meet these criteria.

The three countries represent an interesting cross section of the Arab world. Egypt, the largest Arab nation (estimated 1976 population, 38 million), has traditionally had "the most influential and quoted press in the Arab world" (Mowlana 1976, 467). Its seven daily newspapers have a combined circulation of 1,333,000 (1976 figures) (Rugh 1979, 32). By contrast, Tunisia's five small dailies, with a combined circulation of only 139,000 (1976 figures), have virtually no impact beyond her borders (Rugh 1979, 73). Algeria has four dailies with a 235,000 combined circulation (Rugh 1979, 32).

Furthermore, the three countries' media exhibit divergent forms of government control. In Algeria, no private media exist; all reflect the party line and aim to mobilize the citizenry in nation building. The Egyptian press likewise serves as a mobilization tool, but is "not a dull, completely predictable and slavish mouthpiece of the regime akin to Russia's *Pravda*" (Rugh 1979, 43). Tunisian media, which include both party and privately owned newspapers, are much more passive than those of Egypt and Algeria. The press "avoids the language and opinions of aggressive and revolutionary journalism . . . . its news treatment is more likely to be straightforward or even dull" (Rugh 1979, 75).

To provide a contrast with a "free" press, comparable samples from the media of Mexico and Iceland were selected. The Freedom Classification Survey ranks Iceland as 1 (free-no qualifications) and Mexico as 3 (free-some instability) (Nixon 1965, 13). The PICA survey, while not mentioning Iceland, also puts Mexico in category 3 (free-many controls) (Merrill, Bryan, and Alisky 1970, 33).

The Mexican and Icelandic media are listed in the appendix to this book. The Arab world media with 1976 circulation figures (Rugh 1979, Tables 2 and 4) are:

Egypt: *Al Ahram* (520,000), *Al Ghoumhuriya* (60,000), *Al Akhbar* (650,000), Radio Egypt.

Algeria: *El Moudjahid* (French-150,000), *Al Sha'ab* (40,000), Algiers TV.
Tunisia: *Al 'Amal* (27,000), *L'Action* (French-27,000), *La Presse* (French-30,000), TV Tunisia.

Stories coded were those dealing with (1) the home country's activities abroad, (2) events in the home country involving foreign actors or situations, (3) news abroad not involving the home country, and (4) other international news. No purely domestic stories were coded, nor was material from special sections such as sports, travel, or food.

RESULTS

Difference in Treatment of Israel and Egypt. Table 8.1 shows the affect for each mention of an Egyptian or Israeli actor in our target media. The difference in portrayal is significant for all three Arab countries at the <.001 level for Egypt and Tunisia and the <.005 level for Algeria. Thus we can reject the null hypothesis that no difference exists in favor of research hypothesis 1. It is interesting to note the total absence of any positive portrayals of Israel by Algeria and Tunisia.

Table 8.1 Portrayal of Egypt and Israel by Arab media

Actors	Affect					
			Neutral/	Total		
	Positive	Negative	Mixed	%	n	
Egyptian media						
Eyptian	21%	4%	75%	100%	1,342	$x^2 = 59.4$
Israeli	12	14	74	100	377	$p < .001$
					1,719	
Algerian media						
Egyptian	9	57	34	100	158	$x^2 = 11.09$
Israeli	0	62	38	100	119	$p < .005$
					277	
Tunisian media						
Egyptian	3	13	84	100	174	$x^2 = 38.51$
Israeli	0	40	60	100	176	$p < .001$
					350	

Table 8.2. Index of bias in Arab media

Media	Actor	Observed	Theoretical*	x^2
			Mixed/neutral affect	
Egyptian	Egypt	1,010	1,342	82.13
Algerian	Egypt	54	158	68.46
Algerian	Israel	45	119	46.02
Tunisian	Israel	105	176	28.64
Egyptian	Israel	281	377	24.45
Tunisian	Egypt	146	174	4.51

*Theoretical neutral mentions = total mentions of actor

Table 8.3. Portrayal of Egypt and Israel by non-Arab media

Actor	Positive	Negative	Neutral/ Mixed	Total %	n	
		Affect				
Icelandic media						
Eyptian	5%	11%	84%	100%	19	$x^2 = .7$
Israeli	7	5	88	100	40	not sig.
					59	
Mexican media						
Egyptian	7	2	91	100	45	$x^2 = .55$
Israeli	7	5	88	100	104	not sig.
					149	

Bias in Treatment of Egypt and Israel. Table 8.2 shows how well our target countries stand up against a standard of complete neutrality. Here the total number of actual cases was used as the theoretical *N* for the mixed/neutral category. Again we can reject the null hypothesis that no bias exists in favor of research hypothesis 2. (The table has been set up to reflect the successive magnitude of chi-square calculation, with Egypt's portrayal of itself showing the least neutrality and Tunisia's portrayal of Egypt showing the most.)

Portrayal of Egypt and Israel by Free Non-Arab Media. Table 8.3 shows for Iceland and Mexico what Table 8.1 shows for the three Arab countries. There is no significant difference in treatment of Egypt and Israel by either Mexico or Iceland. Thus we can reject the null hypothesis that Arab and non-Arab media are the same in favor of research hypothesis 3a.

Table 8.4. Index of bias in non-Arab media

Media	Actor	Mixed/neutral affect		x^2
		Observed	Theoretical*	
Icelandic	Egyptian	16	19	.47
	Israeli	35	40	.63
Mexican	Egyptian	41	45	.36
	Israeli	92	104	1.38

*Theoretical neutral mentions = total mentions of actor

In contrast to the media of the Arab countries, the media of Iceland and Mexico show no significant bias in Table 8.4. Thus we can reject the null hypothesis in favor of research hypothesis 3b.

DISCUSSION

Having considered the affect associated with 2,346 mentions of Egyptian and Israeli actors in Arab mass media, this study suggests several possible conclusions: (1) the media of individual Arab countries exhibit striking differences, (2) government-controlled media do not slavishly follow government policy, and (3) Arab media tend to conform to certain overarching patterns.

This 1979 study's findings affirm Rugh's earlier assessments of the characteristics of various national press systems. Even under the strain of national and regional upheaval, Tunisia's "news treatment is...straightforward" (Rugh 1979, 75). It avoids coloring its portrayal of both Israel (60 percent neutral/mixed) and, especially, Egypt (84 percent neutral/mixed). (See Table 8.1) Algeria continues to use "the language... of aggressive and revolutionary journalism" (Rugh 1979, 75) by painting a decidedly derogatory picture of its two adversaries (Israel 62 percent negative; Egypt 57 percent negative). Egypt hews to a middle path, with about three-fourths of its coverage neutral/mixed and about one-fourth biased.

If Egypt's media system were a "predictable and slavish mouthpiece of the regime" (Rugh 1979, 43), we would expect Egypt to show toward Israel, with whom a peace treaty had just been signed, a more positive affect than 12 percent. Likewise, we would expect Tunisia to show toward Egypt, with whom it had just broken diplomatic relations, greater negativity than 13 percent.

Looking at Table 8.3, where neutral/mixed affect in Mexican and Icelandic media ranges from 84 to 91 percent, one might conclude that an absence of bias is business as usual. Perhaps most stories are simply pedestrian by nature, unsuitable to injections of positive or negative affect. Such an argument does not hold up, however, when we are looking at actors, and almost all stories include at least one individual or collective actor. This study has dealt with actors precisely because they are so vulnerable to journalistic treatment; in theory, each one could have a positive or, as happens more frequently, a negative epithet or adjective attached to it. The fact that Algeria's *bias count* is so much higher than its *neutral count* (34 percent and 38 percent) shows that journalistic "interpretation" can be done easily. (See Table 8.1)

Some examples demonstrate this kind of "interpretation." The headline of one article in *El Moudjahid* in Algeria on April 23, for example, reads: "Demonstration (erupts) at ElMenia (in Egypt) against the treason of Sadat." An article in *El Moudjahid* on April 17 refers to the "treasonous accord signed by Sadat with the Zionist enemy," a common epithet for Israel. Likewise, in a first-page article in Tunisia's *La Presse* of April 23, Sadat is "condemned" and is criticized for having "buried the feeble hope of Egyptian-Arabic rapport."

Treaty documents notwithstanding, it may be that Israel can never be Egypt's friend. A shift from negative affect to the neutrality we see in Table 8.1 may be as far as deeply intransigent attitudes can "progress." It may also be that Israel will always engender more opprobrium than Egypt could ever evoke, no matter what the Jewish state does.

Arab gatekeepers may thus exhibit a number of patterns of affect:

1. *Arab-to-Arab Affect.* President Sadat referred to the other Arabs' outpouring of criticism against Egypt as a family feud. To Westerners, it may seem that the Arab family has disowned prodigal son Egypt irrevocably. But Sadat just may have been right.

2. *Arab-to-Israel Affect.* In the light of Algeria and Tunisia's complete absence of positive affect toward Israel, we might regard Egypt's positiveness as "artificial"—a forced aberration resulting from a conscious, contrived campaign. That positiveness can be seen as unstable, vulnerable, and sensitive to subtle shifts in thinking.

3. *Arab-to-Other Affect.* The UNESCO data could be used to see if Arabs show a third pattern of affect, and perhaps even a fourth and fifth, toward the East, the West, and the Third World. These patterns could differ from the Arab-to-Arab positiveness and the Arab-to-Israel negativeness where history, culture, and religion have mixed with politics to make neutrality so difficult.

REFERENCES

Abu-Laban, Baha. 1966. Factors in social control of the press in Lebanon. *Journalism Quarterly* 43(3):510–18.

Abu-Lughod, Ibrahim. 1962. International news in the Arabic press: a comparative content analysis. *Public Opinion Quarterly* 26:600–12.

Adams, John B. 1964. Problems of communication in the Arab world. *Arab Journal* 1:83–88.

Almaney, Adnan. 1972. Government control of the press in the United Arab Republic, 1952–1970. *Journalism Quarterly* 49(2):340–48.

Boyd, Douglas A. 1975. Development of Egypt's radio: "Voice of the Arabs" under Nasser. *Journalism Quarterly* 52(4):645–53.

_____ . 1978. A Q-analysis of mass media usage by Egyptian elite groups. *Journalism Quarterly* 55(3):501–7.

Gastil, Raymond D. ed., 1980. *Freedom in the world: political rights and civil liberties, 1980.* New York: Freedom House.

Holsti, Ole. 1969. *Content analysis for the social sciences and humanities.* Reading, Mass.: Addison-Wesley.

Insko, Chester A., and John Schopler. 1972. *Experimental social psychology.* New York: Academic Press.

McFadden, Tom J. 1953. *Daily journalism in the Arab states.* Columbus: Ohio State University Press.

Merrill, John, Carter Bryan, and Marvin Alisky. 1970. *The foreign press.* Baton Rouge: Louisiana State University Press.

Mowlana, Hamid. 1976. The press and national development in the Middle East. *Intellect,* March, 466–68.

Nixon, Raymond B. 1965. Freedom in the world's press: a fresh approach with new data. *Journalism Quarterly* 42(1):3–14, 118–19.

Osgood, Charles E., William H. May, and Murray S. Miron. 1975. *Cross-cultural universals of affective meaning.* Urbana: University of Illinois Press.

Rugh, William A. 1979. *The Arab press.* Syracuse, N.Y.: Syracuse University Press.

United Nations. UNESCO General Conference, Nov. 22, 1978. The Declaration of Fundamental Principles Concerning the Contribution of the Mass Media to Strengthening Peace and International Understanding, the Promotion of Human Rights, and to Countering Racialism, Apartheid and Incitement to War.

Viorst, Milton. 1974. Egypt and Israel: Two nations and their press. *Columbia Journalism Review* (May/June):32–35.

Wynn, C. Wilton. 1948. Western techniques influence party newspaper in Egypt. *Journalism Quarterly* 25(4):391–94.

CHAPTER 9

Greece and Turkey Mirrored

Emmanuel E. Paraschos

IN this highly symbolic mass media world in which we live, perceptions, especially mass-media–generated perceptions, are normally retained by the mass audiences as national images or national stereotypes that eventually shape attitudes and govern behavior.

It is the creation of these national images that is the focus of this chapter —to see what sorts of images of other countries prevail through the news presentations of a national press system.

The 1978 UNESCO declaration on the media says that "the mass media, by disseminating information on the aims, aspirations, cultures, and needs of all people, contribute to eliminate ignorance and misunderstanding among peoples." The world's press, the document continues, sensitizes one country to the needs and desires of others, thus promoting "the respect of the rights and dignity of all nations, all peoples, all individuals" *(United Nations, 1978)*.

It is this perception and its potential translation into foreign policy action that has served as the specific motive for this study. The countries on which this study will focus are Greece and Turkey.

These two countries offer a useful and interesting case study because they have been at each other's doorstep since the beginning of time and they have been at each other's throat since almost the same time. From the days of Homer and Alexander the Great to the era of the Byzantine and Ottoman Empires, their neighborliness went through many tests.

The roots of their current antagonism can be traced as far back as the fall of Constantinople in 1453 and occupation of mainland Greece by the Turks for almost 400 years. The most recent symptom of the ailing relationship was the Turkish invasion of Cyprus (a nation inhabited by Greek and Turkish Cypriots in a four-to-one ratio respectively) in 1974—a conflict still unresolved.

Informal observation of the two countries' major dailies suggests that the image of the "other" country presented by either press system is largely negative. This chapter attempts to document this observation. In particular, the hypotheses are (1) the two press systems would give the "other" country similar play quantitatively (in number of stories, length, and story type), and (2) the media would present a negative quantitative image of the "other" country (through topic selection, and affect toward principal newsmakers).

METHOD. The media analyzed in this study were two of the countries' largest and most important dailies: Greece's *Ta Nea* and Turkey's *Milliyet*, each with a daily circulation of over 200,000. The analysis was done by American faculty with strong ties to those countries. Coverage of Cyprus was included in the data because that country represents a unique common news target for both newspapers.

RESULTS. The general information table on international coverage (Table 9.1) for the two newspapers shows that the Turkish paper covered more foreign countries (52 to 36) than did the Greek paper and ran more international stories (328 to 205). The small difference between the two newspapers' average number of stories per foreign country indicates that the two covered their chosen foreign countries in similar proportions during the period sampled.

In absolute numbers of stories, the Greek paper covered Turkey 60 percent more than the Turkish paper covered Greece, but Turkey covered Cyprus with four times as many stories as Greece covered Cyprus.

The two newspapers treated international news stories in much the same way. The large majority of foreign news was found in the main news section

Table. 9.1. Characteristics of international coverage in *Ta Nea* (Greece) and *Milliyet* (Turkey)

Greek paper		Turkish paper
36.00	Total number of countries covered	52.00
205.00	Total number of international stories	328.00
17.08	Average number of international stories per day	27.33
5.69	Average number of stories per foreign country	6.30
.47	Average number of stories per foreign country per day	.52
16.00	Total number of stories on "other" country	10.00
1.33	Average number of stories on "other" country daily	.83
3.00	Total number of stories on Cyprus	12.00
.25	Average number of stories on Cyprus daily	1.00

of the papers—86.3 percent of the Turkish paper's international news stories and 76.6 percent of the Greek newspaper's international news stories were in the main news sections. Almost all of each paper's stories on the "other" country and Cyprus appeared in the main news sections.

Sources (news agency, own correspondent) of international news items showed some diversity. The Greek paper relied considerably more on the Associated Press (25.4 percent of all its international stories) than on any other single source, while its own correspondents provided 11.2 percent of all international stories. The Turkish paper, on the other hand, relied primarily (36 percent of all its foreign stories) on its own correspondents, with its home country agency providing 23 percent of its stories and the Associated Press providing 14 percent.

Some interesting results were obtained, however, in focusing on the origin of stories about the "other" country. Of the dozen or so story sources utilized by either paper, three were conducive to the use of "bias," if bias was intended to be used by either paper. Those potentially "contaminated" sources were: own correspondent, home country agency, and "no source" given.

Table 9.2 shows that while only 36 percent of the stories on "all foreign countries" in the Greek paper came from potentially contaminated sources, all of the Cyprus stories came from such sources. About one quarter (25.1 percent) of the Greek paper's stories on Turkey came from potentially contaminated sources.

The Turkish paper used considerably more potentially contaminated sources than Greece to cover "all foreign countries." But it used an even higher number of such stories when covering Greece (70 percent) and Cyprus (83.3 percent).

The countries that received most of the coverage in both papers offered some interesting and puzzling results. Unlike the rest of the IAMCR-sampled media that seemed to cover their neighbors more than any other single group of countries, *Ta Nea* and *Milliyet*'s coverage of foreign countries seemed to be based on different criteria than geographical proximity.

Table 9.3 shows that the single most newsworthy country in both papers was the United States, and although there may be a slight preference on the part of the Turkish editors to favor news from the Middle East (half of its countries receiving the most coverage are from that area) that hardly constitutes a pattern. Greece, in fact, has no common border with 11 of its top 13 countries receiving the most coverage.

Table 9.2. Use of home country agency, own correspondent, and no source

	Story Subject		
	All foreign countries	Other country	Cyprus
Greek paper	36%	25.1%	100%
Turkish paper	62	70	83.3

Table 9.3. Distribution of foreign coverage*

Greek paper	%	Rank	Turkish paper	%
USA	22.0	1	USA	12.2
UK	12.7	2	France	6.4
France	11.7	3	Iran	5.8
Turkey	7.8	4	UK	5.5
USSR	6.3	5	West Germany	4.3
West Germany	5.4	6	Cyprus	3.7
Iran	4.4	7	Greece	3.1
Italy	3.9	8	USSR	2.4
Netherlands	2.0	9	Israel	1.8
Yugoslavia	1.5	10	Egypt	1.5
China (Comm.)	1.5		Hungary	1.5
Cyprus	1.5		Switzerland	1.5
Israel	1.5			
Total	82.2		Total	49.7

*Countries mentioned less than 1 percent have been omitted.

The topics the two papers chose to print presented some interesting results. Of the IAMCR-generated categories of topics given the coders, three of the top five mostly utilized by each paper were the same. The Turkish paper's favorite international story topics were Diplomatic Activity (30.2 percent of all international stories), Internal Crisis (10.4 percent), Economic Aid (7.6 percent), Elections/Government Change (5.5 percent), and Sports (5.2 percent). The Greek paper covered Diplomatic Activity (14.6 percent), Internal Crisis (12.2 percent), Science/Medicine (8.3 percent), Sports (5.9 percent), and Human Interest (5.8 percent).

Ten of the 47 topic categories included in the study clearly were loaded with negative implications and could lend themselves to negative image creation if one intended to so use them: Armed Conflict, Civil Suits, Crime/Political, Crime/Nonpolitical, Crime/Other-Legal, Disasters/Accidents, Internal Crisis, Other Military/ Arms Deals, Weapons and Bases, Pollution and Social Problems. These topics used in a primary or secondary position in a story can only convey a mainly negative image of the country of their origin.

Table 9.4 focuses on those negative-topic stories as they were used by the Greek and Turkish papers in covering "all foreign countries," the "other" country, and Cyprus. In particular, Table 9.4 shows that in the Greek paper, 35.1 percent of the stories on "all foreign countries" had a negative main topic and 30.9 percent had a negative secondary topic. Of the Greek paper's stories on Turkey, however, 75 percent had a negative main topic and 46.1 had a negative secondary topic. Of the Turkish paper's stories on "all foreign countries" 19.8 percent had negative main topics, and of the stories on Greece 20 percent

Table 9.4. Percentage of stories with negative topics

	Main Topics			Secondary Topics		
	All foreign countries	Other country	Cyprus	All foreign countries	Other country	Cyprus
Greek paper	35.1%	75%	33.3%	30.9%	46.1%	0%
Turkish paper	19.8	20	25	38.5	60	27.2

had negative primary topics. The Turkish paper's secondary topic selection showed that 38.5 percent of the stories on "all foreign countries" were negative but 60 percent of the stories on Greece were negative.

Cyprus was covered by the Greek paper in much the same manner as "all foreign countries" in main topics, but it received no negative coverage by the paper in secondary topics. The Turkish paper gave Cyprus more negative coverage than "all foreign countries" in main topics (19.8 percent to 25 percent) but less negative coverage than "all foreign countries" in secondary topics (38.5 percent to 27.2 percent).

Coverage of each other's main news "actors" also tended to be negative.

DISCUSSION. Our quantitative hypothesis, which said the two papers would cover the "other" country similarly, met with mixed results. The two papers covered the world in general and the "other" country in particular primarily through news stories. The large majority of these stories was found in the general news sections of the papers.

Perhaps the most important similarity between the two papers was in the selection of countries and topics to be covered. Three of each paper's most covered topics were the same, with sports being an unsurprising popular subject in both.

Since the Turkish paper's five most covered topics occupied 58.9 percent of all international stories and the Greek paper's five top topics occupied 46.8 percent of all international stories, it might be said that the latter exhibited more diversity in topic selection than the former.

Another significant similarity is the two papers' lists of most coverd countries. About two-thirds of their lists are identical and there is little to suggest that geographical proximity was the key factor in that grouping (Table 9.3). The relationship of both Greece and Turkey with the United States must have played a key role in the latter's topping the two lists.

Story origin showed another difference between the two papers. The Turkish paper's heavy reliance on its own correspondents showed a considerable interest in foreign affairs and might have said something about the paper's financial status. The Greek paper relied primarily on the AP and printed a large number of stories with no origin attribution, a point with ethical implications.

The qualitative hypothesis, which expected that the coverage of the "other" country by the two papers would have been negative, fared well. Table 9.4 clearly shows the two papers' biases.

CONCLUSION. This chapter makes several comparisons and offers some observations. The bottom line is the image *Ta Nea* and *Milliyet* present of the "other" country and Cyprus. Mostly it was negative.

Of course, we do not know if these images reflect those already held by public opinion or shape it. We do not know if these images are the ones government wants diffused or if they are the basis of government action. What can be said with some certainty is that *Milliyet* and *Ta Nea* in our sampled period did exhibit signs of shortsightedness in their handling of news from the "other" country.

One might expect that papers of their size, circulation, and prestige would perform at a higher level of responsibility when covering issues of such national importance. Since a large number of their respective newspaper-reading publics gets information from these two papers, it should be incumbent upon them to use more restraint in covering the "other" country thus minimizing the possibility of contributing to conflict and feeding the feud.

REFERENCE

United Nations. UNESCO General Conference, Nov. 22, 1978. The Declaration of Fundamental Principles Concerning the Contribution of the Mass Media to Strengthening Peace and International Understanding, the Promotion of Human Rights and to Countering Racism, Apartheid and Incitement to War.

CHAPTER 10

Leaders and Conflict in the News in "Stable" vs. "Pluralistic" Political Systems

Donald L. Shaw and Robert L. Stevenson

WALTER LIPPMANN in the 1920s described the role of the press in providing readers with a view of the "unseen environment" (Lippmann 1922). For most, the world is filtered through the news of newspapers, television, or radio. We have little alternative, a concern to many "developing" nations whose leaders feel that their countries are not being mentioned either enough or fairly in the news (MacBride 1980). Our views of other nations, the chances for peace, the need for stronger national defense, and many other topics are based in part upon foreign affairs news. Such news is our window to the world.

Yet this chapter asks whether countries that emphasize social stability and tighter control over their citizens provide an emphasis in foreign news rather different from countries that are more pluralistic and open in approach to internal political life. The views of the world that one would obtain by reading newspapers of these contrasting government-press systems would suggest important, although subtle, differences. Relatively speaking, one world is peaceful and the other is less so.

Such differences in coverage are important to the extent they show how newspapers generally reflect the political-economic systems in which they operate. We share more than we often admit. Journalists have an important job in constructing our views of foreign affairs regardless of political system. We no longer allow news to "just happen."

STABILITY VS. PLURALISM: TRADITIONAL FRAMEWORKS FOR COMPARISON. In the midst of the United States-Soviet Union cold war in the 1950s, three American scholars developed a typology of the world's press systems (Siebert, Peterson, and Schramm 1956). They found four types of press theories: authoritarian, libertarian, social responsibility, and Soviet Communist. This typology soon powerfully fixed itself upon the Western scholarly mind. The typology provides an appropriate starting point for comparison of "pluralistic" and "stable" government-press systems. These systems did not develop in a historical vacuum.

Authoritarian Theory. The authoritarian theory characterized the early days of the American colonial press, a time in which kings still were vested (by themselves at least) with divine authority and in which the press by contrast had little power or authority. Licensing of printers, creation of "official" printing companies, taxes, and finally the threat of seditious libel pushed the ingenuity of printers to find ways to reach literate audiences with, first, religious and philosophical books and then news books, racy books, and finally, in England in the seventeenth century and America in the eighteenth century, newspapers. In this unequal struggle of printing press against government, from the late seventeenth to the late eighteenth centuries, stability reigned.

Libertarian Theory. By the middle of the eighteenth century, the press was more than just a threat to authority, although many still mainly so perceived it. The press was a business, often a very profitable one. The press dealt in information and ideas and what could be a more important "product"? The rhetoric of John Milton, soon to be supplemented with the voices of others, characterized the predominant theory of the early U.S. press and also evidenced eighteenth century faith in reason. Born in the eigtheenth century, buffeted by events of the Revolution and the hostile first party period immediately following, the U.S. press entered the new mechanical nineteenth century committed to the great experiment that John Milton had urged. The United States, our example in this brief historical trip, embraced libertarianism. Truth would have the best chance of emerging from a plurality of voices. Stability (within reason) would have to move aside.

Social Responsibility Theory. But the small-scale economic arrangements of the early nineteenth century did not last. As economic lord, William Randolph Hearst matched with newspapers what John D. Rockefeller did in oil and Andrew Carnegie did in steel. By the middle of the twentieth century, press consolidations, which had been under way at least since 1880 (Emery 1972, 442), had altered the many press voices of the nineteenth century. Spotlights were replacing fireflies. So few any more were throwing wheat *or* chaff into the wind.

What was to be done? *Time* magazine and *Encyclopaedia Britannica* supported a commission composed of distinguished scholars who in the middle 1940s studied press performance and, in their 1947 report on balance, found the American press wanting (Commission on Freedom of the Press 1947). The report reflected new economic realities. As e pluribus unum described the political nation, it also held in local economic communities for newspapers. It was becoming difficult for a community to support competing newspapers.

There was not, said the Commission, enough diversity, enough about minorities, enough plain digging into the news behind the news (Rivers and Schramm 1969, 47–48). Only a press cognizant of its social responsibilities could provide the depth needed. The press would have to *simulate* the diversity that the economic order of things could no longer generate upon its own. The press would have to spotlight events from all angles and seek the why of events. The journalist has a responsibility for picking and shaping events. Only active journalism could ensure the pluralism that an open social system needed. Pluralism requires effort.

Soviet Communist Theory. A special responsibility also is imposed upon the journalist in the Soviet Union but there the responsibility is to the party system and goals (Hopkins 1970). If the Communist party has identified social goals and organized the state to support them, the press must also play a supportive role. Lenin himself gave the press a positive function. Where authoritarianism sought mostly to control the noisy and disruptive press, the Soviet Communist theory places a special responsibility upon the press for social organization. The journalist must place events within the proper context. The emphasis is upon continuity. Stability also requires effort.

Brief Comparison. The social responsibility theory is really the libertarian theory in which the press, so far, has been left on its own to find a positive role by seeking out all angles for a wide range of stories. The press must generate the diversity and seek out a plurality of voices that no longer can be expected to happen naturally. There are no longer enough competing newspaper voices.

The Soviet Communist theory rests upon stability, as does authoritarian theory, and the Soviet journalist has a positive obligation to relate events to party doctrine. Are these differences in kind or merely degree? Whatever the difference, journalists of all political systems are expected to play an active role in generating information of use to the social system in which they live.

When comparing government-press systems, it is easy to be pejorative. Yet John Merrill (1965) has warned us that judgments of press systems are generally made from the comfortable platform of one's own political and social system. The book by Siebert, Petersen, and Schramm, *Four Theories of the Press* (Urbana: University of Illinois, 1956), is still very useful and leaves little doubt as to which theories are "good" and which "bad." It obviously is an American study. While arguments about which press-government system is best cannot be "won," a system's perspective provides a useful framework for analysis. Data always must be analyzed from some perspective.

STUDY FOCUS. This chapter combines findings from the UNESCO content analysis with results of an independent assessment of the relative freedom of press systems. With these data, the study contrasts the foreign affairs news coverage in a sample of newspapers from countries that have adopted a relatively "pluralistic" approach to internal political freedoms and civil rights with the same type coverage in newspapers in countries that have developed more "stable" approaches to those freedoms. The newspapers of countries with an approach between these two ("mixed" systems) demonstrate patterns between those of pluralistic and stable systems. These adjectives are intended merely as labels, not values.

METHOD

Newspaper Data. This chapter used the newspaper data gathered as part of the larger study of world news patterns. For each story, coders determined subject and theme, main actors, whether or not quotes were used, and a variety of other variables. These variables were used in comparing nations with different types of government-press systems.

National System Data. The study also "borrowed" the 1978 press freedom rankings done annually by Freedom House, a New York–based organization (Gastil 1979). This ranking represents a U.S. view and is used, with qualifications, as an analytical starting point. All national system rankings must take some perspective into account.

The ranking of world press systems by Freedom House takes into account the evaluation of political rights, civil liberties, and the overall performance of the political and economic systems of individual nations. The Freedom House process results in a final judgment of press systems as "free," "partially free," or "not free." While one might quibble with the labels—final judgments depend upon your perspective—most would agree that the factors that Freedom House takes into account are significant.

Examples are:

Evaluation of Political Rights

1. Are leaders chosen, or decisions made, on the basis of an open voting process?

2. Are there multiple parties or are there candidates who are not selected by the government?

3. Are polling and vote counting done without coercion and fraud?

4. What share of power is exercised by elected representatives?

Evaluation of Civil Liberties

1. Does the average person have the right to express views openly?

2. Can one discuss political issues without fear?

3. Can one belong to an independent private organization that is free of government supervision?

4. Is there an independent judiciary with a right of fair trial?

From the evaluation of political rights plus civil liberties, each country was ranked from 1 (the "good" side) to 7 (the "bad" side), resulting in a theoretical total score ranging from 2 to 14, with most countries falling in between. However defined, the condition of being "free" or "not free" is dynamic and falls on a continuum along which one only can estimate the position of a given press system at a given moment. Freedom House systematically and annually measures what long has interested other scholars (Nixon 1960).

The 16 countries of the UNESCO study analyzed here "scored" from 2 to 13, as Table 10.1 shows, with Iceland and the United States first and the Soviet Union and Zaire last. Such anyway is a ranking consistent with U.S. values.

Table 10.1. Comparative press freedom survey

Country	Political rights	Civil liberties	Total	Overall ranking
Iceland	1	1	2	Free
United States	1	1	2	Free
Turkey	2	3	5	Free
Mexico	4	4	8	Partly free
Brazil	4	5	9	Partly free
Egypt	5	4	9	Partly free
Indonesia	5	5	10	Partly free
Kenya	5	5	10	Partly free
Zambia	5	5	10	Partly free
Ivory Coast	6	5	11	Not free
Tunisia	6	5	11	Not free
Thailand	6	5+	11+	Not free
Argentina	6	6–	12–	Not free
Algeria	6	6	12	Not free
Soviet Union	7	6	13	Not free
Zaire	7	6	13	Not free

Note: Rankings vary from 1 (least constraint placed upon political rights or civil liberties) to 7 (most constraint). Any improvement less than a full step since the previous year in either of these two areas is indicated by a " + " while a deterioration is indicated by a "-."

Those countries with "low" scores are most likely to encourage a plurality of public voices. Those with "high" scores are most likely to promote stability, with less emphasis upon diverse points of view. Countries with scores in the middle are most likely to demonstrate aspects of both plural and stable systems. These assumptions formed the basis for the study questions. In general these assumptions were substantiated.

Fig. 10.1 sketches the hypothesized dynamics of press performance that this study follows. In the "free" or, less judgmentally, "plural" press systems, government and press stand independently serving the public. The government can, and sometimes does, communicate directly with the citizens, as with information regarding taxes. The public can speak back with meaningful votes and by exercising real choice. But the press is the main avenue of information and even most official information flows through it. Press and public officials constantly jockey to determine the "proper" agenda of issues. Most often the government holds the upper hand, but sometimes, as in the U.S. Watergate imbroglio, it does not. There is give and take.

The same potential for pluralism is lacking in stable systems. If the press identifies with governmental interests, the circles overlap. Complete overlap eliminates completely the press as a source of independent observation. Public ability to speak back is diminished. From country to country, the degree of overlap varies and it also varies over time. In times of internal tension or international threat, the circles move closer together while in less tense times they may drift apart (Siebert 1952, 10). Beneath political and economic systems there apparently are social system survival instincts.

FINDINGS AND DISCUSSION

Main Actors in Foreign Affairs News. Across the 16 countries, the main actor (the major person around whom the story revolved) came from the executive branch of the government. This included all types of executive leaders, from symbolic heads of state to ambassadors, ministers, and cabinet officers, but in most stories it was the chief executive who predominated. (The results of radio and television coverage, not included here, show even more striking executive dominance.) Chief executives usually are charged with responsibility for foreign affairs and when they travel or speak, their words readily lend themselves to national stories. For the moment at least, they *are* their nation.

Across the 16 nations, executive leaders accounted for at least one of every three foreign affairs stories in home country coverage. (See Table 10.2.)

In nations judged stable, executives accounted for about four of every ten home country foreign affairs stories. "Mixed" systems fell in the middle. Coverage of foreign leaders in the stories about other countries, on the other hand, was about the same by all three "types" of press systems, one of every three stories.

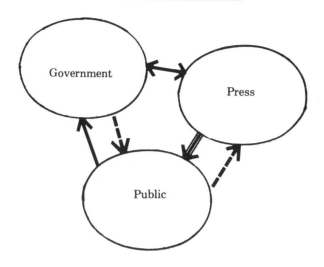

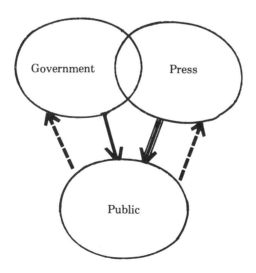

Fig. 10.1: Model of press-government relationships

Table 10.2. Executives as main actors in own country and other country foreign news

Type country	Home country		Other country	
	%	n	%	n
Free/pluralistic				
Iceland (2)	9	93	19	631
United States (2)	29	826	29	1,797
Turkey (5)	53	73	53	242
Total	29	992	29	2,670
Partly free/mixed				
Mexico (8)	22	238	24	1,714
Brazil (9)	21	201	45	771
Egypt (9)	45	441	40	1,243
Indonesia (10)	35	117	36	696
Kenya (10)	30	91	26	515
Zambia (10)	35	63	34	329
Total	33	1,151	31	5,268
Not free/stable				
Ivory Coast (11)	31	29	42	234
Tunisia (11)	63	212	39	1,256
Thailand (11+)	35	170	29	375
Argentina (12–)	17	335	25	1,184
Algeria (12)	33	162	37	784
Soviet Union (13)	45	301	38	654
Zaire (13)	52	82	42	236
Total	42	1,291	34	4,723

Readers of newspapers in the stable countries would have seen fewer types of people, and those more often executive leaders, dominating their own foreign affairs news. These differences are subtle but they suggest that in stable countries there is less doubt expressed about who is in charge. It also should be remembered that this study deals only with foreign news. In many stable countries, domestic news contains an even higher level of executive dominance.

Use of Quotations. Countries judged pluralistic were much more likely to use quotes from anyone in foreign affairs coverage, nearly one of every two stories, than were countries judged stable or mixed. (See Table 10.3.)

Pluralistic countries were also more likely to use quotes in coverage of other countries. But if anyone in fact were quoted, the stable or mixed countries were much more likely to quote executive leaders. For pluralistic countries, it was one of every three quotes. For the more stable, it was one of every two. The more stable countries also were more likely to quote executive leaders in coverage of other countries. (See Table 10.4.)

Table 10.3. Use of any quotes in own country and other country foreign affairs news

| | Use of Any Quotes in Foreign Coverage of | | | |
| | Home country | | Other country | |
Type country	%	n	%	n
Free/pluralistic				
Iceland (2)	42	93	27	631
United States (2)	49	826	37	1,797
Turkey (5)	40	73	28	242
Total	48	992	34	2,670
Partly free/mixed				
Mexico (8)	31	238	26	1,714
Brazil (9)	40	201	38	771
Egypt (9)	17	441	10	1,243
Indonesia (10)	21	117	21	696
Kenya (10)	23	91	18	515
Zambia (10)	30	63	28	329
Total	27	1,151	23	5,268
Not free/stable				
Ivory Coast (11)	17	29	24	234
Tunisia (11)	35	212	27	1,256
Thailand (11 +)	35	170	23	375
Argentina (12-)	40	335	35	1,184
Algeria (12)	21	162	16	784
Soviet Union (13)	23	301	27	654
Zaire (13)	22	82	29	236
Total	31	1,291	27	4,723

How much is style—quotes are popular, for instance, in Western news—and how much the predilection of a political system to orient on executive power abroad, just as it does at home? At any rate, in the stable and mixed government-press systems, one is more likely to read about an executive leader as a main character in foreign news and *if* there are quotes it is far more likely to come from an executive than from any other type person.

Table 10.5 more directly contrasts the numbers of stories in which anyone is quoted with the number of total quote stories in which the executive is quoted. In general as one "ascends" the freedom scale from 2 (very pluralistic) to 13 (very stable), the tendency is for the quotes that are actually used to come from the top. One can only guess, but it would seem plausible to argue that executive quotes in a system that tended to use fewer quotes anyway would give those that actually appeared more power. Being rarer, quotes would convey authority.

Table 10.4. Use of executive quotes in own country and other country foreign news

Type country	Home country		Other country	
	%	n	%	n
Free/pluralistic				
Iceland (2)	15	39	32	170
United States (2)	35	404	41	662
Turkey (5)	41	29	54	68
Total	34	472	40	900
Partly free/mixed				
Mexico (8)	33	75	42	447
Brazil (9)	39	80	45	290
Egypt (9)	83	75	73	124
Indonesia (10)	64	25	58	146
Kenya (10)	38	21	30	92
Zambia (10)	47	19	46	91
Total	51	295	47	1,190
Not free/stable				
Ivory Coast (11)	80	5	64	55
Tunisia (11)	82	74	66	333
Thailand (11+)	45	60	49	86
Argentina (12–)	25	135	43	408
Algeria (12)	79	34	58	125
Soviet Union (13)	50	70	51	176
Zaire (13)	50	18	57	69
Total	50	396	54	1,252

World of Peace, World of Conflict. For the same countries, the study compared the foreign affairs coverage of internal conflict. This included coverage of political crime (internal political conflict) and coverage of "ordinary" nonpolitical crime or judicial actions (civil conflict). Table 10.6 shows that the pluralistic countries are more likely to cover internal political conflict while all systems cover ordinary crime at about the same rate, although with a bit less emphasis given by the mixed and stable countries. All systems agree, however, about coverage of political and civil conflict in the First World (the economically developed countries of North America, Western Europe, and Japan). There the stable countries do not let up. They do, however, in coverage of political conflict stories in the Second World of Socialist Eastern Europe and the Third World.

If one concentrates only upon news of political conflict, the coverage of their own countries by the more stable countries is very light and coverage of the Second World is not much more. Coverage of political conflict in the Third

Table 10.5. Percentage of stories with any quotes vs. percentage of stories with executives quoted in foreign news

Type country	Home country			Other country		
	Any quote	Exec quote	Diff	Any quote	Exec quote	Diff
Free/pluralistic						
Iceland (2)	42	15	+ 27	27	32	–05
United States (2)	49	35	+ 14	37	41	–04
Turkey (5)	40	41	–01	28	54	–26
Total	48	34	+ 14	34	40	–06
Partly free/mixed						
Mexico (8)	31	33	–02	26	42	–16
Brazil (9)	40	39	+01	38	45	–07
Egypt (9)	17	83	–66	10	73	–63
Indonesia (10)	21	64	–43	21	58	–37
Kenya (10)	23	38	–15	18	30	–12
Zambia (10)	30	47	–17	28	46	–18
Total	27	51	–24	23	47	–24
Not free/stable						
Ivory Coast (11)	17	80	–63	24	64	–40
Tunisia (11)	35	82	–47	27	66	–39
Thailand (11 +)	35	45	–10	23	49	–26
Argentina (12-)	40	25	+ 15	35	43	–08
Algeria (12)	21	79	–58	16	58	–42
Soviet Union (13)	23	50	–27	27	51	–24
Zaire (13)	22	50	–28	29	57	–28
Total	31	50	–19	27	54	–27

World similarly is *relatively* low. Yet if coverage of free/pluralistic countries is taken as a measure, there certainly was conflict in all areas of the world. Only in coverage of the First World does the press of the less-free nations give it both barrels.

Do the news media of the stable and mixed nations score their ideological opponents while demonstrating sympathetic understanding for the problems of the struggling underdeveloped world? Table 10.7 suggests this is not the case. The difference between coverage of political conflict at home and abroad is about the same everywhere, 8 percent to 9 percent. The news media of the mixed and stable systems simply covers political conflict less, except for First World conflict. Conflict is potentially destabilizing; perhaps, therefore, it is best to leave it out, in the view of some editors at least.

Table 10.6. Internal political conflict and civil conflict stories in own country and other country foreign affairs news

Type country	Own coverage			First World			Second World			Third World		
	% IP	% C	Total N	% IP	% C	Total N	% IP	% C	Total N	% IP	% C	Total N
Free/pluralistic												
Iceland (2)	0	1	91	3	5	414	3	0	30	22	1	137
United States (2)	5	3	899	8	4	686	9	5	151	21	3	866
Turkey (5)	2	0	68	6	5	151	0	0	15	34	3	77
Subgroup	4	2	1,058	6	4	1,251	7	4	196	22	3	1,080
Partially free/mixed												
Mexico (8)	1	1	383	3	4	957	3	4	78	16	3	633
Brazil (9)	*	3	329	13	3	367	2	4	54	26	2	287
Egypt (9)	2	3	715	3	3	584	4	2	45	16	3	640
Indonesia (10)	0	3	193	1	2	315	4	4	26	17	3	378
Kenya (10)	5	6	153	6	8	198	0	0	19	26	3	247
Zambia (10)	5	5	112	12	8	119	0	0	7	18	7	190
Subgroup	2	3	1,885	5	4	2,540	3	3	229	19	3	2,375
Not free/stable												
Ivory Coast (11)	0	0	103	2	5	42	0	0	14	13	1	151
Tunisia (11)	0	0	345	5	10	512	4	0	55	12	1	606
Thailand (11+)	1	3	319	3	1	148	0	0	21	10	7	177
Argentina (12–)	*	*	485	4	6	539	0	3	38	18	3	525
Algeria (12)	1	*	316	6	3	259	0	0	38	12	1	456
Soviet Union (13)	1	*	248	4	2	214	3	0	77	18	0	215
Zaire (13)	1	0	112	8	2	64	0	0	10	11	2	147
Subgroup	1	1	1,928	4	6	1,778	2	*	253	14	2	2,227

*Less than .005%.

Table 10.7. Percentage of internal political and civil conflict stories in own country and other country foreign affairs news

	Political conflict			Civil conflict		
Type country	Home %	Other %	Diff %	Home %	Other %	Diff %
Free/pluralistic						
Iceland (2)	0	8	–8	1	3	–2
United States (2)	5	14	–9	3	4	–1
Turkey (5)	2	14	–12	0	4	–4
Total	4	13	–9	2	4	–2
Partly free/mixed						
Mexico (8)	1	8	–7	1	3	–2
Brazil (9)	0	17	–17	3	3	0
Egypt (9)	2	10	–8	3	3	0
Indonesia (10)	0	10	–10	3	3	0
Kenya (10)	5	16	–11	6	5	+1
Zambia (10)	5	16	–11	5	7	–2
Total	2	11	–9	3	3	0
Not free/stable						
Ivory Coast (11)	0	10	–10	0	1	–1
Tunisia (11)	0	9	–9	0	5	–5
Thailand (11 +)	1	7	–6	3	4	–1
Argentina (12–)	0	10	–10	0	4	–4
Algeria (12)	1	9	–8	0	2	–2
Soviet Union (13)	1	10	–9	0	1	–1
Zaire (13)	1	10	–9	0	2	–2
Total	1	9	–8	1	3	–2

The stable countries, furthermore, are likely to cast foreign news coverage into *relational* terms—that is, to carry news that concentrates upon the relationship between states or among groups of states. Through their foreign news coverage, stable nations relate their country to other countries. Table 10.8 shows the amount of foreign news coverage of this type for the 27 nations in the full UNESCO study, the 16 of the nations studied by the U.S. scholars, plus data from 11 additional countries that were obtained by scholars elsewhere as part of the total UNESCO study. As nations become more stable, the amount of news involving or relating to other nations enlarged.

One might hypothesize that more stable nations attempt to provide a context for news, to help their readers see events in a larger perspective. If a government-press system seeks stability, this would be a logical function. Pluralistic systems would not demonstrate the same need to put events into context. Pluralistic nations would leave more up to the reader.

Table 10.8. Foreign news involving relations between states

Type country	%	n
Free/pluralistic		
Australia (2)	25	1,032
Iceland (2)	31	689
Netherlands (2)	39	991
United States (2)	42	1,487
Fed. Rep. Germany (3)	32	3,068
Finland (4)	49	881
Greece (4)	28	205
India (4)	65	1,649
Turkey (5)	59	327
Total	41	10,329
Partly free/mixed		
Mexico (8)	30	1,188
Brazil (9)	34	630
Egypt (9)	74	1,322
Nigeria (9)	39	205
Indonesia (10)	44	811
Kenya (10)	57	501
Zambia (10)	58	516
Total	50	5,173
Not free/stable		
Hungary (11)	48	2,931
Iran (11)	70	453
Ivory Coast (11)	66	390
Poland (11)	40	713
Tunisia (11)	74	1,303
Yugoslavia (11)	56	1,144
Thailand (11+)	35	580
Argentina (12-)	40	1,017
Algeria (12)	80	935
Soviet Union (13)	82	997
Zaire (13)	74	919
Total	59	11,382

SUMMARY AND IMPLICATIONS. "Pluralistic" and "stable" are relative terms in comparing government-press systems. At bottom rests a set of assumptions about the relationships among government, people, and press. Stable systems, in this analysis, appeared to control the amount of conflict in foreign affairs news and to keep a strong focus upon the executive as a leader. News was more often presented in terms that related nation to nation. Such was stability.

Pluralistic systems provided a wider range of news figures, apparently had more access to them (at least provided more quotes by them), did not shy away from internal conflict, and did not provide as much nation-to-nation context for the news. More was left up to the reader. In this study, pluralistic and stable press systems apparently performed as their government-press relationships directed, one with more diversity of sources and more openness to conflict news and one with more stability.

The differences were relative; all systems place a great deal of emphasis upon executive leaders. Yet one news world was in fact more stable while the other revealed a bit more conflict in the world. Which is the more "accurate" view? It depends perhaps upon your assumptions.

REFERENCES

Commission on Freedom of the Press. 1947. *A free and responsible press.* Chicago: University of Chicago Press.

Emery, Edwin. 1972. *The press and America.* 3rd ed. Englewood Cliffs, N.J.: Prentice-Hall.

Gastil, Raymond D. ed. 1979. *Freedom in the world: Political rights and civil liberties, 1979.* New York: Freedom House. (Also see 1980 edition edited by Gastil and published by Freedom House.)

Hopkins, Mark W. 1970. *Mass media in the Soviet Union.* New York: Pegasus.

International Commission for the Study of Communication Problems. 1980. *Many voices, one world.* New York: Unipub.

Lippmann, Walter. [1922] 1960. *Public opinion.* New York: Macmillan.

McCombs, Maxwell E., and Donald L. Shaw. 1972. The agenda-setting function of mass media. *Public Opinion Quarterly* 36(2): 176–87.

Merrill, John. 1965. The press and social responsibility. Freedom of Information Center Publication No. 001. Columbia, Mo.: School of Journalism, University of Missouri.

Nixon, Raymond B. 1960. Factors related to freedom in national press systems. *Journalism Quarterly* 37(1): 13–28.

Rivers, William L., and Wilbur Schramm. 1969. *Responsibility in mass communication.* Rev. ed. New York: Harper & Row.

Shaw, Donald L., and Stephen W. Brauer. 1969. Press freedom and war constraints: Case testing Siebert's proposition II. *Journalism Quarterly* 42(2): 243–54.

Siebert, Fredrick Seaton. 1952. *Freedom of the press in England 1476–1776.* Urbana, Ill.: University of Illinois Press.

Siebert, Frederick Seaton, Theodore Peterson, and Wilbur Schramm. 1956. *Four theories of the press.* Urbana, Ill.: University of Illinois Press.

International News Flow

IN this section, we turn from an examination of national news systems to studies of international news flow. Our focus is on the four major Western news agencies— Associated Press, United Press International, Reuters, and Agence France-Presse. But we also look beyond the gatekeepers to examine how structural factors of economics and politics influence the flow of news among nations.

Even though alternatives are available, as we saw earlier, the "Big Four" are of special interest to our study because of their size and influence. What do they carry to and from the Third World? What elements of the infinitely varied world get into the channels of international news flow?

The four chapters in this section address these questions. Chapter 11, "Foreign News in the Western Agencies," provides the same overview of news agency coverage that earlier chapters provided for national media. The results may or may not be surprising. On one hand, there is little support for the contention that the Western news agencies ignore the Third World: in all of the several regional files to the Third World, the region served received more attention than any other part of the world; even in domestic services to the United States, Third World coverage exceeded that of other parts of the world.

But on the other hand, the weaknesses of foreign news coverage that we observed in national systems— a narrow definition of news and newsmakers, an emphasis on politics—also appear in news agency coverage. The similarity between the quantitative aspects of news agency files and national media content around the world is surprising. Do the Big Four determine the nature of international news flow?

This question is addressed in Chapter 12, "A Test of the Cultural Dependency Hypothesis." It examines the question of news agency influence on national media by reinterpreting the argument of media dependency in the Third World in terms of the popular thesis that the direct effect of mass media is their influence on the salience of events, but not necessarily how they interpret the world around them. In this case, the audience is the national media gatekeeper, and the research question is: does the "menu" of foreign news made available by the Western news agencies influence the "diet" of foreign news selected by the national media gatekeeper?

The answer, on the whole, is "yes," although there are important qualifications. The Latin American media diets closely follow the news agency menus in geographic origin and topics. But when cultural meanings are included—in this study measured by the presence of a set of "themes and references"—the correlation drops. The author suggests a reformulation of the agenda-setting thesis in the international setting: the news agencies influence what parts of the world national media pay attention to and the range of events they consider important; but at the crucial level of cultural interpretation, the national gatekeepers intervene to provide their own perspective. This suggests that our earlier illustration of journalists at work in the African newsrooms editing in their own interpretation of news agency copy could be seen in other parts of the Third World as well (See Chapter 3).

This chapter emphasizes the gatekeeper research tradition, which focuses on individuals in the international news flow who must choose the specific stories to pass on to audiences or other gatekeepers downstream. Of course, the menu of material available to any gatekeeper is not generated spontaneously. It is the product of decisions upstream of what ought to be reported and what can be reported. We typically think of these decisions as questions of journalism, but they are also questions of politics and economics.

Some of the most cogent criticism of Western journalism has emphasized the links between journalism and the political and economic system within which journalists operate. The system is partly national, of course, and we have seen how news almost universally reflects national interests. But the world news system is a part of the world system as well as a reflection of it. The menu of news available to gatekeepers is certainly influenced, if not determined, by an international system in which some nations are dominant in influence over others.

One theory defines this "structural imperialism" as "a sophisticated type of dominance relation which cuts across nations, basing itself on a bridgehead which the center of the center nation establishes in the center of the periphery nation for the joint benefit of both." Chapter 13, "A Test of Galtung's Theory of Structural Imperialism," uses data from the full UNESCO/IAMCR study to examine this theory.

The structural imperialism theory, on the whole, does not hold up. While finding more support for agenda-setting influence of the world news agencies, other expectations derived from the theory were not supported. In particular, hypotheses about the dominance of flow between powerful Western "center" nations and weaker Third World "peripheral" nations and corresponding restricted flows within peripheral regions were not supported.

The author offers three explanations: (1) the international system is more complex than proponents of structural imperialism acknowledge, (2) Third World nations are more active in international news flow than they are given credit for, (3) and generalizations about the flow of economic and political influence cannot necessarily be extended to communication flows.

The final chapter, "Determinants of Foreign Coverage in U.S. Newspapers," attempts to synthesize these two different approaches to the study of international news flow. The author acknowledges the importance of gatekeeper decisions but also recognizes that economic and political factors influence both the quantity and quality of information that will be available to the gatekeeper and the news values that will be invoked in deciding what stories to accept and what to reject.

Using the foreign coverage in the sample of American media as the dependent variable, the author tries to predict the level of coverage of various nations of the world based on a set of economic and political variables that index the countries' political and economic relationships with the United States.

The hypotheses, tested with single- and multistage structural equations, found support for the influence of economic and political relationships on news coverage, although extraordinary events can erupt in countries that do not get routinely heavy attention from the American media.

The chapter deals only with foreign coverage in the United States, although the similarity of news in most countries leads one to suspect that data on other countries would produce similar patterns.

The author finds little hope that changes in news values, which would be implemented by gatekeepers responding more sensitively to pleas for a broader definition of news, are likely as long as Western news agency resources are deployed to cover Western political and economic interests. He does find hope, however, in the expansion of alternative and regional services that would give key gatekeepers in all parts of the world more information and a wider variety of information.

It is appropriate that this section, and the book, end on a positive note. All of the authors agree that it is possible to improve the quality of news coverage around the world, but the task is not simple or easy. If any grand theme runs through these varied probings of this unique data set, it is the importance of the twin pillars of UNESCO declarations: the need for a better-balanced flow of news and information in all parts of the world but also the continuing need for the free flow of information.

CHAPTER 11

Foreign News in the Western Agencies

David H. Weaver and G. Cleveland Wilhoit

ABOUT two-thirds of foreign news in the Third World press and a great proportion in more developed countries originates in the major wire services (Schramm 1980). It is small wonder, then, that the "Big Four" Western services —the Associated Press, United Press International, Reuters, and Agence France-Presse—are singled out for criticism in the debate about world news flow. These four agencies are accused of monopolizing the international flow of news, of failing to serve the needs of the Third World, and of misrepresenting two-thirds of humanity to itself and to the rest of the world.

Definitive histories of the major wire services or explanations of their rise to worldwide influence have yet to be written. (See Schwarzlose 1979; Boyd-Barrett 1980.) One historian, however, correlates the rise of Western-style "objectivity" with the development of wire news in the latter part of the nineteenth century in the United States. Shaw (1967) argues that marketing news to partisan newspapers of widely differing political views led to an emphasis on speed, presentation of facts without elaborate interpretation, and roughly equal attention to different points of view.

Schudson (1978) rejects Shaw's interpretation of the role of the American wire services in fostering objectivity in American journalism. Schudson argues that the notion of objectivity did not emerge as central in journalism until the 1930s, suggesting that the general emergence of logical positivism and the scientific method was the broad social force that produced Western journalistic "objectivity."

In any case, it is clear that news written in the Western wire service style has been widely used around the world. For example, a recent study found that in Yugoslavia—a nation that has been a cradle of many of the ideas supporting a new world information order—press coverage of the United States comes largely from Western news agencies. Becker, Underwood, and Lemish

(1980) found, further, that the Yugoslav papers did very little editing of the original wire copy. In tone and topic, the view of the United States in Yugoslav newspapers was largely that of the Western wires.

Alternative sources to the Western news agencies are widely available, however. Third World editors and national news agency staffs (staple users of the wire services) have access to the Soviet news agency TASS, the Non-Aligned News Agencies pool, and a rapidly increasing number of regional and specialty news services. TASS is used in Eastern Europe and a small number of Third World countries, but the Yugoslav study cited here and a recent study in Asia by Wilbur Schramm and Ervin Atwood (1980) suggest the Western wires are still used substantially in most parts of the world, even in Eastern Europe.

NATIONAL NEWS AGENCIES. Ninety national news agencies, 50 of them controlled by government, are listed in the 1975 UNESCO directory of world communications (UNESCO 1975). All Asian nations from the eastern Mediterranean to the Pacific had news agencies, except Cyprus, Kuwait, Saudi Arabia, Singapore, and Thailand. Of 40 African countries, 13 had no agency. Only five Latin American countries had national news agencies.

Since the publication of the UNESCO directory, dozens of other national and regional agencies have emerged, many with UNESCO encouragement. A recent census by Freedom House counted 104 government news agencies, a figure that represents 68 percent of the world's nation-states (Sussman 1980).

Many of the national news organizations also supply news to other news agencies. For example, according to the UNESCO directory, the national news agencies of Zaire (AZAP), Congo (ACI), Chad (ATP), and the Federal Republic of Germany (DPA) supply news to Cameroon's national news organization (ACAP). The agencies of the German Democratic Republic (ADN), the Federal Republic of Germany (DPA), Romania (AGERPRESS), Czechoslovakia (CTK), and Yugoslavia (TANJUG) supply news to the Egyptian agency (MENA), an important regional wire. The Tunisian news agency (TAP) exchanges with 12 news agencies, and Syria's SANA has agreements with 15 news agencies.

The news agency of the German Democratic Republic in 1975 had contracts with 65 foreign news services (International Organization of Journalists 1969). Romania's AGERPRESS received news from 36 agencies. CTK of Czechoslovakia had 50 agreements. Hungary's MTI had exclusive distribution contracts with 17 foreign agencies. Poland's PAP had 32 external wire sources and had 5,200 subscribers, including 2,000 in foreign countries.

In a study conducted for UNESCO, Phil Harris (1977) noted that the Ghana News Agency used 12 external wires, six of them on a regular basis. Five of the services were from the West, five from socialist countries, and two were services of northern Africa. Harris found widespread Ghanian use of the Western wires, in spite of some annoyance by foreign editors about choices of adjectives in Western wire stories. They easily solved the problem by substituting "nationalist" for "terrorist" or "freedom fighters" for "guerrillas," changes requiring little substantive editing.

A major study of Asian prestige-newspaper use of wire news found heavy reliance upon the Western wires for their foreign news, including news about the Third World. Schramm's research (Schramm 1980) suggested, however, that the Asian newspapers were regional and local in orientation, using an average of only 23 foreign Third World stories on a typical day. Non-Third World news was significantly less. It was clear from Schramm's work that the Western wires were delivering much more foreign news and a great deal more Third World news and Asian news than the Asian newspapers chose to use.

The roughly 100 national news agencies, then, are an important element in world news flow about which little is known. Pinch (1978) found that about three-quarters of the Third World nation-states (with Latin America being the main exception) channel wire service news through their national news agencies. The mass media in those countries, then, are not direct subscribers to external news services, making the national news agency a focal gatekeeper for external wire news.

While little definitive published work is available about the structure and function of the major wire services in world information flow, several conclusions appear plausible: (1) the four major Western wire services supply the great bulk of foreign news used by most of the world's mass media; (2) the Western wires supply a great deal more foreign news than domestic mass media use; and (3) the more than 100 national news agencies, primarily in the Third World, are in a position to play a major gatekeeping and news supply role, although very little is known about the extent to which those roles are exercised in the present world communication picture.

METHOD. Using the coding scheme of the full UNESCO project with modifications appropriate for news agency files, we examined coverage of the following wire service wires:

1. Associated Press (AP) Interbureau (IB) wire to smaller media in the United States
2. United Press International (UPI) state (regional) wire to smaller media in the United States
3. AP wire to three countries of Latin America
4. UPI wire to Latin America
5. Agence France-Presse wire to Latin America
6. Reuters wire to Latin America

7. Reuters wire to the Middle East, edited in Beirut

8. AFP wire to Francophone Africa

Requests were also sent to TASS and the Non-Aligned News Agencies pool for copies of their files. However, neither service responded.

The content sample corresponds to the approach described in the larger report. The sampled days included a continuous six-day week (April 5–10, 1979) and a "constructed" (random sample) week (March 5, April 18, May 2, May 18, June 6, and June 16, 1979) for the AP and UPI regional wires in the United States. Only a continuous six-day week (April 23–28, 1979) was sampled for the other wire service sample.

RESULTS. Tables 11.1 to 11.8 reveal the amount, location, and kind of international news being carried by selected services of the Associated Press, United Press International, Reuters, and Agence France-Presse during sampled days in the spring of 1979. As in the main report on newspapers, radio, and television news, these figures must be interpreted with caution because of the problems inherent in any classification scheme that involves overlapping categories. In spite of such problems, however, these figures do provide a general map of the amounts and kinds of international news flowing through selected services of the Big Four Western news agencies in the spring of 1979.

Table 11.1 provides some idea of the amount of international news reporting available to subscribers of the AP and UPI regional wires in the United States, all four wire services to Latin America, and the services of Reuters to the Middle East and AFP to Francophone Africa. It appears at first glance that AP and UPI provide ten times the volume of international news to Latin America as to small- and medium-sized news organizations in the United States. This is true, however, in large part because the domestic news originating in the United States is coded as foreign, or international, news on the Latin American wires. About one-fourth of the news on the AP wire to Latin America origi-

Table 11.1. International wire news on an average day

	Number of stories	Length (column-centimeters)
AP regional wire to USA	17	250
UPI regional wire to USA	12	236
AP to Latin America	125	2,962
UPI to Latin America	134	2,626
AFP to Latin America	222	3,844
Reuters to Latin America	87	2,010
Reuters to Middle East	59	457
AFP to Francophone Africa	160	2,864

nates in the United States, and nearly one-third of such news on the UPI wire to Latin America is located in the United States. But nearly 40 percent of the news on both these wires is located in Latin American countries. The figures in Table 11.1 suggest that a large amount of international news is available each day for use by subscribers in Latin America and Francophone Africa, a moderate amount to subscribers in the Middle East, and a modest amount to smaller media in the United States.

Judging from these figures, and the other studies referred to earlier in this report, there is little problem with the amount of international news available to various national news agencies and media. In fact, there is evidence from earlier studies that the Western wires supply a great deal more foreign news than domestic media in most countries can, and do, use.

In the analysis of the national data, the press systems with a large amount of international news reporting include those of countries in Latin America and Africa, areas that receive large amounts of wire service international news. The press systems of at least two countries in the Middle East (Egypt and Iran) contain relatively small amounts of international news, matched by small amounts of foreign news in the wires serving those nations. Thus, there does appear to be at least a rough correlation between the amount of Western wire service international news flowing into a region of the world and the amount of international news in the press of that region.

Table 11.2 shows that in the U.S. regional wires of AP and UPI, the bulk of international news reporting concerned foreign news abroad, as was true in the press systems of most of the countries included in the main report. Because the stories of the other wire services were not coded into these categories, it was not possible to tell if this is a common pattern, but the international news content of the press systems analyzed in the main report leads us to suspect that it is. Roughly half of the AP and UPI international news stories concerned relations between states, and the percentage of such news in the U.S. press analyzed in the main report (42 percent) closely reflects that proportion, suggesting again that there is a correlation between the amount of wire service international news and the amount of such news in the press of a given country or region.

Table 11.2. Type of wire service story

	AP regional wire to USA $n = 199$	UPI regional wire to USA $n = 138$
Home news abroad	18%	21%
Foreign news at home	1	0
Foreign news abroad	81	79
Other or uncertain	0	0
Relations between states	41	49

Table 11.3 presents the frequencies for location of international wire service news by region of the world. As is true of the press systems analyzed in the main report, the single most important finding is that the Western wire services going into various other regions (Latin America, the Middle East, and Africa) concentrate on foreign news about the countries of those regions. All four wire services to Latin America contain more news originating in Latin America than in any other region (from 40 percent to 48 percent, as reported in Table 11.3). Reuters to the Middle East contains far more news originating in the Middle East (55 percent) than in any other region. Likewise, AFP to Francophone Africa contains more news originating in Africa (35 percent) than in any other region. The AP and UPI regional wires in the United States do, of course, contain more *overall* news originating in North America than in any other region, but only foreign datelined stories were coded, so the percentages reported in Table 11.3 are negligible for North America. It is noteworthy, however, that the U.S. regional wires carried nearly the same proportions of news originating in Asia and the Middle East as in Western Europe.

Taken together, these findings suggest that the Big Four Western news agencies are not ignoring Third World countries in favor of the more-developed First World countries.

Of course, the selection of the wire services for study must be kept in mind when discussing the relative emphasis of different areas of the world. But there is evidence here consistent with Schramm's (1980) finding that the Western news agencies deliver much more Third World news than the Asian newspapers he studied chose to use. There is also support for the claim, however, that Latin America is largely ignored in the Western wire services flowing into the United States, the Middle East, and Africa. Even though geographical proximity appears to be the prime criterion for determining newsworthiness in the Big Four Western news agencies, just as it was for the press systems studied in the main report, political and economic ties and critical events undoubtedly play an important role in determining news coverage priorities.

COVERAGE OF THE THIRD WORLD IN THE WEST. Few published studies have looked closely at Western wire service coverage of foreign lands, particularly of their coverage of the Third World. Third World critics score Western coverage of their countries as disproportionate and distorted, with too little coverage and too much concentration on the violent, bizarre, and conflictual. Studies that are available suggest that Third World complaints deserve a closer look.

A quarter century ago, Cutlip (1954) analyzed the content and flow of the AP wires in the United States, finding that only about 5 percent to 10 percent of state wire copy dealt with foreign news. Two decades later, Al Hester (1971) found that foreign datelines constituted about 20 percent of the Inter-

Table 11.3. Geographic origin of international news

	AP Reg.	UPI Reg.	AP to L Am	UPI to L Am	AFP to L Am	Reuters L Am	Reuters Mid E	AFP to Africa
n =	199	138	2,250	802	1,326	521	346	944
North America	1%	1%	23%	30%	14%	10%	3%	6%
Latin America	5	7	40	40	47	48	1	3
Africa	13	15	4	3	3	4	13	35
Middle East	18	23	7	7	9	11	55	18
Asia	23	20	3	3	4	6	8	4
Western Europe	28	25	16	14	19	13	18	26
Eastern Europe	11	8	3	3	2	4	3	4
General	1	0	3	1	1	4	0	4

bureau wire. Hester also found evidence that foreign wire news was heavily oriented to European countries and that news about developing countries tended
to emphasize violence, famine, and social disintegration.

Others have argued that wire news is more balanced in foreign coverage
than critics say, and that the problem lies in news selection patterns of mass
media editors (Hamilton 1977). Thus, the background studies suggest a need
for much more extensive baseline data on the performance by wire services in
foreign coverage.

In addition to these studies concerning U.S. wire service coverage of foreign countries, many other studies suggest that general U.S. media coverage
of the rest of the world, especially the Third World countries, tends to be crisis-
oriented and drawn to sensational and atypical happenings. Tatarian (1977)
argues that there is an acknowledged tendency among Western media, including the wire services, to devote greater attention to the Third World in times
of disaster, crises, and confrontation. Aggarwala (1977) concludes that most
of the Third World news is negative and deals with such subjects as famines,
natural disasters, and political and military intrigues. Lent (1977) supports
the crisis orientation of news from the less-developed countries of the world.
Golding and Elliott (1974) argue that much of the coverage of developing nations is centered on nations subject to repetitive crises or military conflicts.

Other scholars suggest that news about the less-developed countries of
the world is likely to constitute a rather small proportion of all Western foreign
news. Hester (1976) found that news concerning Western Europe predominated in the foreign news coverage of U.S. wire services and that TV "news
from Asia, Africa and Latin America was generally little evidenced, unless
U.S. interests were directly involved." Gerbner and Marvanyi (1977), studying
foreign news coverage in nine countries, found that foreign news content constituted about 16 percent of the total news space for the *New York Times* in
1970, as Kayser found in 1951, and that only 3 percent of U.S. press coverage
was devoted to central and southern Africa.

In short, these previous studies and recent complaints of Third World
countries regarding Western news coverage led us to expect the less-developed
countries of the world as a group would receive less of the foreign news coverage in the wire services we studied than would the more-developed countries,
and that the wire service coverage of the less-developed countries would be more
crisis and conflict oriented than would the coverage of the more-developed
countries.

POLITICS IN THE NEWS. Table 11.4 contains the proportions of news from
each wire service devoted to each of 18 major topics. As in the main report,
only the main topic of each story is represented in this table; the detailed subtopics are not reported here. The general finding, as in the main report, is that

Table 11.4. Topics in international news

	AP Reg.	UPI Reg.	AP to LA	UPI to LA	AFP to LA	Reuters LA	Reuters Mid E	AFP to Africa
n =	199	138	2,250	802	1,326	521	346	944
Int'l politics	13%	25%	21%	11%	12%	30%	35%	32%
Domestic politics	21	28	12	14	18	14	18	16
Military, defense	18	14	3	3	3	4	25	11
Economics	8	4	18	18	18	14	7	15
Int'l aid	1	1	1	1	1	1	1	2
Social service	2	0	1	0	1	1	0	1
Crime, legal	11	13	8	9	9	6	7	8
Culture	3	2	1	1	1	0	1	1
Religion	6	4	1	2	1	0	1	0
Science, medicine	1	1	1	3	2	0	0	1
Sports	0	0	19	23	23	19	0	5
Entertainment	1	0	1	1	1	0	1	0
Personalities	2	1	1	2	1	2	0	0
Human interest	6	4	1	1	1	1	0	1
Student	1	0	1	0	0	1	0	1
Ecology	1	0	1	1	1	1	0	0
Natural disaster	4	2	6	6	4	4	5	2
Other	2	1	4	4	3	2	0	3

international wire news reporting equals politics. There is some deviation from this pattern in the four wires to Latin America, where economic matters and sports are emphasized more heavily than in the other wires, but it is clear that political and military matters make up the bulk of Western wire service reporting, leaving little space for cultural, religious, scientific, and medical news. It is also equally clear, however, that the wires do not devote as much coverage to natural disasters and crime as has been claimed by some critics.

It appears that Reuters and AFP emphasize international politics (diplomatic and political activity *between* states) more than do AP or UPI, and the two regional wire services in the United States emphasize domestic politics and military matters more than do the wires to the other regions, except for Reuters to the Middle East, which had the highest proportion of stories about military and defense.

The main report found that the press of the more-developed industrialized nations concentrated less on political, military, and economic matters than did the press of the less-developed countries, but no such difference emerged in our study of the Western wire services. About the same proportion of news was devoted to the first four "hard news" categories by the wire services flowing into the United States as by those flowing into the other areas of the world (roughly 50 percent to 70 percent). Reuters to the Middle East and Agence France-Presse to Africa carried the most such news, and UPI and AFP to Latin America carried the least.

Thus, the topics of international reporting by the Big Four Western wires are quite similar, regardless of their destination. The only noticeable exceptions are more emphasis on economics and sports in the wires going to Latin America, and more emphasis on crime and religion and human interest matters in the regional wires going to media in the United States.

MAIN TOPICS. Table 11.5 provides a profile of the topic of news by the region for each of the eight wire services included in this report. Put another way, Table 11.5 gives us a "news profile" for each region for each wire service. (As in the main report, it must be remembered that no statistical tests are used to analyze these data and many of the percentages are based on very few stories.)

In the regional wires to the United States, there are only five foreign-datelined news stories originating in North America, and these five stories deal mainly with what can be called "hard news"—politics, economics, and crime. In the four wire services to Latin America, the news from North America is mainly about politics, economics, and sports, with little mention of military matters and some coverage of crime and science. This pattern also holds to a large extent for Reuters to the Middle East and AFP to Africa, but with much less coverage of sports by both wires and much more coverage of domestic politics and crime by Reuters to the Middle East.

News coverage of Latin America by AP and UPI regional wires in the United States focuses heavily on domestic politics, with some coverage of international politics, crime, science, and natural disasters. In the four wires going to Latin America, however, there is much less emphasis on domestic politics in Latin America and much more coverage of Latin American economics and sports. Latin America is nearly invisible in the Reuters wire to the Middle east; and in AFP's African wire, the coverage of Latin American countries focuses on politics, economics, crime, and natural disasters.

Turning to news coverage of Africa, it is apparent that coverage in the U.S. regional wires deals mainly with military matters and domestic politics. Whereas military and defense were nearly ignored in Latin American coverage, these topics constitute nearly one-half of the coverage about Africa in the AP and UPI wires going to smaller media in the United States. But for some unknown reason, the AP and UPI wires to Latin America concentrate much less on military matters in their coverage of Africa, and the same is true for Reuters and AFP to Latin America. There is considerable emphasis on African domestic politics in all the wires to Latin America and generally more coverage of international politics and sports from Africa than in the American regional wires.

Reuters' Middle East wire covered Africa almost entirely in terms of politics and military matters; and AFP's African wire concentrated more on economics and noticeably less on domestic politics in its coverage of Africa than did the other Western news agency wires. This pattern of focusing less on domestic politics and more on economics in covering the region to which the wire service is directed is also evident in Latin America. Perhaps there is so much coverage of domestic politics in the media indigenous to a given region or in the national wire services that the Western wires do not wish to compete with, or duplicate, such coverage. Or perhaps such coverage is politically more sensitive when directed toward the region to which it refers. It must be remembered, too, that in terms of absolute numbers of stories, there is *not* actually less coverage of domestic politics in those regions to which the wires are directed. Because of the larger number of total stories devoted to the "home" regions by each wire service, it is only the *proportions* of news about domestic politics that are less, not the number of stories.

Coverage of the Middle East by the American regional wires concentrates on politics, military matters, and crime. This pattern is generally repeated in the other Western wire services studied here. With the exception of AFP to Africa, it is clear that international politics is more heavily emphasized in coverage of the Middle East than in coverage of North America, Latin America, or Africa. And in all eight wires, international politics is the most heavily covered topic in the Middle East, a finding that is not surprising in view of the Middle East peace negotiations between Israel and Egypt and the Iranian revolution. This finding is also consistent with the coverage of the Middle East in

Table 11.5. Main topic by region for eight wire services

AP REGIONAL WIRE TO UNITED STATES

	N Am	L Am	Africa	Mid E	Asia	W Eur	E Eur	Gen
n =	3*	11*	26	35	46	55	22	1*
Int'l politics	0%	9%	0%	31%	4%	11%	27%	0%
Domestic politics	33	45	35	23	17	16	4	100
Military, defense	0	9	42	26	26	5	0	0
Economics	33	9	4	6	13	9	5	0
Int'l aid	0	0	0	0	2	0	0	0
Social services	33	0	4	0	2	3	0	0
Crime, legal	0	0	4	11	11	20	9	0
Culture	0	0	0	0	4	3	9	0
Religion	0	0	0	3	2	12	14	0
Science, medicine	0	0	0	0	0	3	4	0
Sports	0	0	0	0	0	0	0	0
Entertainment	0	0	0	0	2	2	0	0
Personalities	0	9	4	0	2	2	0	0
Human interest	0	9	8	0	7	9	5	0
Student	0	0	0	0	2	0	0	0
Ecology	0	0	0	0	0	2	0	0
Natural disaster	0	0	0	0	6	2	14	0
Other	0	9	0	0	0	2	9	0

*Although small *n*'s are more likely to produce misleading percentages, we report the percentages here and in other tables for the sake of tabular consistency.

UPI REGIONAL WIRE TO UNITED STATES

	N Am	L Am	Africa	Mid E	Asia	W Eur	E Eur	Gen
n =	2	10	21	32	28	34	13	0
Int'l politics	0%	10%	9%	34%	21%	18%	69%	0%
Domestic politics	0	40	43	31	29	21	0	0
Military, defense	0	0	48	13	11	3	8	0
Economics	0	10	0	3	0	9	0	0
Int'l aid	0	0	0	0	4	0	0	0
Social services	0	0	0	0	0	0	0	0
Crime, legal	100	20	0	13	14	18	0	0
Culture	0	0	0	3	0	6	0	0
Religion	0	0	0	0	0	9	15	0
Science, medicine	0	10	0	0	0	0	0	0
Sports	0	0	0	0	0	0	0	0
Entertainment	0	0	0	0	0	0	0	0
Personalities	0	0	0	0	4	0	0	0
Human interest	0	0	0	0	11	9	0	0
Student	0	0	0	0	0	0	0	0
Ecology	0	0	0	0	0	0	0	0
Natural disaster	0	10	0	3	0	0	8	0
Other	0	0	0	0	4	3	0	0

Table 11.5 (continued)

AP TO LATIN AMERICA

n =	N Am 574	L Am 828	Africa 91	Mid E 157	Asia 88	W Eur 443	E Eur 52	Gen 9
Int'l politics	11%	18%	24%	48%	44%	18%	65%	0%
Domestic politics	6	14	46	11	13	11	0	0
Military, defense	1	1	9	19	13	4	2	0
Economics	26	18	1	3	10	16	0	56
Int'l aid	3	1	1	0	1	1	2	0
Social services	1	1	0	0	1	1	0	0
Crime, legal	7	7	10	15	0	8	11	0
Culture	1	1	0	1	0	2	2	0
Religion	1	1	0	0	0	2	2	0
Science, medicine	2	1	0	0	0	2	0	0
Sports	24	23	3	1	6	21	6	11
Entertainment	1	1	0	0	0	3	0	0
Personalities	1	1	0	0	0	1	0	0
Human interest	1	0	1	0	2	2	0	0
Student	1	1	1	0	0	0	0	0
Ecology	2	1	0	0	0	1	0	0
Natural disaster	7	8	2	0	7	4	2	0
Other	4	3	1	1	3	3	8	33

UPI TO LATIN AMERICA

	N Am	L Am	Africa	Mid E	Asia	W Eur	E Eur	Gen
n =	237	320	23	57	25	110	26	0
Int'l politics	5%	11%	9%	35%	16%	13%	26%	0%
Domestic politics	8	15	39	32	28	9	4	0
Military, defense	1	1	9	26	12	4	0	40
Economics	26	18	4	0	12	17	0	40
Int'l aid	1	0	13	0	0	0	0	0
Social services	0	1	0	0	0	0	0	0
Crime, legal	8	9	4	4	8	12	22	0
Culture	1	1	0	0	0	2	0	20
Religion	1	1	0	0	0	4	4	0
Science, medicine	6	1	0	0	0	1	9	0
Sports	28	26	17	0	8	21	13	0
Entertainment	1	0	0	0	8	3	0	0
Personalities	4	1	0	0	0	1	0	0
Human interest	1	3	0	0	4	1	0	0
Student	1	1	0	0	0	0	0	0
Ecology	1	1	0	0	0	0	4	0
Natural disaster	4	8	4	3	0	8	4	0
Other	3	4	0	0	4	4	13	0

Table 11.5 *(continued)*

AFP TO LATIN AMERICA

	N Am	L Am	Africa	Mid E	Asia	W Eur	E Eur	Gen
n =	188	615	34	124	58	250	30	15
Int'l politics	9%	11%	18%	31%	9%	9%	20%	0%
Domestic politics	13	18	35	23	22	13	23	0
Military, defense	4	2	15	27	22	2	3	0
Economics	17	20	0	2	15	17	0	93
Int'l aid	5	1	0	2	2	0	3	0
Social services	0	1	0	0	0	1	3	0
Crime, legal	6	9	9	11	3	8	10	0
Culture	1	1	0	0	2	2	0	0
Religion	0	1	0	0	0	4	0	0
Science, medicine	6	1	3	0	2	2	10	0
Sports	28	23	12	1	21	28	23	7
Entertainment	0	1	0	0	0	4	0	0
Personalities	3	1	0	0	0	0	0	0
Human interest	1	1	0	1	0	2	0	0
Student	1	1	0	0	0	0	0	0
Ecology	2	11	0	0	0	1	0	0
Natural disaster	3	6	3	0	2	2	3	0
Other	1	2	6	2	0	5	0	0

REUTERS TO LATIN AMERICA

	N Am	L Am	Africa	Mid E	Asia	W Eur	E Eur	Gen
n =	56	256	19	59	34	83	12	0
Int'l politics	21%	23%	47%	59%	41%	28%	42%	0%
Domestic politics	9	14	26	15	6	21	8	0
Military, defense	5	2	5	15	3	2	0	0
Economics	13	21	0	3	15	4	8	0
Int'l aid	2	1	0	0	0	0	0	0
Social services	0	1	0	0	3	0	0	0
Crime, legal	5	7	11	5	3	6	0	0
Culture	0	1	0	0	3	0	0	0
Religion	0	0	0	0	3	1	0	0
Science, medicine	0	1	0	0	0	0	0	0
Sports	25	19	5	0	18	29	33	0
Entertainment	0	1	0	0	0	1	0	0
Personalities	7	1	0	0	0	1	0	0
Human interest	2	1	0	0	6	1	0	0
Student	0	1	0	0	0	0	0	0
Ecology	2	1	0	0	0	1	0	0
Natural disaster	3	5	5	0	0	1	8	0
Other	4	1	0	2	0	4	0	0

Table 11.5 *(continued)*

REUTERS TO MIDDLE EAST

	N Am	L Am	Africa	Mid E	Asia	W Eur	E Eur	Gen
n =	9	2	44	192	29	61	9	0
Int'l politics	0%	0%	30%	40%	42%	26%	56%	0%
Domestic politics	56	0	25	16	4	23	0	0
Military, defense	0	0	25	31	17	16	0	0
Economics	11	0	5	5	17	7	22	0
Int'l aid	0	0	2	0	0	2	0	0
Social services	0	0	0	0	0	0	0	0
Crime, legal	22	0	4	4	7	13	22	0
Culture	0	0	0	0	3	2	0	0
Religion	0	0	2	1	3	2	0	0
Science, medicine	0	0	0	0	0	0	0	0
Sports	0	0	0	0	0	0	0	0
Entertainment	0	0	0	0	3	2	0	0
Personalities	0	0	0	0	0	0	0	0
Human interest	0	0	0	0	0	2	0	0
Student	0	0	0	0	0	0	0	0
Ecology	0	0	0	0	0	0	0	0
Natural disaster	11	50	7	3	3	6	0	0
Other	0	50	0	0	0	0	0	0

AFP TO AFRICA

	N Am	L Am	Africa	Mid E	Asia	W Eur	E Eur	Gen
n =	56	29	332	172	35	251	39	31
Int'l politics	27%	7%	43%	38%	46%	16%	56%	7%
Domestic politics	20	10	15	13	11	22	5	3
Military, defense	3	4	9	30	6	3	13	6
Economics	16	10	10	3	6	30	0	55
Int'l aid	3	0	3	1	3	1	0	0
Social services	0	7	2	0	6	1	0	0
Crime, legal	2	24	6	10	3	8	10	3
Culture	2	4	1	0	0	1	0	0
Religion	0	0	1	0	0	1	0	0
Science, medicine	3	4	1	0	0	1	0	0
Sports	9	0	2	0	11	10	3	26
Entertainment	0	0	0	0	0	1	0	0
Personalities	2	7	0	0	0	0	0	0
Human interest	4	0	1	0	0	1	0	0
Student	4	0	2	0	0	1	0	0
Ecology	0	3	1	1	0	0	0	0
Natural disaster	5	17	2	1	3	1	10	0
Other	0	3	2	3	6	3	3	0

171

the press systems of other regions, as revealed in the main report, and suggests that the emphases in Western wire services are reflected to some extent in the press systems of other countries.

U.S. regional wire service coverage of Asia concentrated on political, military, and crime matters, as was true for Middle Eastern coverage, but more attention was paid to human interest material in Asia than in the Middle East. The same general pattern was followed by the four wires to Latin America, with more coverage of sports by AFP and Reuters than by AP or UPI. The picture of Asia presented to the Middle East by Reuters featured international politics, military, and economic news, with a sprinkling of crime. AFP covered Asia mainly in terms of international politics, domestic politics, and sports for its African customers.

Western Europe was covered mainly in terms of politics and crime by the American regional wires of AP and UPI, and there was noticeably more reporting on religious news than in the five regions discussed thus far. In the four wires to Latin America, coverage of Western Europe focused on politics, economics, and sports, as it did in the AFP wire to Africa. Only in the Reuters wire to the Middle East was military and defense news from Western Europe emphasized much. These findings are at odds with the conclusion in the main report that the Western European media systems show a far greater spread of interest in "softer" news items than is apparent in either the socialist or developing worlds. And this discrepancy suggests that the Big Four Western news agencies are not very effective agenda-setters of news for the Western European media systems, perhaps because there are so many other sources of international information available to these diverse media systems.

News coverage of Eastern Europe concentrates heavily on international politics and religion in the U.S. domestic wires, and on international politics, crime, and sports in the four wires to Latin America. Economic news from Eastern Europe is stressed more by Reuters to the Middle East than by the other wires, and military matters are stressed more by AFP to Africa. The emphasis on international politics by the Western wire services parallels the emphasis on international politics by the domestic media of the eastern European region, and is in line with Becker, Underwood, and Lemish's (1980) finding that the Yugoslav press relied strongly on Western news agencies for its coverage of the United States.

Aside from news of these seven regions, there is really no coverage of other parts of the world in the AP and UPI regional wires to the United States, and in Reuters' wires to Latin America and to the Middle East. The AFP wires to Francophone Africa and to Latin America carry the most coverage of other areas of the world, and this coverage deals mainly with economic matters and to a lesser extent with sports events. This pattern is partly reflected in the AP and UPI wires to Latin America, but UPI offers no coverage of sports and replaces that gap with news about military and cultural matters.

Thus, the major finding from all these cross-tabulations is that the Western news agencies consider politics to be the most newsworthy topic in news from all areas except Africa (where military matters prevail) and the general world category (where economics dominate). Close behind politics are military, economic, and crime news, regardless of the destination of the wire services. Once again, the evidence suggests that the topics of international news reporting by the Western news agencies are quite similar.

For some reason, however, there is generally more coverage of sports from most regions in the wires directed to Latin America than in the wires directed to other areas. And there is a trend of more coverage of economics and less coverage of domestic politics of countries in the region to which a wire service is directed, perhaps because the press of a given region already contains much coverage of domestic politics or because such material is more politically sensitive than other kinds of news.

Finally, there is evidence that the Big Four Western news agencies are agenda-setters for the various national press systems, except in western Europe where there appears to be much more "soft" news (dealing with cultural, scientific, and human interest subjects) than is carried by the Western wires.

NEWS LEADERS. Just as the topic of politics dominates Western international news reporting, so politicians are the most frequently mentioned actors in the news, as Table 11.6 illustrates. Government figures are especially prominent in Reuters' wire to the Middle East and in Agence France-Presse's wire to Africa. Thus, the conclusion from the main report that international news in the press systems of 29 countries is made up of political news with political actors is supported by this analysis of eight Western wires.

The only other actor categories to receive double-digit percentages were those of military figures (especially irregular military or terrorists in the U.S. wires), sports personalities (in the wires to Latin America), and ordinary people (in the U.S. wires). Ordinary people were also featured in the reporting of the press of Australia, the Soviet Union, West Germany, Greece, Iceland, the Netherlands, the United States, and Thailand, as pointed out in the main report. Such ordinary people and citizens included Vietnamese refugees, the Harrisburg, Pennsylvania, inhabitants, and Iranian demonstrators.

These parallel findings once again suggest that what is emphasized in the Western news agencies is also, to some extent, what is emphasized in the press systems of many countries. Whether this is because the press systems take the lead from the wire services, or because the wires pick up stories from the press systems, is not clear from our data, which have been collected for a single period in time. But it seems likely from past studies and from our knowledge of how wire service news is used, that the wires have more influence on the press systems than vice versa. The main report to UNESCO (Sreberny-Mohammadi

Table 11.6. Actors in wire service news

	AP to USA	UPI to USA	AP to L Am	UPI to L Am	AFP to L Am	Reuters to L Am	Reuters to Mid E	AFP to to Afr
n =	199	138	2,250	802	1,326	521	346	944
Head of state/ govt.	17%	28%	7%	6%	6%	8%	15%	14%
Other leading govt.	10	15	17	13	18	20	42	29
Nonlegitimate oppos.	1	0	1	1	1	0	0	1
Other legit. govt.	2	7	3	3	3	4	2	4
Local govt. official	1	0	1	1	1	1	0	1
Diplomat/ ambassador	1	1	2	2	4	5	1	3
Regular military	5	6	4	4	4	8	11	6
Irregular military	12	11	2	2	2	2	5	2
Industry	2	0	8	6	5	6	4	4
Workers, union	1	1	3	5	3	3	1	1
Pressure groups	1	1	3	1	1	1	1	1
Religions	3	1	1	1	2	1	2	1
Sports	0	0	21	24	20	18	0	5

Media	4	1	3	3	2	3	2	3
Academics, scientists	3	1	2	3	3	2	1	2
Police	0	1	1	2	1	1	1	1
Judiciary/lawyer	1	1	1	1	1	1	1	1
Criminal/prisoner	3	1	2	2	1	3	2	1
Celebrities/show biz	1	1	1	1	3	1	0	1
Aristocracy/royalty	1	1	1	1	1	1	1	
Nation(s)	1	3	3	2	4	0	1	0
United Nations	1	0	1	1	0	3	1	0
Other intergovt.	3	1	1	1	1	1	1	3
Other int'l bodies	0	0	0	1	1	1	1	2
Citizens	19	15	6	6	5	5	1	1
Other	2	1	2	3	6	1	1	2
No human actor	4	3	4	4	2	1	2	8

1981) showed that only four of the 29 nations analyzed obtained more than 50 percent of their international news from the Big Four Western news agencies (Mexico, Iran, Egypt, and Indonesia), and most of the rest received 20 percent to 50 percent from them. This is considerably less than the figure of two-thirds reported by Schramm (1980). But a lot of the material credited to the national news agency or not credited at all apparently is derived from the Western agencies. (See Harris 1977.) There is a kind of "two-step" flow from the Big Four Western agencies to home news agencies to various media that masks the true influence of the Western wires.

COVERAGE OF TWO WORLDS. We also carried out a more detailed comparison of the coverage of the more-developed and less-developed countries, using only the AP and UPI regional wire service sample to media in the United States. The data for this comparison were obtained in the same manner as the other data analyzed in this report, and a "pretest" sample from February 20, 22, 26, March 7 and 16, 1979, was also included. This "pretest" sample represented one consecutive five-day week chosen randomly from the first two months of 1979, and one constructed week sample chosen from the first three months of the year.

In order to compare the amount and kind of regional wire service coverage of more-developed and less-developed countries of the world, it was necessary to divide the 91 countries included in our study into these two groups. This is, of course, a somewhat problematic and challenging task, given the absence of any "official" list to serve as a baseline. Our classification was based primarily upon a North-South geographical dimension, with the more-developed countries tending to fall into the Northern Hemisphere and the less-developed countries tending to fall into the Southern Hemisphere. This classification follows the logic behind the first North-South dialogue conference on international economic cooperation held in Paris in December of 1975.

We decided to put the countries of Europe and the USSR, North America, Japan, Australia, and South Africa in the more-developed (Northern) category because of their economic development status and because both Japan and Australia were members of the North group in the Paris conference. We also included Greece in the more-developed group because of its ties with the Western world. (See Table 11.7.)

In the less-developed (Southern) category, we included Africa (minus South Africa), Asia (minus the Eastern USSR), South America and Oceania (minus Australia). Yugoslavia was also included in this group, although it is a European country by any geographical standard, because of its leading role in the new world information order debate and in the Non-Aligned Movement, and its membership in the South group at the 1975 Paris conference.

Other debatable cases—especially Turkey, Israel, Hong Kong, and Por-

Table 11.7. Frequency of U.S. regional wire service coverage

	February–March sample $n = 194$	April–June sample $n = 336$
More-developed countries (n = 25)		
Australia	0.5%	0.9%
Austria	0.5	4.2
Belgium	0.0	0.6
Canada	0.5	0.9
Czechoslovakia	0.0	0.6
Denmark	0.0	0.0
France	1.5	4.2
Germany (DR)	0.0	0.0
Germany (FR)	0.0	1.2
Great Britain	10.8	6.2
Greece	0.0	0.3
Hungary	0.0	0.0
Ireland	0.5	0.9
Italy	8.8	5.0
Japan	3.6	3.0
Norway	1.0	0.3
Poland	0.0	1.5
Portugal	0.5	0.0
South Africa	0.0	0.9
Spain	0.0	0.9
Sweden	0.0	0.0
Switzerland	1.0	0.3
United States	0.5	0.6
USSR	2.6	7.1
Vatican	2.6	1.8

	February–March sample $n = 194$	April–June sample $n = 336$
Less-developed countries (n = 66)		
Afghanistan	0.5%	0.6%
Algeria	0.0	1.8
Argentina	0.0	0.0
Brazil	1.0	0.3
Burma	0.0	0.3
Cambodia	1.5	0.3
Chad	0.5	0.3
China (PR)	3.1	3.6

Table 11.7 *(continued)*

	February–March sample *n* = 194	April–June sample *n* = 336
Less-developed countries (n = 66)		
Colombia	0.0	0.6
Cuba	0.0	0.0
Cyprus	0.5	0.6
Dominican Republic	0.0	0.0
Ecquador	0.5	0.0
Egypt	2.6	4.2
El Salvador	1.0	0.0
Ethiopia	0.0	0.0
Fiji Islands	0.0	0.0
Ghana	0.0	0.9
Guyana	1.5	0.0
Hong Kong	1.5	1.2
India	0.5	0.9
Indonesia	1.0	0.3
Iran	19.1	8.3
Iraq	0.0	0.0
Israel	3.1	5.0
Jordan	0.5	0.9
Kenya	0.0	0.0
Korea (N)	0.0	0.3
Korea (S)	0.5	0.9
Kuwait	0.0	1.2
Laos	1.2	0.0
Lebanon	2.1	0.6
Liberia	0.0	0.6
Libya	0.0	0.0
Malaysia	0.5	1.2
Maldive Islands	0.5	0.0
Mauritania	0.0	0.0
Mexico	1.0	1.5
Mongolia	0.0	0.0
Nepal	0.0	0.3
Nicaragua	0.0	3.0
Nigeria	0.0	0.0
Pakistan	0.5	2.7
Palestine	0.0	0.0
Panama	0.0	0.6
Peru	0.0	0.0

Table 11.7 *(continued)*

	February–March sample	April–June sample
	n = 194	*n* = 336
Less-developed countries (n = 66)		
Philippines	2.1	0.6
Portugal	0.0	0.0
Puerto Rico	0.5	0.0
Saudi Arabia	0.0	0.0
St. Lucia	0.5	0.0
St. Vincent	0.0	0.3
Sudan	0.5	0.0
Syria	0.0	0.3
Taiwan	0.5	0.0
Tanzania	0.0	0.0
Thailand	1.0	2.1
Tunisia	0.0	0.0
Turkey	1.0	0.0
Uganda	1.5	7.4
United Emirates	0.0	0.3
Vietnam	5.7	2.1
Yemen (N)	0.5	0.3
Yemen (S)	0.0	0.0
Yugoslavia	1.5	0.6
Zimbabwe	1.5	2.1

tugal—were classified according to their concern with the UNESCO-sponsored debate on the new world information order. Of these four, only Portugal was classified as a more-developed country. Israel was classified as a less-developed country because of its comparative newness, its concern with developmental problems, and its sensitivity to the issue of cultural imperialism, especially in the form of imported television programming.

The most frequently covered less-developed countries in the "official" wire service sample were Iran, Uganda, Israel, Egypt, China, and Nicaragua. And the same was generally true for the pretest sample as well, with Iran dominating the list and Vietnam replacing Nicaragua and Uganda. The frequencies of stories about the less-developed countries of the world in Table 11.7 also suggest that most of these 66 countries received some coverage during the four weeks we studied, even if this coverage was rather sparse.

Among the 25 more-developed countries included in our study, Austria, France, West Germany, Great Britain, Italy, Japan, and the Soviet Union received the most frequent coverage. As with the less-developed countries, most of the more-developed countries received some coverage in either the pretest or official samples. In fact, we were surprised at the number of countries receiving some coverage in the AP and UPI regional wire services during the four weeks we studied. There were considerably more countries represented (69) than we expected to find in such a relatively short time period on the regional services that supply state and national news as well to smaller daily papers.

The AP and UPI carried significantly more foreign news stories from the less-developed countries than from the more-developed countries in the official two-week sample period, with UPI carrying almost twice as many stories from less-developed countries as from more-developed countries. (See Table 11.8.) And the same was true for the pretest sample, where 117 stories were located in less-developed countries and 74 were located in more developed countries. The other three stories were located in "noncountries," such as the United Nations.

Table 11.8. Comparison of U.S. regional wire service coverage—number of stories

	Less-developed	More-developed	Total	
AP	54%	46%	100%	($n = 198$)
UPI	65	35	100	($n = 138$)
Total	59	41	100	($n = 336$)

Chi-square = 3.74, df = 1, p = .05.

However, it should be remembered that the less-developed countries in our study outnumbered the more-developed countries nearly three to one, so one would expect nearly three times as much coverage of the less-developed countries as of the more-developed countries, if an equal number of stories were carried about each country. But this seems to us to be an unreasonable demand to place upon the wire services, when many of the less-developed countries of the world are far less populated than are the more-developed countries.

In short, the sheer numbers of foreign datelined stories carried by the regional wire services do not support the claim that the U.S. wire services are ignoring the less-developed countries of the world in favor of the more-developed countries in their foreign news coverage.

Both AP and UPI carried foreign news stories that were, on the average, longer when located in the less-developed countries of the world than when located in the more-developed countries. (See Table 11.9.) This was especially true for AP, where the average length in column-centimeters of the foreign news stories about the less-developed countries was one and one half times as great (17.1) as the average length for the more-developed countries (12.1). (We could not compare the pretest sample with the official sample because length was not measured for the pretest stories.)

Table 11.9. Comparison of U.S. regional wire service coverage average story length (column-centimeters)

	Less-developed	More-developed	F-test signif.
AP	17.1	12.1	$p = .002$
UPI	20.1	18.9	$p = .56$
Total	18.5	14.4	$p = .001$

In short, the average lengths of the foreign news stories in our sample do not support the claim that U.S. wire services are devoting more foreign news coverage to the more-developed countries of the world than to the less-developed countries.

As explained in the methodological appendix, each story was coded into one main topic and into no more than three subsidiary topics. The comparison of the subject matter of stories from more-developed and less-developed countries that follows is based on main and subsidiary topics combined. All differences noted between more-developed and less-developed countries are significant to the .05 level or beyond, as measured by the chi-square test.

The bulk of the regional wire service coverage for both more-developed and less-developed countries was about diplomatic and political activity between states, internal conflict or crisis, armed conflict or the threat of it, peace moves and negotiations, elections and campaigns, crime, human interest, and odd happenings. (See Table 11.10.) In short, the wire services concentrated mostly on "official" news, that which flows mainly from government and military sources.

There was very little news dealing with social problems, culture, education, health, family planning, and other social services. And there was very little wire service news dealing with international aid and economic matters, especially agricultural projects.

Overall, then, the subject matter of the regional wire service stories in general supports the claim that the Western news agencies do not report much about social and economic development as compared to political and military events. But is this tendency more pronounced in news from the less-developed countries of the world as compared to the more-developed countries?

The comparison of the 139 stories from the more-developed countries with the 197 stories from the less-developed countries in Table 11.10 indicates that stories from the less-developed countries are significantly more likely than are stories from more-developed countries to be about diplomatic/political activity between states, internal conflict or crisis, armed conflict or the threat of it, military aid, and political crime.

Wire service stories from the more-developed countries of the world, on the other hand, are significantly more likely than stories from the less-developed countries to be about nonpolitical crime, religion, human interest, or odd happenings.

Table 11.10. Comparison of subject matter (stories) of U.S. regional wire service foreign coverage

	More-developed	Less-developed	Total
$n =$	139	197	336
Diplomatic/political activity between states	34.5%	48.3%	42.6%**
Internal conflict	13.7	46.7	33.0**
Elections, govt. changes	15.1	10.1	12.2
Other politics	1.4	3.0	2.4
Armed conflict or threat	10.8	41.6	28.9**
Peace moves	10.8	17.3	14.6
Other military/defense	4.3	2.5	3.3
Agreements on trade	3.6	3.5	3.6
International trade	4.3	2.5	3.3
Capital investment	0.7	0.0	0.3
Stock exchange activities	0.0	0.0	0.0
Economic performance	2.2	0.5	1.2
Prices, inflation	0.7	1.0	0.9
Industrial projects	4.4	1.5	2.7
Agriculture	0.0	0.5	0.3
Industrial/labor relations	3.6	1.0	2.1
Monetary questions	3.6	0.0	1.5**
Other economic	0.0	2.0	1.2
Disaster/famine relief	0.0	2.5	1.5
Aid for economic purposes	1.4	1.0	1.2
Military aid	0.7	7.1	4.5**
Other aid	0.7	0.5	0.6
Social problems	3.6	1.5	2.4
Education	0.0	0.5	0.3
Health	0.7	0.0	0.3
Family planning	0.0	0.0	0.0
Other social services	0.0	0.5	0.3
Nonpolitical crime	14.4	3.6	8.1**
Political crime	9.4	17.8	14.2**
Noncriminal legal	0.0	0.5	0.3
Other crime/legal	2.9	0.0	1.2
Culture, arts	5.7	3.0	3.2
Religion	10.8	1.0	5.1**
Science, medicine	7.9	3.0	5.1
International sports	0.0	0.0	0.0
Domestic sports	0.0	0.0	0.0
Entertainment	0.7	1.0	0.9

Table 11.10 *(continued)*

	More-developed	Less-developed	Total
n =	139	197	336
Sports personalities	1.4	1.0	1.2
Entertainers	0.0	1.0	0.6
Other personalities	0.7	2.0	1.5
Human interest	22.3	4.5	11.9**
Student affairs	0.7	2.0	1.5
Energy conservation	1.4	0.5	0.9
Pollution	0.0	0.0	0.0
Other ecology	0.7	0.0	0.3
Natural disaster, accident	2.2	3.6	3.0
Other	4.3	2.0	3.0

*All three columns will total more than 100% because stories were coded into one main topic and up to three subsidiary topics; columns are based on multiple codings.

**Difference between more-developed and less-developed significant at .05 by chi-square test.

The trends are generally supported by the pretest data. Significantly more stories from the less-developed countries focus on elections, political violence, internal conflict or crisis, and armed conflict than do stories from the more-developed countries. And significantly more stories from the more-developed countries concentrate on prices, labor relations, and culture than do stories from the less-developed countries. In addition, there are very few stories in the categories of social problems, education, health, the family and other social services from either the less-developed or the more-developed countries of the world.

In short, our data on the subject matter of U.S. regional wire service foreign news coverage in the spring of 1979 supports those who claim that Western coverage of the less-developed Third World countries tends to concentrate on conflicts and crises. The largest differences we found between wire service coverage of the more-developed and less-developed countries were on the topics of internal conflict or crisis, and armed conflict.

As mentioned earlier, previous studies and more recent charges by Third World countries led us to expect that the less-developed countries would receive less of the foreign coverage of the regional wires we studied than would the more-developed countries. But our data on number and length of wire service stories did not support this expectation. In fact, there were more foreign news stories from the less-developed countries than from the more-developed countries in both the AP and UPI regional wires, and these stories were, on the average, longer than those from the more-developed countries. And in the four weeks we studied, 69 different countries were reported on, 48 of them "less-developed."

Some will argue that this finding is not typical because of the time period we studied. The Iranian revolution, the conflict between Israel and some of her Arab neighbors, and the fighting in Uganda, Vietnam, and Nicaragua did increase the number (and probably the length) of many wire service stories from less-developed countries of the world. But we would argue that it is difficult to find a time period when such events are not occurring somewhere in the world. Because of this tendency for armed conflict to be occurring somewhere in the world at any given time, our findings are probably more typical than they might appear at first.

Although our data do not support the claim that the less-developed countries of the world are neglected in favor of the more-developed countries in the foreign coverage of the two U.S. regional wire services, our findings do support the claim that Western news agencies focus on conflicts and crises when covering the less-developed or Third World countries. This may be true, however, because there simply is more open, armed conflict and crisis in these countries than in the more-developed countries.

But even in the more-developed countries, the bulk of the wire service stories we analyzed concentrated on political and military activity and crime. Economic matters, international aid efforts (except for military aid), social services, culture, scientific and medical achievements, and ecological issues such as energy and pollution were all but neglected in the coverage of *both* less-developed and more-developed countries of the world in favor of the more "official" news from governmental and military authorities.

These findings suggest that basic questions of news values among Western editors and reporters may be more fundamental and, in the long run, more important than is the amount and kind of coverage of less-developed and more-developed countries of the world. Radically different definitions of news than those that exist today might help greatly in promoting not only international but also intranational understanding and cooperation.

REFERENCES

Aggarwala, Narinder. 1977. Third World news agency. Paper presented at Tufts University conference, Third World and Press Freedom, New York.

Becker, Lee B., Paul Underwood, and Dafna Lemish. 1980. Coverage of the U.S.: A study of the Yugoslav press. Paper presented to International Association for Mass Communication Research, meeting in Caracas, Venezuela.

Boyd-Barrett, Oliver. 1980. *The international news agencies.* Beverly Hills, Calif.: Sage Publications.

Cutlip, Scott M. 1954. Content and flow of AP news. *Journalism Quarterly* 31(Winter): 434–46.

Gerbner, George, and George Marvanyi. 1977. The many worlds of the world's press. *Journal of Communication* 27(1): 52–66.

Golding, Peter, and Philip Elliott. 1974. Mass communication and social change: The imagery of development and development of imagery. In *Sociology and Development*, eds. E. de Kadt and G. Williams. London: Tavistock.

Hamilton, John Maxwell. 1977. Ho-hum, Latin America. *Columbia Journalism Review* 16(May–June): 9:10.

Harris, Phil. 1977. News dependence: The case for a new world information order. Leicester: University of Leicester. Mimeo.

Hester, Al. 1971. An analysis of news flow from developed and developing nations. *Gazette* 17: 29–43.

——————————. 1976. Foreign news on U.S. television: Through a glass darkly or not at all. Paper presented to International Association for Mass Communication Research, meeting in Leicester, United Kingdom.

International Organization of Journalists. 1969. *Handbook of news agencies.* Prague: IOJ.

Kayser, Jacques. One week's news: Comparative study of 17 major dailies for a seven-day period. Paris: UNESCO, 1953.

Lent, John. 1977. Foreign news in American media. *Journal of Communication* 27(1): 46–51.

Pinch, Edward T. 1978. A brief study of news patterns in sixteen Third World countries. Medford, Mass.: Fletcher School of Law and Diplomacy, Tufts University.

Schramm, Wilbur. 1980. Circulation of news in the Third World. In *Mass communication review yearbook,* eds. G. Cleveland Wilhoit and Harrold De Bock. Beverly Hills, Calif.: Sage Publications.

Schramm, Wilbur and Erwin Atwood. 1981. Circulation of news in the Third World—A study of Asia. Hong Kong: The Chinese University Press.

Schudson, Michael. 1978. *Discovering the news: A social history of American newspapers.* New York: Basic Books.

Schwarzlose, Richard Allen. 1979. The American Wire Services: A Study of Their Development as a Social Institution. New York: Arno Press.

Shaw, Donald L. 1967. News bias and the telegraph: A study of historical change. *Journalism Quarterly* 44(1): 3–12.

Sreberny-Mohammadi, Annabelle. 1981. *The world of the news: the news of the world.* Report submitted to UNESCO. Mimeo.

Sussman, Leonard. 1980. Press control: Is there a middle ground? Paper presented at World Communications Conference II, Ohio University, Athens, Ohio.

Tatarian, Roger. 1977. News flow in the Third World. Paper presented at a conference on the Third World and Press Freedom at the Edward R. Murrow Center for Public Diplomacy, Fletcher School of Law and Diplomacy, Tufts University, Medford, Mass.

UNESCO. 1975. *World communications.* New York: Unipub.

Test of the Cultural Dependency Hypothesis

Jere H. Link

CULTURAL dependency has become a serious international issue over the past two decades, partly because of the forum that UNESCO has provided for the increasing number of proponents of a "balanced flow" of international news. The MacBride Commission (International Commission for the Study of Communication Problems 1980) came out in favor of those advocating a more balanced flow of international news:

> The media in developing countries take a high percentage of their cultural and entertainment content from a few developed countries. . . . Local imitations of imported culture and entertainment do not improve the situation; they too lead to the imposition of external values. The connecting thread in this process is a commercial approach to culture, operating to the detriment of true values. Transnational companies are playing an ever-more-active role in the worldwide provision of communication infrastructures, news circulation, cultural products, etc. Although their role in extending facilities for cultural development has been considerable, they also promote alien attitudes across cultural frontiers.

Whatever one might say against this notion of an alien culture contaminating pristine, indigenous cultures, the theory of cultural dominance and dependency is popular. Perhaps the most vocal proponents of this idea are the Latin American *dependencia* theorists. Somavia (1976) agrees with the MacBride report that the commercial nature of international news distorts it for receiving markets; Diaz Rangel (1967) relates cultural to economic dependence in Latin America; and Beltran (1978, 185) presents probably the most ideological statement of the *dependencia* theory in this regard. He maintains that "cultural imperialism through communication is not an occasional and fortuitous event . . . . it is a vital process for 'imperial' countries to secure and maintain economic domination and political hegemony over others." That this is not merely a fashionable leftist sentiment in Latin America is clear from a 1969 statement by the bishops of Peru (Novak; 1982, 69):

> Like other nations in the Third World, we are the victims of systems that exploit our natural resources, control our political decisions, and impose on us the cultural domination of their values and consumer civilization. . . . News agencies and the communications media, which are controlled by the powerful, do not express the rights of the weak; they distort reality by filtering information in accord with vested interests.

The Latin American case may indeed not be unique to the Third World, but its early independence from direct colonial rule and other factors certainly make it a special case worth a separate study.

Gerassi (1965, 13, 41–42), who sympathizes with Latin America, nonetheless says that its "social and economic structure is decadent, corrupt, immoral and generally unsalvageable." He contends that the Latin American press, "from which most U.S. correspondents copy the information they send us to read at home, is usually a party press—an organ of political parties that, in turn, represent the oligarchies." Whatever the extent of corruption in the Latin press, Reyes Matta (1976, 42) lays the blame, not so much on the ruling oligarchies, as on the wire agencies that feed the media:

> There is a bedazzlement which conditions the practice of editors and wire-men. The old inertia makes them follow certain editorial patterns. The persistence of the stereotyped behavior confirms the news agencies in their belief that "this is what the media wants." So the vicious circle of domination perpetuates itself, condemning Latin America to ignorance of its own affairs and cutting it off from the profound changes that are unfolding in the Third World.

This "bedazzlement" is more conventionally referred to as modeling by the Latin American elites on foreign models. If charges that the Latin American media are subservient to foreign interests have any truth, then the content of their media should closely resemble that of the foreign wires they subscribe to. And if we understand the process of cultural domination to be analogous to agenda-setting, then modeling, or dependence, can be shown by means of comparative content analysis: the more dependent a receiver medium, the more its agenda of topics and themes will resemble the agenda of the foreign wires.

We may make certain reasonable assumptions on what we would expect of agenda-setting in the Latin American media. Let us first separate the news into two components: the topics, which represent the objective facts of the story, and the themes, which represent subjective overtones or labels closer to opinion than fact. Given this admittedly arbitrary distinction, we could expect an independent newspaper with access to divergent sources to reject *themes* in wire copy more often than a "dependent" newspaper, that is, one that had access only to the major wires or that had modeled its agenda on the wire agenda, for whatever reasons of ideology, prestige, or necessity. From neither dependent nor independent papers would we expect a rejection of wire topics, which, after all, are the substance of the news. Here we would expect that the structural factors of news values and traditional content would have most nearly approximated what Tunstall (1977) has called the common international agenda.

Theoretically, at least, cultural values would clash more on the level of themes than topics, which are governed by more mundane newsroom values. This is not to say that a newspaper will not present a unique blend of topics with respect to local news or non-news events and discussions: indeed, this would be precisely the place where indigenous cultural values would be most logical and appropriate. It is only in foreign news that we expect a common international agenda, due to the preponderance of the major news wires. Whether topical or thematic agendas are rejected or accepted is at the heart of news and cultural dependency. If both wire topics and themes are accepted by a medium, then there is a case for cultural dependency; if themes are rejected, then a case for cultural independence. In both cases we must try to correlate the degree of independence with the number of sources used. Presumably, the more sources used, the more independent.

METHOD. The Latin American newspapers included in the study were: *Excelsior* and *El Universal*, two leading dailies in Mexico City; *O Estado de Sao Paulo* and Rio De Janeiro's *Jornal do Brasil*, the leading dailies of Brazil's two major cities; and *Cronica*, *Clarin*, and *La Opinion*, all dailies in Buenos Aires. As of 1979, *Cronica* had the largest circulation of any paper in Argentina. Both *Cronica* and *Clarin* follow the tabloid format; all other sampled papers follow more reserved newspaper style (Pierce 1979). For the sake of economy of words, these papers will be referred to as the Mexican, Brazilian, and Argentine media, respectively; but we must not generalize findings beyond the capital cities where they have the bulk of their circulation. For some correlations, the papers' frequencies have been collapsed into aggregates that might be considered the "capital city" agenda (in Brazil's case, "leading cities" agenda), but this again is only a concession to the requirements of statistical analysis, and is thus in no way meant to apply as a generalization beyond the papers aggregated. But since these are leading Latin American dailies, their examples must be considered seriously in any study of *dependencia*.

With regard to news sources, the linchpin of agenda-setting, only the two Mexican newspapers gave attribution to nearly all their stories. As Table 12.1 shows, the Argentine media gave some attribution to the four major wires, but almost none to the commentary of their own journalists, whereas the Brazilian papers credit their own correspondents, but not the major wires.

Table 12.1. Attributed sources in Latin American newspapers

	El Universal	*Excelsior*
MEXICO		
Home country agency	2	1
UPI	225	0
AP	1	239
AFP	162	181
TASS	0	3
Other agency	4	9
Own correspondent	59	127
Other medium, home	2	7
Other medium, foreign	0	15
Other source	56	84
No source	110	226
Multiple sources	3	4
EFE (Spain)	166	115
ANSA (Italy)	31	62
New York Times Service	0	69
WashPost-LA Times	0	24
DPA (Germany)	1	26
TPI (Argentina)	1	0
NEA (US)	1	0
ACI (Congo)	1	0
Prensa Latina (Cuba)	0	30
Inter Press Service	0	16
LATIN-Reuter	0	54
LATIN	0	35
Washington Star	0	2
Total cases	825	1,329

	Clarin	*La Opinion*	*Cronica*
ARGENTINA			
Reuters	0	1	0
UPI	15	19	66
AP	27	0	54
AFP	41	28	86
Other agency	37	0	23
Own correspondent	1	6	6
Other medium, home	0	0	1
Other medium, foreign	9	2	0
Other	126	0	20

Table 12.1 *(continued)*

	Clarin	*La Opinion*	*Cronica*
No source	165	542	67
Multiple sources	49	0	5
EFE (Spain)	17	6	88
ANSA (Italy)	0	14	51
TAP (Tunisia)	1	0	0
DPA (Germany)	0	0	34
LATIN-Reuter	0	21	0
LATIN	0	8	0
Total cases	488	647	501

	O Estado de Sao Paulo	*Jornal do Brasil*
BRAZIL		
UPI	8	0
AFP	0	1
TASS	1	1
Own correspondent	61	49
Other medium, foreign	12	14
Other	85	111
No source	349	393
Multiple sources	17	1
New York Times Service	1	0
Total cases	534	570

Notes: Two sources could be coded for each story, but only the first source is included here. Reuters and LATIN-Reuters are the same agency, but the coders were given both options, because papers did not code the agency always in the proper manner: Reuters-LATIN. "Multiple sources" was an option in cases of more than one agency, but in some cases coders chose to code the first agency under its own name, then use the multiple sources code in the Source 2 position. Only the Mexican papers and *Estado* offered this problem of multiple coding.

Because of erratic attribution of sources and the problem of low numbers of cases for some data manipulations, the statistical analysis were kept simple. To avoid low n's of cases, aggregation had to be used in two ways: (1) aggregation of the papers into an artificial "country" aggregate, and (2) aggregation of the several types of foreign news (news items from the wires, commentary by local correspondents, editorials) into the aggregate of "foreign news."

Based on this strategy of data analysis, the research hypotheses concerning news dependence were operationalized as follows:

1. All four wires will have similar topical and thematic agendas.
2. All the Latin American newspapers will accept the topical agenda of the wires (to be tested by means of AP and AFP, known to be used by all papers).
3. If a newspaper rejects the thematic agenda of a wire service, it will also prove to attribute more sources than papers that do not reject the wire agenda.

Based on charges of a Western wire agenda and Latin American dependence on that agenda, these are the most reasonable hypotheses. The third represents the criteria for cultural independence in the works of two prominent libertarians: *On Liberty* (John Stuart Mill) and *Public Opinion* (Walter Lippmann). According to them, access to divergent sources increases the independence of the person from the power of any one source of opinion. Of course, it is possible that a history of exposure to one source of opinion (e.g., AP or UPI) could have conditioned a receiver against new sources of information, but this possibility must be considered unlikely in a climate of opinion so favorable to more cultural independence as that which prevails in Latin America.

Testing these hypotheses required several examinations of the data that cannot be presented here. The data presented had to conform to the special shortcomings in source attribution in each of the three countries, so the strategy followed was this:

1. An examination was made of each of Mexico's sampled newspapers separately for agenda-setting. Presumably, the own-correspondent comments would tend to be more independent than copy credited to a wire; and in either case, the own-correspondent copy would tend to reject themes from the wires.
2. A table was compiled to show correlations of newspapers intracountry, for the sake of collapsing the individual papers into a country aggregate.
3. An examination was made of the collapsed Brazilian and Argentine papers (compared to the AP and AFP agendas) with respect to their peculiarities; that is, for Brazil, the own-correspondent and no-source copy were examined separately, and for Argentina, wire-attributed copy and no-source copy (there being no own-correspondent copy).
4. A full table was constructed comparing the collapsed "foreign news" agenda of each paper with the agenda of each of the four wires, even though some of the papers (e.g., the Argentine) may not have subscribed to all four wires.

After the final table, a calculation was made correlating degree of independence with number of sources attributed. This was done to show whether divergent news sources make a newspaper less dependent, and to provide a basis for the interpretations and conclusions to follow.

RESULTS

Mexico. As is clear from Table 12.1, the Mexican newspapers provided the best data for testing the agenda-setting theory cross-culturally, since they usually attributed the source of the news item and also featured by-lined commentary. Adapting the agenda-setting model to the wire-newspaper relationship, we can posit the following line of diminishing source influence:

Wire agenda ► wire attributed copy ► own correspondent copy ► editorials

The number of editorials was insufficient for all papers to run a Spearman's correlation. And only for the two Mexican papers was it possible to test the first part of this agenda-setting line. As predicted, Table 12.2 shows that the two papers accept the topical agenda of the U.S. wire that each took (UPI for *El Universal*, AP for *Excelsior*).

Table 12.2. Agenda-setting in Mexican newspapers (Spearman's correlations)

	Topics		Themes	
El Universal				
UPI with UPI-run copy	.7832	($p = .001$)	.6189	($p = .028$)
UPI with own-correspondent copy				
	.7622	($p = .002$)	–.1250	($p = $ NS)*
UPI-run copy with own-correspondent copy				
	.8252	($p = .001$)	.1083	($p = $ NS)
Excelsior				
AP with AP-run copy	.7553	($p = .002$)	.3210	($p = $ NS)
AP with own-correspondent copy				
	.8869	($p = .001$)	.3242	($p = $ NS)
AP-run copy with own-correspondent copy				
	.8369	($p = .001$)	.1048	($p = $ NS)
Interwire				
UPI with AP	.9842	($p = .001$)	.8842	($p = .001$)
Between wire-attributed copy				
UPI-run copy with AP-run copy				
	.8084	($p = .001$)	.6259	($p = .026$)
Between own-correspondent copy for the two papers				
Universal own-correspondent with *Excelsior*				
own-correspondent copy				
	.8925	($p = .001$)	.6333	($p = .025$)

*Nonsignificant

If the mix of topics does carry cultural values of the wires, as some critics contend, then even topical agenda-setting (indicated here) means a degree of cultural dependency; but it seems more reasonable to expect a different mix of topics for local news and local commentary, than for foreign news. The issue here is cultural dependence on foreign news sources, and that is better represented by the coding category of themes. Here both Mexican newspapers rejected the wire agenda and presumably offered one of their own. Notice first that the two U.S. wires have similar thematic agendas, as do the two Mexican papers (as represented by the intracountry, own-correspondent and wire-attributed correlations at the bottom). Though *El Universal* accepts the UPI thematic "line" in its UPI-attributed copy, neither paper accepts the wire agenda in its own-correspondent copy, a clear sign of cultural independence.

Brazil. For Brazil, two wires (AP-to-Rio and AFP) were compared to the own-correspondent copy (collapsed for both papers) and the no-source copy, likewise collapsed. This was done to see whether the no-source copy, probably representing a majority of the wire stories, would not correlate differently from the own-correspondent copy, which would presumably, if independent, have a different agenda from either of the two test wires. Table 12.3 shows to the contrary:

Table 12.3. Agenda-setting for aggregated Brazilian newspapers (test wires— AP-to-Rio and AFP-LATIN)

	Topics		Themes	
Interwire				
AP with AFP	.9091	$(p = .001)$	.7477	$(p = .006)$
AP				
AP with own-correspondent copy				
	.6620	$(p = .010)$	.6483	$(p = .021)$
AP with no-source copy	.8531	$(p = .001)$	.7073	$(p = .011)$
AFP				
AFP with own-correspondent copy				
	.6550	$(p = .010)$	.6646	$(p = .018)$
AFP with no-source copy	.8741	$(p = .001)$	.6991	$(p = .012)$
Domestic				
Own-correspondent with no-source copy				
	.8581	$(p = .001)$	.7615	$(p = .005)$

For topics and themes, for own-correspondent and no-source copy, the two Brazilian papers proved to have agendas similar to both the AP and AFP agendas, at least for foreign news. None of this analyis is meant to insinuate that any of these papers may not pursue an independent editorial line domestically; in fact there is ample evidence for criticism of the local government by Brazil's two papers sampled here, Mexico's *Excelsior*, and Argentina's *Clarin* and *La Opinion* (Pierce 1979). But for papers not of the stature or power of *O Estado* or the *Jornal do Brasil*, it is the consensus that domestic censorship takes its toll on independent thought. Maldonado (1976) considers Brazil's domestic censorship "ironclad," but sarcastically adds that neither AP, UPI, nor the Western European agencies have had any problem distributing their news in Brazil, which obeys the principle of the free flow of information. Clearly we must distinguish between domestic news coverage, where several of these papers are independent, and foreign news reporting, where other factors operate.

Argentina. In the Brazilian case it was possible to infer cultural independence from the by-lined own-correspondent alone, without the desirable link of wire-attributed copy to show the connection with wire agendas; but in the Argentine case, even this means of inference is lacking. Though there is some wire attribution, there are almost no own-correspondent stories and enough no-source stories to make us suspicious of the consistency with which the three papers attribute foreign news items. Another problem is the lack of warrant to aggregate the three papers, as shown by the nonsignificant Spearman's correlations in Table 12.4. Given these drawbacks, Table 12.4 still shows some interesting agenda comparisons for AP-to-Buenos-Aires and AFP-LATIN, the two test wires.

Whereas AP themes do not correlate with the aggregated thematic agenda for AP-attributed copy, AFP themes do, in the corresponding case. And whatever the no-source copy represents, it has more in common with the AP, than with the AFP thematic agenda. So there is tentative evidence that the Argentine papers do exhibit some cultural independence, albeit in a very selective way. This will become clearer in a paper by paper agenda comparison.

The similarity of topical and thematic agendas across the four wires has been indicated in previous correlations. This would lead us to believe that a newspaper that accepted AP and AFP themes would accept those of UPI and Reuters as well; but we do not know whether each of these papers takes all four wire services (Table 12.2 helps in some cases, not all), we are speaking here not of acceptance so much as similarity of wire and paper agendas. This is called agenda-holding here to distinguish it from the agenda-setting that we found did not hold in the Mexican case. The results of comparing, then, every paper's collapsed "foreign news" agenda with every wire's agenda are given in Table 12.5.

Table 12.4. Agenda-setting for aggregated Argentine newspapers (test wires —AP-to-Buenos Aires and AFP-LATIN)

	Topics		Themes	
Interwire				
AP-Argentina with AFP	.9441	$(p = .001)$	.8303	$(p = .001)$
AP				
AP with AP-run copy	.5105	$(p = .045)$	.2580	$(p = NS)$
AP with no-source copy	.7483	$(p = .003)$	.6687	$(p = .017)$
AFP				
AFP with AFP-run copy	.8652	$(p = .001)$	.7561	$(p = .006)$
AFP with no-source copy	.7692	$(p = .002)$	.4559	$(p = NS)$
Domestic correlations				
AP-run copy with no-source	.4126	$(p = NS)$	.5619	$(p = .045)$
AFP-run copy with no-source	.6900	$(p = .007)$	.6269	$(p = .026)$

Table 12.5. Agenda-holding for all four wires and the eight newspapers (general foreign news)

	Topics		Themes	
MEXICO				
El Universal with:				
AP	.7180	$(p = .004)$	.2970	(NS)
AFP	.7902	$(p = .001)$	.2796	(NS)
UPI	.7483	$(p = .003)$	.1281	(NS)
Reuters	.6760	$(p = .008)$	−.1515	(NS)
Excelsior with:				
AP	.6095	$(p = .004)$	.5000	(NS)
AFP	.6573	$(p = .010)$	.2446	(NS)
UPI	.6434	$(p = 0.12)$	.3252	(NS)
Reuters	.4098	(NS)	.4817	(NS)
BRAZIL				
O Estado de Sao Paulo with:				
AP	.7483	$(p = .003)$	.6942	$(p = .013)$
AFP	.7692	$(p = .002)$	.8338	$(p = .001)$
UPI	.7413	$(p = .003)$	.8160	$(p = .002)$
Reuters	.7040	$(p = .005)$	.4634	(NS)

Table 12.5 *(continued)*

	Topics		Themes	
Jornal do Brasil with:				
AP	.6713	(p = .008)	.6646	(p = .018)
AFP	.7273	(p = .004)	.6220	(p = .027)
UPI	.7063	(p = .005)	.6116	(p = .030)
Reuters	.6550	(p = .010)	.0000	(NS)

ARGENTINA

Clarin with:				
AP	.5954	(p = .021)	.7234	(p = .009)
AFP	.7776	(p = .001)	.8232	(p = .002)
UPI	.7461	(p = .003)	.6300	(p = .025)
Reuters	.5825	(p = .023)	.4377	(NS)
La Opinion with:				
AP	.7972	(p = .001)	.6121	(p = .080)
AFP	.7762	(p = .001)	.4255	(NS)
UPI	.7343	(p = .003)	.7195	(p = .009)
Reuters	.7531	(p = .002)	.7455	(p = .007)
Cronica with:				
AP	.4308	(NS)	.1539	(NS)
AFP	.5709	(p = .026)	.3797	(NS)
UPI	.6165	(p = .016)	.4489	(NS)
Reuters	.4140	(NS)	-.0862	(NS)

INTERWIRES

Other thematic intercorrelations

	AP-Mex	AP-Rio	AP-Arg	UPI	AFP
UPI	.8842 (p = .001)	.8828 (p = .002)	.9025 (p = .001)		
AFP	.7964 (p = .003)	.7195 (p = .009)	.8268 (p = .002)		
Reuters	.4909 (NS)	.5410 (NS)	.5515 (p = .049)	.4939 (NS)	.2310 (NS)

*All Spearman's for topics significant to the $p = .001$ level, for all permutations. Also, the three AP services intercorrelate highly as to themes ($p = .001$ for all).

As the interwire correlations show, Reuters proved to be the only maverick: with every wire service except AP-Argentina it shows a nonsignificant thematic correlation. Clearly Reuters is sending across a different mix of themes from the other three wires. So it is doubly interesting to see that only *La Opinion* of Argentina has a thematic agenda similar to that of Reuters; and compared with *Clarin*, *La Opinion* emerges as the more Anglophile of the two, whereas *Clarin* could be considered more Francophile, based on these data. *Cronica*'s independence from wire themes would seem inexplainable, were it not for the fact that *Cronica* is a sensational tabloid, which seems to slant its news, foreign and domestic, accordingly.

The Mexican papers run true to form, rejecting all wire themes, just as the two Brazilian papers have thematic agendas similar to everywhere except the maverick Reuters. This would lead us to believe that the earlier tables with their aggregations were not far off the mark in their pictures of cultural dependency or independence. Consequently, based on these data, we can rank Mexico's elite papers as the most culturally independent of wire influence, Argentina's papers as next most independent, and Brazil's two elite papers as most culturally dependent, in the area of foreign news.

DISCUSSION. The three hypotheses fared as follows:

1. "All four wires will have similar topical and thematic agendas." This was not borne out, even though it was true that AP, UPI, and AFP all had similar agendas. The presence of Reuters as a thematic anomaly in the supposedly monolithic "Big Four" world wires was a surprise, and should be investigated further. If divergent voices are the desideratum in the Latin American news system, then a turn to Reuters might be a step in the right direction.

2. "All the Latin American newspapers will accept the topical agenda of the wires." Counsulting Table 12.5, we see that this hypothesis is also not strictly borne out, though most newspapers do show remarkable topical similarity to the wire agenda. Both *Excelsior* and *Cronica* have agendas dissimilar to Reuters', and *Cronica* even shows topical dissimilarity to the AP service going to Buenos Aires. The reasons for these anomalies are not apparent from the data, and deserve further investigation.

3. "If a newspaper rejects the thematic agenda of a wire service, it will also prove to attribute more sources than papers that do not reject the wire agenda." This can be tested by the following strategem. The number of divergent sources used (d) can be estimated from Table 12.1 if we use the following equation with n = number of stories attributed to a source, t = total number of stories, and s = total number of sources:

$$(n/t)s = d$$

From this equation the uncredited stories are absent because they represent either lack of sources or disinclination to name them. Using this formula, the coefficient of source diversity can be specified for each paper. (See Table 12.6.) This rank order roughly corresponds with the order derived from Table 12.5: Mexico most independent, Argentina next, and Brazil least independent. The exceptions are the Argentine paper *Cronica*, which attributes a high number of sources, and *La Opinion*, which does not.

Table 12.6. Diversity of sources

		Coefficient of source diversity	Rank
Excelesior	(Mexico)	16.5	1
El Universal	(Mexico)	13.0	2
Cronica	(Argentina)	8.7	3
Clarin	(Argentina)	7.3	4
O Estado	(Brazil)	2.4	5
Jornal	(Brazil)	1.9	6
La Opinion	(Argentina)	1.8	7

If we look at the number of rejections/acceptances of wire agenda in Table 12.5, then we see that three newspapers hold agendas dissimilar to all four wire-theme agendas (*El Universal*, *Excelsior*, and *Cronica*), whereas the other four newspapers reject only one wire's thematic agenda. Since on the scale of source diversity the top three ranks are the same as the top three in this rough measure of cultural independence, we may accept the hypothesis as confirmed. It does seem that the more sources are attributed in a newspaper, the more it will tend to print a thematic agenda dissimilar from those of the wires. Whether this reflects genuine cultural independence or sheer editorial perversity remains to be shown.

These few signs of cultural/news independence in Latin America should not blind us to the fact that most of the Latin American dailies probably take only AP or UPI, as Diaz Rangel (1967, 28) points out when he says that "an ideal daily in Latin America would be that which would publish in its pages telegraphic information from UPI or AP, from one European agency such as Reuters or AFP (preferably the latter), and from one Latin American agency (Prensa Latina), and dispatches from some of its correspondents in some of the more important Latin American countries." Anthony Smith has already noted a trend in some Latin American newspapers to use fresh sources of material and treat agency material less mechanically; this was also noticed by Reyes Matta, who singled out *Excelsior* in Mexico, *O Estado de Sao Paulo* in Brazil, *El Nacional* in Caracas, and *Clarin* in Buenos Aires.

Another ideal for the Latin American press system would be a genuine news agency for the whole region, since Cuba's Prensa Latina agency, though touted in some quarters, suffers from ideological predispositions. But this ideal is perennial and has been voiced since 1926, according to Knudson (1977), most vocally by countries such as Bolivia and Cuba that have thrown off dependence on AP and UPI. In any event, the mere presence of a diversity of sources would be unavailing, as Smith (1980, 43) points out, unless news content was "intrinsically admired, or trusted, or needed." Given the anti-imperialist climate in much of Latin America today, the only answer to this problem may well be a UN-funded regional news agency to compete with the existing news agencies, or at the very least some form of subsidies to Latin American papers so that they may subscribe to some of the lesser European agencies (EFE, ANSA, DPA) and Prensa Latina, which were significantly used by the two Mexican newspapers sampled in this study.

REFERENCES

Beltran S., Luis Ramiro. 1978. Communication and cultural domination: USA-Latin American case. *Media Asia* 5(4): 183–92.

Diaz Rangel, Eleazar. 1967. *Pueblos subinformados.* Caracas: Universidad Central de Venezuela.

Gerassi, John. 1965. *The great fear in Latin America.* New York: Collier Books.

International Commission for the Study of Communication Problems. 1980. *Many voices, one world.* New York: Unipub.

Knudson, Jerry. 1977. U.S. coverage since 1952 of Bolivia: The unknown soldier of the cold war. *Gazette* 23(3): 185–97.

Maldonado, Alberto. 1976. Federacion Latinoamerica de periodistas. In *La circulacion de noticias en America Latina,* ed. Eleazar Diaz Rangel. Caracas: Imprenta Nacional.

Novak, Michael. 1982. Why Latin America is poor. *Atlantic Monthly,* March, 66–75.

Pierce, Robert N. 1979. *Keeping the flame: Media and government in Latin America.* New York: Hastings House.

Reyes Matta, Fernando. 1976. The information bedazzlement of Latin America. *Development Dialogue* 2:29–42.

Smith, Anthony. 1980. *The geopolitics of information.* New York: Oxford University Press.

Somavia, Juan. 1976. The transnational power structure and international information. *Development Dialogue* 2:15–28.

Tunstall, Jeremy. 1977. *Mass media policies in changing cultures.* New York: Wiley-Interscience.

CHAPTER 13

Test of Galtung's Theory of Structural Imperialism

Robert D. Haynes, Jr.

IN Galtung's (1971) theory, the world consists of developed "center" states and undeveloped "periphery" states. Each, in turn, possesses a "core"—a more highly developed area—and a "periphery". Employing these concepts, Galtung defines structural imperialism as a "sophisticated type of dominance relation which cuts across nations basing itself on a bridgehead which the center of the center nation establishes in the center of the periphery nation for the joint benefit of both" (1971, 81). The structural relationship is one in which there is

1. a harmony of interests between the center of the center and the center in the periphery nation
2. more disharmony of interest within the periphery nation than within the center nation
3. a disharmony of interest between the periphery in the center nation and the periphery in the periphery nation (1971, 83)

In other words, there exists in developing countries a dominant group whose interests coincide with the interests of the developed world. Thus, this "center" provides a means by which the core can maintain its economic and political domination. In terms of values and attitudes, the bridgehead group is more like groups in the developed world than they are like groups in their own periphery. There is a striking similarity between Galtung's conception of structural imperialism and the implicit structure of Schiller's definition of cultural imperialism.

Both maintain that the structure of political and economic domination exercised by the center over the periphery results in the re-creation of certain aspects of the center's value system in the periphery. Periphery-center linkages are reinforced by role transfers occurring through increased information flows, through reproduction of economic activities, and, in general, through the process of modernization. In turn, these role transfers create institutional linkages that function to serve the interests of dominant groups both in the center and the periphery (*cf.* Apter 1976). Institutions in the periphery, mirror, at least within the center of the periphery, those of the developed world and thus promote linked and compatible value systems.

Galtung defines five types of imperialism that depend upon the type of exchange between center and periphery nations: economic, political, military, communication, and cultural. Of these, communication imperialism is more germane to the issue at hand, although the five form a syndrome of imperialism, and interact, albeit by different channels, to reinforce the dominance relationship of center over periphery. In Galtung's view, communication imperialism is intimately related to cultural imperialism. In fact, for Galtung, news communication is a combination of cultural and communication exchange (1971, 93).

That communication imperialism is related to other economic and political structures seems to be consistent with the findings of research on other social levels. Communication patterns are intimately involved with other forms of social and political activity. Galtung's views coincide with those of Schiller (1978, 1979a, 1979b) and Pronk (1978); the international communication order is intimately tied to the economic order.

The basic mechanism of structural imperialism revolves around the interaction structures. Galtung argues that there is a "vertical" interaction principle and a "feudal" interaction principle. The vertical principle maintains that relationships are asymmetrical; that the power relationship in a dyad flows from the more-developed state to the less-developed state while the benefits of the system flow up the scale, from the less-developed states to the core states. The feudal principle states that "there is interaction along the spokes, from the periphery to the center hub; but not along the rim; from one periphery nation to another" (1971, 89).

Communication and information flow from the core to their periphery and back again. Developing states receive information about the core but little information about fellow developing countries. In terms of communication, Galtung states: "As to...communication imperialism, the emphasis in the analysis is turned towards the second mechanism of imperialism: the feudal interaction structure" (1971, 93). The feudal interaction structure reinforces the inequalities produced by the vertical interaction structures. There are four rules that define feudal interaction and these may be taken as empirical expectations of relationships between core and periphery.

1. Interaction between center and periphery is *vertical*.
2. Interaction between periphery and periphery is *missing*.

3. Multilateral interaction involving *all three* is *missing*.

4. Interaction with the outside world is *monopolized* by the center, with two implications: (a) periphery interaction with other center nations is missing; and (b) center as well as periphery interaction with periphery nations belonging to other center nations is missing (1971, 89).

Galtung's feudal model in its broad outlines is structurally similar to more generalized cybernetic models of communication flows. Feedback, an information flow from recipient back to the communicator, is a necessary ingredient of these models since it allows for checking actions against results and thus facilitates the maintenance of centralized control over outcomes. Likewise, in a structural imperial relationship, feedback becomes crucial to maintaining the center's dominance. In terms of news flows, feedback—the gathering and reporting of news from the Third World nations to core via multinational wire services—allows the core to judge and to adapt to changing local circumstances in order to maintain its preeminent position. Information flows structured according to the feudal principle and the judicious use of feedback reduce the necessity of overt or drastic political or military action. Galtung implies the potential impact of the feudal mode when he asks:

> How could—for example—a small foggy island in the North Sea rule over a quarter of the world? By isolating the periphery parts from one another, by having them geographically at sufficient distance from each other to impede alliance formation, by having separate deals with them to tie them to the center in particularistic ways, by reducing multilateralism to a minimum with all kinds of graded memberships, and by having the Mother country assume the role of window to the world (1971, 90).

As window to the world, the mother country interprets events and processes for the peripheral country and thereby structures the "cognitive world" of the elite with whom she communicates. This cognitive world is structured in a manner that resembles the cognitive world of the mother country. In terms of communication, "this is done by training journalists to see events with center eyes, and by setting up a chain of communication that filters and processes events so that they fit the general pattern" (1971, 93).

SIMILARITIES OF CULTURES. Galtung's theory of structural imperialism argues that the harmony of interests between the cores of the dominant and peripheral states creates similar cognitive worlds. That is, the elite in the metropolis and the elite in the periphery would have similar interests and views and interpret messages transmitted via the news media similarly. Although cultural differences may create barriers to cross-cultural communication, the cultural similarities in terms of values and interests guarantee that these barriers are minimized.

Research from diverse intellectual viewpoints indicates that the members of the periphery's core have a more modern outlook than the rest of the country (Schramm 1963; Fisher 1979), are better educated and more literate than the periphery and thus more capable of making use of the press (Schramm 1963; Pool 1963), have greater access to the news media and rely more on the news media for information (Frey 1973), and are oriented more toward the developed world than are the "traditional" sectors of the society (Lerner 1958).

These factors coupled to Galtung's bridgehead concept would mean that the images of the developed world are reproduced in the context of the underdeveloped world. Maletzke (1970, 484) writes about "intercultures" that grow up between the elite in the developed and the developing worlds: "When members of the elite in developing countries join such intercultures, then the danger exists that they are only increasing that process of alienation from their own country which in turn only strengthens the dubious dualism (between center and periphery already noted)." Hence the similarities of culture and interest stimulate the demand for the goods and services displayed in the media as well as create demand for similar types of media coverage. Thus the media are an important link for the transference of the values of one culture to another.

The emphasis on the cultural ramification of international news flows is in keeping with the emphasis placed on this aspect in the UNESCO forum. Third World delegates claim that news, along with the values it transmits, is a threat to the cultural sovereignty of the nation (Masmoudi 1978; Schiller 1979; Sauvant 1979). Information flows originating outside the cultural domain create values and desires that are derived from the "global village"—a common cultural sphere that links the most modern and cosmopolitan elements of the states—and reflect the dominance of the developed countries. These conflict with those of the national culture. Conflicting value orientations, in turn, make the processes of political and economic development more difficult. Nations argue that they reserve the sole right to define their own culture and to provide bulwarks against media imperialism.

SETTING THE AGENDA. Newsgathering agencies located in the developed countries are economic actors that must take into consideration the demands of their potential audience. In other words, there is always the market factor to be considered in the allocation of the time and energies of the newsgathering agencies. The prime market for the wire services is the developed, industrialized countries of Europe and North America (UNESCO 1980, 152).

The cultures of the developed world define what is of news value to themselves. Topicality, audience interest, the estimation of the impact of happenings on the society, and the norms and values of a society are factors that go into deciding what is a relevant event to be reported by the press. Developing countries maintain that this produces a bias toward the developed countries and does not take into consideration that the interests of the Third World do not necessarily coincide with the interests of the audience of the developed world. Accordingly, it is claimed that

> even important news may be deliberately neglected by the major media in favor of information of interest only to public opinion in the country to which the media in question belong. Such news is transmitted to the client countries and is indeed practically imposed on them despite the fact that readers and listeners in these countries have no interest in them (Masmoudi 1978, 10).

This type of newsgathering, collecting news in light of developed market forces, has produced an emphasis on events—the momentary and transitory happenings that are timely in the sense that they are a "break from the normal flow of events: an interruption of the expected" (Abel 1978, 4)—and a neglect of the coverage of processes such as development that are of long-term duration and not as topical. This alleged ability to create a particular type of news and impose it upon developing countries would be in agreement with Galtung's theory of the existence of a vertical imperialist structure in the international order.

If the core actors are defining news according to the criteria and demand for news in the developed world market, then the demand for and criteria of news will be similar in the center of the peripheral nation. This is perhaps what observers mean when they speak about the "agenda-setting function" of the international press. Information is transferred to the developing elite in such a way that primary importance is attached to the same issues the developed world sees as important. The identity of interests between the center of the center and the center of the periphery greatly influences the acceptance of an international agenda.

DIRECTION OF FLOW: THE FEUDAL STRUCTURE. Galtung maintains that the emphasis of communication imperialism is on the feudal interaction structure in which the periphery states are tied to the center in particularistic ways. Information, therefore, does not flow from the core in general but from differing core states in different proportions. The dominant criteria for determining the core-periphery linkage are capital and trade flows and colonial ties.

The patterns of news flows will exhibit the same vertical and feudal patterns of the structural imperialism paradigm: news flows from the core to the periphery via the newsgathering world agencies while reporters gather information in Third World countries that is eventually retransmitted for the world agencies. The effect of this feudal structure is that Third World nations know virtually nothing about events in neighboring countries that have not been filtered through the lenses of the developed media systems.

Compare this to Galtung's claim that the mother country acts as a window to the world for the underdeveloped country and therefore has a substantial impact on the resulting interpretation of the world. Following Galtung, this interaction structure means that (1) there exist interactions, news flows, between center and periphery; (2) interaction between periphery and periphery is missing; and (3) periphery interactions with other centers are missing.

Furthermore, decisions about what type of news goes where are made in the headquarters of the wire service. The major news agencies retransmit information to Latin America dealing with Latin America but very little about Africa or Asia. The entire wire service output does not go in its entirety to the developing countries. Weaver and Wilhoit elsewhere in this book report that of the news in the four major wire services to Latin America, about 45 percent was about Latin America while only about 3 to 4 percent was about Africa or Asia. Similar patterns are repeated for information sent to Africa and Asia. This structure reinforces the asymmetry between the center and periphery created by vertical structures.

POLITICAL INTERVENTION IN NEWS FLOW. Once the wire service output reaches the subscriber, the entire output still does not find its way to the population of the country. The "gatekeeper" determines what will and will not be passed on to the newspaper. Gatekeepers define what becomes news in the context of the developing countries. "Governments and community elite," according to Deutsch and Merritt (1965, 136), "are the managers of public messages about events, selecting out of the mass of competing messages those that they will transmit, those that they will give special attention and those that they will suppress."

The efficacy of the actual intervention in news flows by gatekeepers, however, has been the subject of conflicting interpretations. On the one hand, there are those such as Masmoudi who stress the dominance of the Western news-gathering agencies and give little attention to the effects of decisions made by editors, publishers, or ministers about what will actually be printed. On the other hand, there are those such as Abel who stress the intervention of the information elite into the news flow.

The four world news agencies, all based in the West, are the primary sources of international news. In some cases in the Third World, the transnational news agencies are directly subscribed to by other news agencies such as local newspapers. However, the growing trend in underdeveloped countries is for the government to be the main subscriber. Abel (1978, 3) makes the following observation:

> Of the 85 nonaligned countries in the sample, AP makes direct sales to 23%, UPI to 18%, and Reuters (the largest direct supplier of the three) enters 73% of these countries only through government or government-controlled channels. The respective figures for the other agencies are—AP, 77% and UPI, 82%. Thus the

nonaligned countries and their populations are by no means "passive recipients" of unwanted foreign information. Their governments are, and have long been, in firm control.

Direct sales to news agencies is most prevalent in Latin America where individuals and parties have traditionally owned the independent newspapers. Abel's data show that only Reuters makes sales to governments and then only in two instances in Latin America. The latter case, sales to governments, is most likely to be found in the less-developed nations of Africa and Asia. In most cases the government either directly owns the media of information transmission, newspapers, radio, and television, or places direct controls over gathering and disseminating the news through ministries of information (Tunstall 1977, 147).

Decisions about what becomes news are affected by the relationships between the particular newspaper and the government of the country. The concentration or dispersion of decision making reflects differing conceptions of the purpose and responsibilitiy of the press.

In Latin America, for instance, the press operates much as the press in the developed world as opposition to government. To a certain degree this opposition is tolerated by the government. There are, however, certain economic controls that the government may exercise in order to "deter" the complete independence of the press. Such controls take the form of import controls on newsprint, tax structures, licensing, and so forth, as a means to put a lid on independent press activity. While the press still conceives of itself as an opposition or watchdog, there is a certain level of opposition above which editors and publishers will not venture. Self-censorship, albeit in the face of government power, is the norm.

In African and Asian countries, the press is considered to be much more of a partner in development. Ministries of information control the output in order to further the economic and political plans of the government. Tunstall (1977) writes that during the colonial days there was a tradition of opposition to colonial rule that had to be brought under control after liberation. The establishment of ministries or the nationalization of newspapers was an effective means of bringing this opposition to heel.

The press is presently viewed as an important conduit between the central decision-making authorities and the inhabitants. In these nations, the press takes on a more functional role: as a tool of education, as a voice of national planning, and as a means to achieve the legitimacy of the national elite (Schramm 1964). Furthermore, a centrally directed press is involved with establishing a national identity, homogenizing and integrating the society, and mobilizing the society for concerted political and economic action (Schramm 1964; Pye 1963).

Therefore, differences between countries in which the press is privately owned and countries in which the press is managed by the government can be expected. Specifically, in the latter countries, the profiles of the press will be indicative of the more functional approach. The data set allows differences in the quantity of attention paid to the outside world and the representation of the countries' interests to be investigated.

Expectations are that for countries in which the press has government-directed roles, more attention will be given to international news and that this international news will concentrate on the countries' interests abroad. Both of these measures are taken in order to maintain the stability of the government by diverting attention elsewhere and create a sense of national identity among different cultural groups and a sense of government legitimacy by stressing the government's involvement in international affairs.

ANALYSIS. In broad outlines, five areas in the UNESCO/IAMCR foreign news study can be used to test the relationships developed here:
1. the sources of international news,
2. the feudal structure of the news flow,
3. the direction of the flow or vertical structure,
4. effects of political direction on the news,
5. the case for agenda setting.

SOURCES OF INTERNATIONAL NEWS. Table 13.1 presents the data on sources of international news as coded from the by-line on news stories, using data from all of the Third World countries included in the full project. Foremost among the findings is the underrepresentation of the "Big Four" news agencies. Nowhere are the levels of domination by the international news agencies as high as the 80 percent claimed by Masmoudi. The data do not reflect the level of dependence. Only four countries, in fact, get over 50 percent of their international news from the agencies—Mexico, Iran, Egypt, and Indonesia. The finding has to be tempered, however, by the large number of unidentifiable sources. Developing nations on the whole tend not to report the sources of their news stories or rewrite news agency stories and attribute them to a national agency local staff. Missing sources range as high as 92 percent for Tunisia, 80 percent for Zaire, and 84 percent for the Ivory Coast. In Latin America, Brazil did not attribute 70 percent of its stories. Conceivably, many of the unidentified news items could have the MNC's at its ultimate source.

A number of countries—Turkey, Algeria, and Zambia for instance—have active national news agencies. Coupling the trend in news agency growth with the involvement of the newspapers' own staffs in reporting indicates that Third World newspapers, contrary to theoretical suppositions, are not passive consumers of news from the developed world. Rather they appear to be very actively involved with the reporting and dissemination of news stories.

Table 13.1. Sources of international news

Country	Home agency	Reuters	UPI	AP	AFP	TASS	Other Agency	Staff	Other	Unidentified
USA	4	6	9	22	...	...	...	36	8	11
Argentina	...	...	11	8	14	...	20	1	12	40
Brazil	...	1	...	...	...	...	...	13	16	70
Mexico	...	...	19	13	22	...	30	12	14	8
Algeria	32	4	...	...	8	...	...	4	2	54
Ivory Coast	...	2	...	...	2	...	1	13	1	84
Kenya	2	3	6	6	3	...	...	11	19	44
Nigeria	2	3	1	2	13	...	...	9	19	52
Tunisia	2	...	...	...	3	...	...	1	1	92
Zaire	2	...	...	...	...	...	1	10	1	87
Zambia	40	24	...	...	9	...	1	11	12	40
Egypt	5	4	4	5	9	...	3	12	24	35
Iran	4	12	5	19	17	1	15	2	8	20
Australia	26	19	11	7	1	...	1	41	5	16
India	21	15	...	15	9	1	3	21	16	8
Indonesia	26	5	2	13	31	...	4	27	6	16
Thailand	1	...	...	28	5	...	...	18	16	34
Turkey	42	3	...	14	13	...	3	36	7	4

Very few nations use material supplied by TASS, the Soviet
two, Iran and India, report using any TASS material. As for t.
news pool, data were lumped together under "other agency,"
include national news agencies from other countries, second-le
mentary services such as the *Washington Post* service and Deutsche-Presse-
Agentur, as well as the nonaligned news pool. It is difficult to determine to
what extent Third World agencies rely on the pool. However, Pinch's suggestion (1978, 165) that the non-aligned news pool has very little impact seems
warranted.

In general the data reveal that Third World newspapers rely on a multi-
tude of sources for their information. The major Western agencies are supplemented by the newspapers' own network of sources. Hence Third World newspapers are presented with many choices among sources of news. While the
world agencies may in fact be the largest supplier in terms of the number of
stories delivered, there is little reason to suspect that gatekeepers are dominated
by the agencies or that the transnational agencies are most prevalent because
there is little alternative.

FEUDAL STRUCTURE OF THE NEWS FLOW. According to Galtung, the
flow of news will exhibit a feudal structure. That is, news flow should reflect
the vertical patterns of structural imperialism and there will be little or no information about other regions. Table 13.2 reports the location of international
news stories as reported in national news media.

Overwhelmingly the news in developing areas reflects an emphasis on the
region in which the country is located: Asian newspapers report about Asia,
African about Africa, and Latin American about Latin America. What is evident, however, is the continental lines of demarcation. Latin American newspapers report very little about Africa and so forth. Cultural isolation is defined
in continental rather than national terms. The continental lines of demarcation
are reinforced by the world agencies' propensity to funnel regional news to
various areas rather than news about other developing areas.

While the news services reinforce regionalism, several interregional factors also interact to insure that these items are given prominence. First, the
similarity of the elite culture across various states of Latin America and Africa
influences the selection of the news. Second, the growing regional cooperation
in matters of economics and politics through continental mutilateral organization increases the interregional importance of states to each other. Third, as
will be seen in later parts of the analysis, geographically proximate states will
tend to loom larger in national news coverage.

Table 13.2. Geographic location of foreign news (in percentages)

Country (n)	Region in News						
	N Am	L Am	Afr	Mid E	Asia	W Eur	E Eur
USA (1,487)	26	7	10	16	14	16	6
Argentina (1,016)	13	32	5	20	3	18	3
Brazil (630)	12	29	5	14	10	23	6
Mexico (1,188)	23	30	5	10	7	16	3
Algeria (935)	3	3	50	21	3	13	5
Ivory Coast (390)	3	2	56	11	5	11	5
Kenya (501)	8	1	46	13	7	11	4
Nigeria (205)	8	5	50	11	13	8	0
Tunisia (1,302)	7	2	36	24	6	16	4
Zaire (419)	5	2	53	16	4	12	3
Zambia (516)	8	1	46	17	6	14	3
Egypt (1,322)	13	2	12	48	8	13	2
Iran (453)	10	6	8	49	10	12	5
Australia (1,032)	20	2	10	9	32	22	4
India (1,649)	15	2	8	12	40	17	4
Indonesia (811)	9	3	7	15	46	13	3
Thailand (500)	8	2	7	11	51	13	4
Turkey (327)	13	3	3	16	6	52	5

COVERAGE OF AREAS—VERTICAL STRUCTURES. Communication is supposed to follow both trade and capital flows and old colonial ties. The data suggest that colonial ties are the stronger of the two. Expectations were that Latin America would have coverage skewed towards the United States while African and Asian states would show similar skewness towards Europe. Contrary to this, data show that the region covered most by Latin Americans is western Europe. Only Mexico, an immediate neighbor of the United States, shows a pattern of news coverge coinciding with trade flows. One can surmise that the European heritages of many of the people of Latin America (especially Argentina and Brazil) and the existence of European language similarities provide the attraction for the newspapers.

Africa devotes its secondary coverage to the Middle East. Western Europe ranks only third among those areas covered. North America ranks fifth in area coverage competing with general news coverage.

In general, propinquity appears to be the most significant determinant of the coverage of various areas in international news. Evidence shows that Mexico covers the United States more than other Latin Americans cover the United States; that African countries cover the Middle East more than western Europe; and that Iran and India—both bordering or linked to the Soviet Union —are the only countries to use material from TASS. The exception appears to be the Middle East. Middle Eastern newspapers cover western Europe and North America more than they cover either Africa or Asia.

The data again indicate that developing countries cover extracontinental developing countries very little. More is known by developing countries about western Europe and North America than is known about other developing cultures.

The data also illustrate the unevenness of information transfers. The developing nations cover the developed world at a greater rate than North America or Europe cover the peripheral world. There is indeed an imbalance in the coverage between North and South as claimed by Third World states.

EFFECTS OF POLITICAL DIRECTION. Table 13.3 illustrates the attention paid to international news on the part of national newspapers. Column 1 indicates the percentage of news items in which the country's interests were represented while column 2 refers to the percentage of news involving either domestic politics in another country or relations between two other states.

Table 13.3. Self-interest in international news items

Country	Self-interest	International
USA	32%	59%
Argentina	9	74
Brazil	4	78
Mexico	16	71
Algeria	37	63
Ivory Coast	25	70
Kenya	19	74
Nigeria	11	36
Tunisia	30	70
Zaire	35	64
Zambia	18	77
Egypt	38	61
Iran	41	51
Australia	18	83
India	30	67
Indonesia	27	71
Thailand	52	63
Turkey	27	58

Note: Mean of self-interest-category of countries in which news is privately owned, 18.25%; mean of countries in which news is government controlled, 32.4%. Mean of international category of countries in which news is privately owned, 66–67%; mean of countries in which news is government controlled, 62.3%.

For nations where government plays an active role in the selection of news, there tends to be a higher concentration on the country's interests abroad— 18.25 percent for countries in which the news is privately owned compared to 32.4 percent for countries in which the government controls the selection of items.

According to the theory tested here, this can be interpreted as representing the political utilization of the news to foster the status quo. The news is used as a tool of socialization and legitimization of the current regime. By stressing the involvement of the nation in international politics, the government can increase its perceived stature among the population and create some form of legitimacy. Further, by combining this with the regionalization of news, the government can use the national press to promote itself as a regional political leader.

It can also be seen that a higher percentage of the space available for news is consigned to international news in those countries in which the government exercises control over the media. These countries turn the focus of the press from domestic matters to international matters. This however cannot be taken too seriously since the mean differences are relatively slight—32.2 percent for private ownership vs. 36.7 percent for government. The means are for relatively few countries and the differences are so narrow that they might not be meaningful. (See Table 13.4.)

In general, however, the findings appear to coincide with the theoretical suppositions. Developing countries actively intervene in the flow of news in order to further the political stability of the regime. That also is suggested in Chapter 10 by Shaw and Stevenson.

AGENDA-SETTING. Finally, the idea of agenda-setting should be addressed. Tables in Chapter 3 and Chapter 12 show the similarity of news among national media and between national media and the Western news agencies. What is readily apparent is the overwhelming identification of international news with political topics. The trend is repeated cross-nationally for all the countries in the sample. Political relations between states and domestic politics in other states are the primary foci.

Economic matters, which one would believe are more important to developing countries than domestic politics in other countries, appear to get much less newspace. One suspects, however, that economic news and information may be supplied through different channels to a particular audience. The amount of attention paid to cultural stories, religion, sports, and entertainment also appears to have cross-national similarities.

In quantitative terms, there appear to be many similarities in what is considered to be news interest to an audience. That audiences appear to have similar tastes and attach similar importance to various topics coincides with ideas of the existence of an international agenda. Cultural similarities are at once created by the flow of news and influence the flow of news so that audiences worldwide receive a fairly homogeneous diet of international news stories. This, however, represents only about 35 percent of the total news package that the audience receives. The rest is composed of domestic news and stories about which no inferences from the data are possible.

A reasonable expectation is that if international news is used as a tool of socialization and maintenance of the status quo then domestic news will also resemble the pattern and show a high content of positive aspects of the regime's accomplishments and a very low content of criticism.

It seems, as Galtung suggests, that Third World newspeople have readily absorbed the journalistic lessons of the developed world. Events (happenings above the routine) constitute news. There is reason to believe that long-term processes such as economic and social development have little place in the news of the underdeveloped world. In this sense, while the developed world may not dictate specific stories, it has certainly influenced directly the style of reporting and indirectly the choice of particular types of news stories. It would appear that some vertical dominance does exist but it is neither as direct nor as pervasive as the theory would suggest.

Table 13.4. Percentage of newshole devoted to international news

Country	Ownership/Control*	%**
USA	Private	31
Argentina	Private	40.3
Brazil	Private	30.5
Mexico	Private	38
Algeria	Government	44
Ivory Coast	Government	51
Kenya	Private	40.5
Nigeria	Mixed (2 of 14 by gov't)	11.3
Tunisia	Government	63.5
Zambia	Government	62
Zaire	Government	27
Egypt	Government	18
Iran	Government	17
Australia	Private	34.3
India	Private	24.2
Indonesia	Government	32
Thailand	Government	16
Turkey	Private	33

Note: Mean of newshole for private, 32.2%; mean of newshole for government press, 36.7%.

*Data from Arthur S. Banks, ed. (1978), *Political handbook of the world 1977*.

**Data from Sreberny-Mohammadi (1981).

DISCUSSION. It can be seen that the structure of international news flows does not conform completely to the theoretical expectations. While there is some reason to believe that in quantitative terms the international agenda is being established through the process of transmitting news from the center to the periphery, the expectations of the density of these flows, the directionality, and the particularness of the flows do not hold up under analysis.

Galtung's expectations were that interaction between center and periphery would be vertical, interaction between periphery and periphery would be missing, and that periphery interaction with other center nations would be missing. The empirical examination of the data did not support these expectations.

Specifically, in terms of vertical interaction, there exist additional interaction structures among regional partners that soften the dominance of center over periphery. Secondly, and arguing directly from the preceding, it can be seen that there is interaction between peripheral states that Galtung would not expect. There is, however, little interaction between blocs of states defined in continental terms. Finally, contrary to expectations, the pattern of interaction between center and periphery did not hold; the periphery did interact with center nations other than "their" center state.

The first question that should be asked is: Why didn't the data support the theory? Three reasons can be advanced for the lack of substantive verification: (1) the complexity of the international system, (2) the myth of developing world passivity, and (3) misplaced generalizations from communication flows. The three interact to create problems for analysis.

The findings indicate that the international system is not a simple feudal structure as Galtung suggests. Communication flows, especially news flows, do not necessarily follow the same lines as other types of structural relations. The diverse types appear to possess structures of their own that, using the language of determinism, have different underlying determinants. News flows, for instance, respond to cultural, linguistic, and geographic determinants rather than to the flows of investment and trade, thereby creating a situation in which periphery nations interact with other center nations. This situation is especially evident in Latin America where the European heritages of the elite news audience are reflected in the amount of attention they give to that part of the world.

The conclusion to be drawn is that dependency in a particular functional sphere does not coincide with dependency in cultural spheres. This conclusion gives some tentative support to the argument that cultures produce, select, and channel information while societies produce, select, and channel goods and services.

Although there may be similarities of production in the societal sphere that would allow for the specification of valid cross-national models to study economic and political-economic activity, the creation of information and flows of communication have a cultural input that reduces the applicability of a single mode. Thus it would seem that structural theories of the international system that are directed towards the societal tasks of production and allocation of goods and services, both in political and economic terms, have little to say about the flows of information that are influenced by specific cultures. This certainly raises questions about the applicability of models and techniques borrowed from economics for the study of communication and information flows.

Secondly, many researchers have employed the political equivalent of supply-side economics to their analysis of the relationship between the center and the periphery. In this view the developing countries are relatively passive accepters of communication flows that, to paraphrase Masmoudi (1978), they are neither interested in nor in need of. This analysis suggests that, on the contrary, developing countries are very actively involved in the creation of news flows. Home-country agencies, newspaper staffs, and ministries of information operate much like their equivalents in the developed world. They are actively engaged in finding and reporting the news and redistributing this news via agencies with links to regional affairs or to the nonaligned news pool. The eventual structure of news flows is thus being created by the work of Third World agencies as well as the developed-world news agencies.

Evidence also suggests that governments are creating bulwarks against the communication flows in order to enhance their own position vis-à-vis the domestic and international political systems. Reporters returning from Third World assignments report the increasing number of attempts to manipulate the international press into providing a more positive picture of the activities of their regime (Rosenblum 1977). Additionally, theories stemming from the structural imperialist and dependency school of analysis denigrate the activities of gatekeepers and ministries in exercising rights of choice in accordance with their own values or the political realities within the developing nation. Adequate conceptualization of news flows and effects must certainly take into consideration that both developed and developing nations have influence on the evolution of a more equitable and just communication order.

REFERENCES

Abel, Elie. 1978. Communication for an interdependent, pluralistic world. Document No. 33 submitted to the UNESCO International Commission for the Study of Communications Problems.

Apter, David E. 1965. *The politics of modernization.* Chicago: University of Chicago Press.

Banks, Arthur S., ed. 1978. *Political handbook of the world 1977.* New York: McGraw-Hill Co.

Deutsch, Karl, and Richard L. Merritt. 1965. International events and national images. In *International behavior: A social-psychological analysis,* ed. Herbert C. Kelman. New York: Holt, Rinehart and Winston.

Fisher, Glen. 1979. *American communication in a global society.* Norwood, N.J.: Ablex.

Frey, Frederick W. 1963. Political development, power and communication in Turkey. In *Communications and political development,* ed. Lucien W. Pye. Princeton: Princeton University Press.

──────────. 1973. Communication and development. In *Handbook of Communication,* eds. Ithiel de Sola Pool, et al. Chicago: Rand McNally.

Galtung, Johan. 1971. A structural theory of imperialism. *Journal of Peace Research* 8(2): 81–117.

Lerner, Daniel. 1958. *The passing of traditional society.* New York: Free Press.

Maletzke, Gerhard. 1970. Intercultural and international communication. In *International Communication,* eds. Heinz-Dietrich Fischer and John C. Merrill. New York: Hastings House.

Masmoudi, Mustapha. 1978. The new world information order. Document No. 34 submitted to the UNESCO International Commission for the Study of Communication Problems.

Pinch, Edward T. 1978. Flow of news: An assessment of the nonaligned news agencies pool. *Journal of Communication* 28(3): 163–71.

Pool, Ithiel de Sola. 1963. Mass media and politics in the modernization process. In *Communication and political development*, ed. Lucien W. Pye. Princeton: Princeton University Press.

Pronk, Jan. 1978. Some remarks on the relation between the new international economic order and the new international information order. Document No. 35 submitted to the UNESCO International Commission for the Study of Communication Problems.

Pye, Lucien W. 1963 Model of traditional, transitional and modern communication systems. In *Communications and political development,* ed. Lucien W. Pye. Princeton: Princeton University Press.

Rosenblum, Mort. 1977. Reporting from the Third World. *Foreign Affairs,* 55(July): 815–36.

Sauvant, Karl P. 1979. Socio-cultural emancipation. In *National sovreignity and international communication,* eds. Kaarle Nordenstreng and Herbert I. Schiller. Norwood, N.J.: Ablex.

Schiller, Herbert I. 1978. Communication accompanies capital flows. Document No. 47 submitted to the UNESCO International Commission for the Study of Communication Problems.

──────────. 1979a. Transnational corporations and the international flow of information: Challenge to national sovereignty. *Current Research on Peace and Violence* 2: 1–11.

──────────. 1979b. Transnational media and national development. In *National sovreignity and international communication,* eds. Kaarle Nordenstreng and Herbert I. Schiller. Norwood, N.J.: Ablex.

Schramm, Wilbur. 1963. Communication and the development process. In *Communications and political development,* ed. Lucien W. Pye. Princeton: Princeton University Press.

──────────. 1964. *Mass media and national development.* Stanford, Calif.: Stanford University Press.

Sreberny-Mohammadi, Annabelle. 1981. *The world of news: news of the world.* Final report of the foreign images study undertaken by the International Association for Mass Communication for UNESCO. Mimeo.

Tunstall, Jeremy. 1977. *The media are American.* New York: Columbia University Press.

UNESCO. 1980. International commission for the study of communication problems, 1980. *Many voices, one world.* New York: Unipub.

CHAPTER 14

Determinants of Foreign Coverage in U.S. Newspapers

Thomas J. Ahern, Jr.

BETWEEN 1965 and 1974, a number of theoretical studies of international news flow proposed that the economic, social, political, and geographic characteristics of nations helped determine the amount of coverage one country received in the press of another (Galtung and Ruge 1965; Ostgaard 1965; Hester 1973; Rosengren 1974). While differing considerably in many respects, these studies shared the fundamental assumption that the influence of these characteristics made news flow stable and predictable over time. They predicted that further studies would reveal patterns in news flow attributable to these characteristics.

Empirical research based on these theoretical studies has begun to uncover such patterns. Using 11 national characteristics in regression analysis, including population, per capita income, and foreign stock residing in the United States, Dupree (1971) was able to account for 41 percent of the variance in coverage of different countries in *Atlas*, an American digest of foreign news. Rosengren (1974, 1977) found that gross national product, trade data, population, and geographic distance accounted for between one-third and two-thirds of the variance in foreign election coverage by three elite European newspapers. De Verneil (1977), studying newspapers from 15 nations, found trade data a significant predictor of foreign coverage in the press of fourteen of the nations studied. Intelsat circuitry was a significant predictor of coverage for 13 countries, and a population-distance ratio was significant for nine.

In these studies, both internal characteristics of nations (such as population and gross national product) and characteristics involving the relations of countries with other nations (such as trade data) were used successfully as predictors of news flow. In the discussion that follows, characteristics of nations, whether internal or relational, will be referred to collectively as national variables.

Given that these variables function well as predictors of news coverage, how is their predictive power to be explained? In the eyes of the gatekeepers of international news, do national characteristics function as generalized factors of newsworthiness, conferring upon all stories reported from large, wealthy, and populous nations a higher level of newsworthiness than stories from smaller nations? Or is their influence exerted outside the day-to-day gatekeeping process, perhaps through their effects upon the logistics of newsgathering by major news agencies?

The following study seeks to answer these questions by looking at how, and how much, national economic, political, social, and geographic characteristics influence the international flow of news. The context is news flow into the United States. First, the study focuses on how national variables influence news flow, drawing on previous research to determine the mechanisms through which such variables affect coverage. Second, seven national variables are organized into a model showing their effects on foreign news coverage. The parameters of this model are then estimated from empirical data and tested for significance using a combination of ordinary least-squares and two-stage least-squares modeling techniques.

This analysis differs from previous research on national variables in a number of respects. It seeks to develop a detailed explanation for the influence of variables on coverage. In so doing, it uses explanation oriented modeling techniques in place of the simple predictive techniques used in previous studies. Finally, it examines coverage of virtually all nations of the world in one of the world's most influential news channels, the elite newspapers of the United States.

TWO APPROACHES. Researchers have studied news flow using two distinct approaches. The more common one is grounded in social psychology and centers on the gatekeeper paradigm. The other, more recent and more diffuse, examines the economic and physical logistics of newsgathering, emphasizing the economic and political conditions under which coverage takes place.

In the gatekeeper model, events are transformed into news as a succession of editors decide to relay items to the news audience. Each successive gatekeeper scans a "universe of events," selects those items newsworthy under personal or institutional criteria, and forwards them along the chain to generate a new universe of events for the next decision maker. Gatekeeping studies focus on the process of news selection. The aim for such studies is to determine what factors cause an event to be selected as newsworthy.

In the logistics approach, newsgathering by correspondents is a production rather than a selection process. With the exception of TASS, the major wire services are commercial organizations that must produce, with limited resources, daily quantities of salable information. They deploy their correspondents and equipment under constraints imposed by their markets and the dictates of operational efficiency. In thus committing resources, they do not so much passively scan a universe of events as actively create one. Studies following this tradition focus on the economic, political, and social factors affecting newsgathering. The key research goal is to determine what characteristics of a country cause news to flow from it in greater or lesser degrees.

If one regards the approaches as complementing one another, the question of how national characteristics affect news flow could be answered from four perspectives:

1. National characteristics have no effect. If news flow is predictable, other factors are responsible.
2. The influence of national variables is psychologically mediated through the decisions of gatekeepers. Gatekeepers use national characteristics as criteria of newsworthiness in determining which events will be reported.
3. The influence of national variables is exerted through their effects on the logistics of newsgathering.
4. National variables influence news flow at both the gatekeeper and logistics levels.

In the following sections the gatekeeping and logistics oriented literature will be reviewed for evidence with which to evaluate these four perspectives.

GATEKEEPER PERSPECTIVE. The gatekeeping paradigm, originally proposed by Lewin (1947), was applied to news flow in pioneering studies by White (1950), Cutlip (1954), and McNelly (1959). Gatekeepers of foreign news reaching an American newspaper reader include the overseas bureau chiefs, central desk staffers, trunk wire editors, and state wire editors of one or more news services; the newspaper wire editor; and finally the reader. Through their decisions to cover, relay, or attend to some events and to reject others, each member of the channel has the ability to alter the quantity and composition of news flow. Understanding the alterations they impose, to paraphrase Lewin (1947, 3), is equivalent to understanding the selection criteria of the various gatekeepers.

Selection criteria for international news proposed in recent theoretical studies (Galtung and Ruge 1965; Ostgaard 1965; Hester 1971) are listed in Table 14.1. These selection criteria, or news factors as Galtung and Ruge term them, can be classified as either intrinsic or extrinsic to a given news event (Cooper 1981).

Table 14.1. Gatekeeper selection criteria for international news

News factors	Galtung / Ruge (1965)	Ostgaard (1965)	Hester (1971)
Intrinsic			
Event duration	X	X	
Magnitude	X		X
Unambiguity, simplification	X	X	
Consonance with previous frame of reference	X		
Continuation of ongoing event	X	X	
Elite actors	X	X	
Personification	X	X	
Unexpectedness, sensationalism, or human interest	X	X	X
Negativity	X		
Extrinsic			
Gatekeeper socialization			
Personal political views		X	
Western culture		X	
Reader/client feedback		X	
Media constraints			
Story origin/type relative to other stories that day; or space available	X	X	
Timeliness of report		X	X
Event context			
Meaningfulness (cultural proximity, relevance); or cultural affinity shared language, migration between countries, colonial heritage)	X	X	X
Elite nation focus; or perception of national strength or weakness	X		X
Geographic proximity		X	

Intrinsic factors of newsworthiness are unique to each event and pertain directly to what happened, how, and when. A border confrontation, for example, possesses a degree of magnitude based on the number of troops involved and a degree of negativity based on the level of conflict. These characteristics are inherent in confrontations regardless of where they occur and the identity of the people involved.

While the intrinsic characteristics of an event are important in bringing about its selection as news, the theoretical studies cited also specify a number of selection factors extrinsic to the event itself that figure in an event's equation of newsworthiness. These extrinsic factors can be classified under the headings of gatekeeper socialization, media constraints, and event context.

A gatekeeper's professional, political, and cultural socialization, and the time and space constraints of the medium in which he or she works, could be expected to influence materially the selection of a given event as news. Of particular interest to this study, however, are event context factors.

Event context factors supply the backdrop against which individual events occur, and pertain to the questions of where the event took place and who was involved. Confrontations equal in terms of magnitude and intensity of conflict vary in newsworthiness depending on the economic and military power of the participants. Earthquakes of equal strength and destructiveness vary in newsworthiness depending on the geographic and cultural proximity of their victims.

As may be noted in Table 14.1, the context factors proposed as influencing news selection are in many cases identical to national variables known to be predictors of news coverage. Gatekeeping theory thus includes national characteristics as extrinsic factors in news selection. Perspective 2 acquires a sharper focus: national strength, distance, and cultural proximity influence the flow of news, and at least part of their influence is mediated through the decisions of gatekeepers.

The latter part of the perspective is of key importance. National variables have already been identified as strong predictors of news flow volume, but have they been shown to function also as selection criteria in gatekeeping decisions?

The data offered by Galtung and Ruge (1965) in support of their news factor theory, perhaps the most elaborate and formally developed theory of international gatekeeping yet put forward, was criticized on this point by Rosengren (1974). Rosengren maintained that news factors could not be shown to operate as selection criteria without a comparison between events reported and events rejected. Galtung and Ruge had assumed, without empirically confirming, that characteristics of published news accounts distinguished them from events not published, and caused gatekeepers along the channel to select them.

A number of studies, however, have convincingly demonstrated the use of national variables as selection criteria in gatekeeping decisions. Gatekeeping contexts are established in these studies through a variety of methods. Some compare media reports with the event universe from which they were drawn. Some set up controlled decision-making situations for experimental manipulation. Some rely on field interviews with foreign news gatekeepers.

Three studies based on content analysis (International Press Institute 1953; Cutlip 1954; Hester 1971) traced foreign news through wire services into U.S. newspapers. Since the newspapers in these studies selected their foreign news almost entirely from the wire services, wire service content provided a universe of events against which newspaper content could be compared. Studying the use of AP state wire news in four Wisconsin newspapers, Cutlip was able to show that newspaper editors overselected news concerning U.S. foreign relations relative to their wire service input. The more detailed International Press Institute study also reported this trend and showed it to favor selection of news from some countries over others. In practice, this political selection factor translated into extensive newspaper coverage of U.S. alliances in Europe, with heavy emphasis on "the official acts and attitudes of the United Kingdom, France, Germany, Italy, and one or two other countries, expressed individually or in connection with the activities of the UN or NATO" (International Press Institute 1953, 25).

In Hester's study, foreign relations news was overshadowed by war news from Vietnam, and parallels with the earlier studies are difficult to draw. Hester's tables did show a tendency for newspaper editors to overselect news from elite nations. Such news made up 70 percent of the Wisconsin AP wire space but 75 percent of the space in Wisconsin newspapers.

Several survey-based, quasi-experimental studies have identified national variables influencing news selection by gatekeepers. Two of these were readership studies. MacLean and Pinna (1958) found a strong correlation between geographic proximity and news interest among Italian newspaper readers. In a survey of newspaper readers in Syracuse, New York, Sparkes and Winter (1980) noted higher interest in elite and culturally familiar nations.

Another study of this nature was conducted by Peterson (1979), who surveyed stringers, correspondents, and editors of the *Times* of London with a questionnaire designed to identify both news selection factors and gatekeeper socialization effects. Cultural proximity and national elitism were found to operate as selection factors at all levels of the organization.

Finally, Hester's (1971, 1974) studies of news flow into the United States via the Associated Press provide interview data with gatekeepers. Respondents in the 1974 study, which reported interviews with AP correspondents in Latin America and central desk editors in New York, ranked direct involvement of U.S. interests as a key criterion of newsworthiness for foreign news reports.

The 1971 study, which reported interviews with AP Interbureau wire editors and Wisconsin newspaper wire editors, was more specific. The Interbureau editors believed their clients to be "more interested in news from foreign nations which share a common cultural and ethnic background with the United States" and reported that "they would give first priority to stories from developed Anglo-Saxon nations over items from non-Anglo-Saxon developing countries if news values were held constant" (Hester 1971, 37). Newspaper wire editors felt their readers cared little about news from the developing world and were interested primarily in areas with which they had common ethnic and cultural ties.

Overall, these studies indicate that a nation's level of political dialogue with the United States, level of elitism expressed in economic terms, degree of cultural proximity, and, in some cases, geographic proximity, influence selection of news items from that nation by media gatekeepers and readers.

LOGISTICS PERSPECTIVE. National variables function as selection criteria that influence editorial decisions and thus the flow of news. Do they also influence news flow outside the gatekeeping process?

Several recent theoretical studies say they do, either in conjunction with the gatekeeper paradigm or in place of it. Hester, for example, speculated that "not only do perceptions of dominance or weakness in the hierarchy of nations have effects upon information flow, but so do the resources and activities of the nations themselves" (1973, 242). Ostgaard, too, included "economic factors which directly influence the flow of news" (1965, 43) in addition to gatekeeper-mediated factors. Rosengren, on the other hand, called for the outright replacement of "the psychological theory of Galtung. . . by an economic, political, and sociological theory of the flow and structure of international news" (1974, 154). National variables proposed in these studies as exerting direct effects upon news flow are listed in Table 14.2.

Lacking from these studies are the mechanisms by which national variables might directly affect news flow. With the exception of transmission costs and location of bureaus, direct connections between the variables in Table 14.2 and news flow are not immediately obvious. The studies propose such connections, then leave their nature largely unelaborated.

This question can be addressed indirectly, however, by juxtaposing two further groups of studies. The first group deals with the influence of wire service bureau location on news flow. The second deals with the influence of economic, political, and social variables on the location of wire service bureaus.

Table 14.2. Factors influencing news flow outside the gatekeeping process

Factors	Ostgaard	Hester	Rosengren
Government news management (direct or indirect)	X		
Transmission costs	X		
Location of agency bureaus	X		
National rank in international hierarchy (area, population, economic development, political stability); or gross national product	X	X	X
Trade between nations		X	X
Distance between nations			X

Ostgaard identified both bureau location and transmission costs as factors likely to influence the flow of news directly. The influence of transmission costs, however, has diminished rapidly as access to communication satellites has become more widespread. Hester (1974) and Larson (1979) documented large increases in news flow from Third World countries following installation of earth stations. The days when developing countries communicated over cable connections routed through London or Paris are virtually over.

Bureau location, however, remains capable of influencing news flow due to the continuing dominance of the major wire services. Boyd-Barrett (1980), reviewing some 25 recent wire service studies, concluded that the four major Western agencies continue to provide the majority of the world's international news and to set the agenda for smaller agencies.

Wire service news comes from wire service bureaus. The distribution of bureaus thus establishes the geographic boundaries of the wire service universe of events. Larson (1979) found a .55 rank-order correlation between coverage of nations by CBS Evening News and the presence of bureaus for the major wire services and international newspapers in those nations. The presence of bureaus was found to be a stronger predictor than the presence of national news agencies, Intelsat ground stations, or even CBS News permanent bureaus.

The quantity of news flow from various regions within the wire service universe is conditioned by bureau size. A number of studies (Rubin 1977; Lent 1977; Smith 1980) link the quantity of news flow into the United States with the number of correspondents deployed by American media overseas. There is a limit to the number of reports a correspondent can file in a day, regardless of how many newsworthy events may occur in his or her area of coverage. In the absence of crisis, when additional reporters would be provided, correspondent productivity sets a maximum limit on wordage reported from a country.

Conversely, regardless of how few newsworthy events may occur during a slow news spell, correspondent professionalism sets a minimum level for daily output. In the absence of hard news, features will be produced and forwarded. Hester's (1971) data for the Associated Press trunk wires showed Canada, Japan, and China, which received little A-wire coverage, with high levels of feature coverage on the B wire.

The location and staffing of wire service bureaus would thus appear to exert a powerful direct influence on the quantity of news flow. The studies cited bear out Ostgaard's hypothesis that "the countries where the agencies are already well established, are apt to provide a larger outgoing service, all other things being equal, not necessarily because what happens in the country is especially 'newsworthy,' but simply because there are large bureaus and/or many well-paying clients there" (1965, 43). The next question to consider is what factors influence the establishment and staffing of bureaus.

Recent studies by Tunstall (1977) and Boyd-Barrett (1980) address this problem. Tunstall adopted a historical approach to show how the spread of

Anglo-American influence in television, radio, cinema, and news services paralleled the growth of American political influence, economic interests, and technological innovation. While acknowledging this historical dimension, Boyd-Barrett stressed the commercial nature of the wire services themselves, and showed how their present-day operations are constrained by market considerations.

Boyd-Barrett listed a number of factors influencing bureau location and size. Principal among these was a nation's potential as a market for wire service products. Revenue considerations dictate "the distribution of agency resources in favor of privileged markets" (1980, 43). Also included were a nation's potential as a center for the production of news, and its logistical potential as a center for coverage of wider geographic areas.

These factors are clearly related to economic and political variables. In the absence of political restrictions on news flow, nations with large gross national products are likely to be richer media markets than less prosperous countries. A nation's ability to generate the political and economic events that comprise much of foreign news coverage is proportional to its economic productivity and its activity in international politics. Finally, a nation's capacity to support newsgathering operations depends on the development of its communication system and travel facilities, which in turn depend on its overall level of economic development.

In general, support is provided for the hypothesis that national variables influence news flow independent of day-to-day gatekeeping processes. National variables are closely related to a nation's ability to serve as market, news center, and logistic base for the major wire services, and thereby influence the siting and staffing of bureaus. Wire service correspondent deployment, in turn, is strongly related to the quantity of news flow from a given country. The influence of national variables on news flow would thus appear to be mediated through wire service organizational structure.

Previous research provides considerable evidence bearing on the four perspectives regarding the influence of national variables enumerated earlier in this study. The "no effects" hypothesis was not supported. A number of studies offer evidence for the psychological mediation of national variable influence through the decisions of gatekeepers; others provide evidence that the influence of national variables is exerted through their effects on the stucture of the newsgathering media. Together, these studies provide indirect support for the fourth hypothesis, which proposed that national variables influence news flow at both the gatekeeper and logistics levels.

NATIONAL VARIABLE INFLUENCE: A CAUSAL MODEL. Causal modeling requires convincing evidence for the presence of causal operators capable of translating change in independent variables into change in dependent variables. Two such operators linking news flow with national variables have now been established. The gatekeeping chain and foreign correspondent deployment are implicitly included in the model that follows as the mechanisms by which the influence of national variables is exerted.

In the following model, the quantity of coverage a nation receives in the U.S. press is hypothesized to depend primarily on three things: that nation's economic productivity, its trade with the United States, and the scope of its political relations with the United States. These three variables are thought to affect coverage directly by influencing gatekeeper decisions and correspondent deployment and indirectly through causal relations with each other.

A nation's economic productivity causally affects both the size of its trade and the scope of its political relations with the United States. Expanding productivity generates additional export trade goods and provides capital to finance additional import trade. Further, expanding productivity is likely to generate a broadening of economic, political, military, and cultural contacts with the U.S. government.

Trade, on the other hand, causally affects a nation's economic productivity and the scope of its political relations with the United States. Expanding trade could be expected to fuel productivity and to broaden the economic agenda with Washington.

The range of a nation's political relations with the United States is considered to have little effect (short of transitions from belligerence to nonbelligerence and vice versa) on productivity or trade.

This system may be more formally set out through flow graph representations and structural equations; Fig. 14.1 shows the directions of the hypothesized relations. Let a represent the structural coefficients that indicate how change in a given variable is converted to change in another. Let U represent unspecified disturbances that produce the variance unaccounted for by the specified variables. With economic productivity represented as E, trade as T, scope of political relations as P, and coverage as C, the system may be defined in terms of the following equations:

$$E = a_2 T + U_E \tag{14.1}$$
$$T = a_1 E + U_T \tag{14.2}$$
$$P = a_3 E + a_4 T + U_T \tag{14.3}$$
$$C = a_5 E + a_6 P + a_9 T + U_C \tag{14.4}$$

As now specified, it is possible to test this theory by estimating and testing its structural coefficients using empirical data.

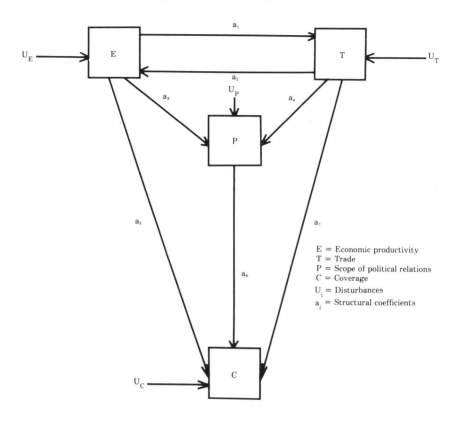

Fig. 14.1: Model of foreign news coverage in elite U.S. newspapers

DATA. Data suitable for testing the theory were collected in a 1979 multinational study of foreign news coverage. For purposes of this study, articles were considered "foreign coverage" if they concerned events occurring within the borders of nations other than the United States. The *New York Times*, *Washington Post*, and *Los Angeles Times*, the elite newspapers selected for use in this study, together featured 1,106 such articles over the sample period.

Analysis of relations between the economic and political characteristics of nations and their coverage in the American press required that nation, rather than article, be used as the unit of analysis. Accordingly, coverage data were summarized for each nation and paired with each nation's predictor data to form the new cases. Nations included the membership of the United Nations as of spring 1979, together with Taiwan, North Korea, South Korea, South Africa, and Switzerland, for a total of 151.

The following variables were used in testing the model:

1. quantity of coverage, measured as the number of articles for which each nation was coded as the main event location (Coder reliability of this measure was 94 percent.)
2. economic productivity, measured as gross national product (GNP) for each nation for 1975 (United Nations 1978)
3. trade, measured as the sum of each nation's import and export trade with the United States for 1977 (U.S. Bureau of the Census 1978)
4. scope of political relations, measured as a difference score representing the scaled distance between the maximum levels of conflict and cooperation in a nation's relations with the United States over the last six months of 1978. Higher scores on this variable were taken to indicate greater scope in political contacts.

The political relations variable was derived from data stored in the Conflict and Peace Data Bank (COPDAB), a computerized source of information on political transactions (Azar 1980). COPDAB holds records of international and domestic political events occurring in 135 countries over the past 30 years. The records are derived from content analysis of some 60 news publications from all regions of the world.

Among the variables coded for each event is the degree of conflict or cooperation involved. Events are assessed on a 15-point scale, with a score of 1 representing maximum cooperation, a score of 15 representing full-scale warfare, and a score of 8 representing a neutral point between. Participants in international events are characterized as "actor nations" or "target nations," depending on the character of their participation.

To generate the political dialogue variable, U.S. interactions both as actor and target with each of the other 134 nations in the data base for the last six months of 1978 were examined, and the maximum levels of conflict and cooperation between the United States and each nation identified. The cooperation score was then subtracted from the conflict score; the resulting value represented a nation's political dialogue variable. This variable could range from zero, representing a stable, virtually unidimensional relationship with the United States, to 14, representing a rapidly changing and unstable dialogue. In practice the maximum for the dialogue value was 9.

The rationale behind this variable was the expectation that the more varied and wide ranging a nation's dialogue with the United States became, the less predictable it would be and the more surveillance, in the form of news coverage, it would generate.

Estimation of the relations between GNP and trade, which jointly determine each other, required the use of additional instrumental variables (Heise 1975). A variable could serve as an instrument for GNP in specifying the effect of GNP on trade, for example, if it did not affect trade directly, did affect

GNP directly, was not affected by GNP or trade, and if no unspecified variable affected both the instrumental variable and trade.

Variables considered to meet these criteria for GNP were (1) area (World Almanac 1980) and (2) population (World Almanac 1980). Variables thought to meet instrumental criteria for trade were (1) distance from the United States, measured border to border (2) political system, scaled for degree of similarity to the Western democratic model. Politicial system was measured on a scale of 2 to 14, with 14 representing liberal democracy. It was derived from 1978 ratings for worldwide political and civil liberties (Freedom House 1978).

The correlation matrix for all variables in the model, together with their means and standard deviations, is presented in Table 14.3.

ANALYSIS. The structural coefficients for equations 14.3 and 14.4 were estimated using ordinary least-squares regression. Coefficients for equations 14.1 and 14.2, which define a jointly dependent relationship, were estimated using the methods of two-stage least squares.

If two variables, X and Y, are jointly dependent, the unspecified causes of Y will affect X through Y, biasing estimates of X's effect on Y. Two-stage least-squares estimation first isolates variance in X unrelated to unspecified causes of Y, and vice versa. Estimated values of X, uncontaminated by disturbance variance of Y, are then used to obtain estimates of the structural coefficient relating X to Y. The structural coefficient from Y to X is estimated in similar fashion.

The technique employed to obtain uncontaminated values of X and Y is regression of each variable on instrumental variables assumed to be unrelated to the disturbance term of the other. The regression equations obtained yield predicted values of X and Y theoretically free of influence from each other's disturbance term. Ordinary least-squares regression of Y on the uncontaminated values of X, and of X on the uncontaminated values of Y, is then conducted. The regression coefficients obtained for the uncontaminated X and Y values are the estimates of the structural coefficients between X and Y.

In the present study, uncontaminated estimates for trade and GNP were obtained by regressing these variables on area, population, distance, and political system, the four variables designated above as instruments for the joint trade-GNP relationship. The predicted values of trade and GNP yielded by these regressions were substituted into equations 14.1 and 14.2, together with the appropriate instruments, to obtain estimates of the structural coefficients a_1 and a_2. Equations 14.1 and 14.2 were thus replaced by

$$E = a_2 T + b_1 A + b_2 P + U_E \tag{14.5}$$

$$T = a_1 E + b_3 D + b_4 S + U_T \tag{14.6}$$

Table 14.3. Instrumental, source, and dependent variables

Descriptive statistics	Unit of measure	Mean	Standard deviation	Coverage n = 151	GNP n = 151	Trade n = 101	Political relations n = 93	Area n = 151	Population n = 151	Distance n = 151	Political System n = 151
Coverage	articles	7.33	15.85	1.0							
GNP	$ (millions)	31,039	86,568	0.72**	1.0						
Trade	$ (millions)	2,525	6,478	0.55**	0.46**	1.0					
Political relations	14-pt. scale	3.62	2.83	0.49**	0.38**	0.37**	1.0				
Area	square miles	314,163	896,563	0.49**	0.63**	0.31**	0.17*	1.0			
Population	thousands	24,737	86,888	0.34**	0.46**	0.12	0.16	0.50**	1.0		
Distance	great circle degrees	65.30	30.67	-0.12	-0.16*	-0.20*	0.02	0.09	0.02	1.0	
Political system	14-pt. scale	7.15	4.00	0.18*	0.19*	0.30**	0.03	-.06	0.00	-0.32**	1.0

*$p < .05$
**$p < .01$

where *A* represents area, *P* represents population, *D* represents distance from the United States, and *S* represents political system.

Results of the analysis are presented in Fig. 14.2. The findings indicate that an increase in trade with the United States is likely to produce an increase in a nation's GNP, and vice versa. An increase in trade with the United States, in GNP, or in both, will broaden the scope of a nation's political dialogue with the United States. With regard to the relationships of primary interest, increase in GNP, trade, and scope of political dialogue all produce increases in a nation's coverage in elite U.S. newspapers. GNP exerts the most powerful influence on coverage. Trade is next in importance, followed closely by political relations. Together these variables account for 59 percent of the variance in foreign coverage.

QUALIFICATIONS. At any given time, some nations are receiving far greater coverage than would have been predicted from their levels of GNP, U.S. trade, and political relations with the United States. Such instances are generally due to short-term coverage of events of extraordinary intrinsic newsworthiness. Over a year or two such coverage would tend to even out. Restriction of the sample period to three months could be expected to reduce the predictability of foreign coverage from national variables. The inclusion of a continuous week as part of the sample reduces predictability still further. The equations derived above are thus time specific, applicable to periods of a few months. The disturbance variance in coverage for a model based on a year's data might well be considerably less.

Within the model, the values of the estimated structural coefficients are highly dependent on proper specification of relationships between variables and the availability of suitable instruments for estimating these relationships. In the present case, perhaps the greatest likelihood of misspecification lay in the omission of a relationship from political relations to trade. Instances where political changes have affected trade are not unknown. It was assumed that such instances are relatively rare, occurring only during radical alterations in political dialogue. Preliminary testing for this relationship using a number of possible instruments failed to yield significant results, and it was omitted from the final model.

The adequacy of the instruments used to specify the joint trade-GNP relationship was partially testable. Using a procedure developed by Namboodiri, Carter, and Blalock (1975), one of the two instruments for GNP could be tested for a direct relationship with trade, and vice versa. Population was tested for evidence of a direct relationship with trade, and political system for a direct relationship with GNP. Estimated structural coefficients for these relations did not differ significantly from zero at the .05 level, indicating that in this model, population and political system at least partially fulfill the criteria for suitability as instruments.

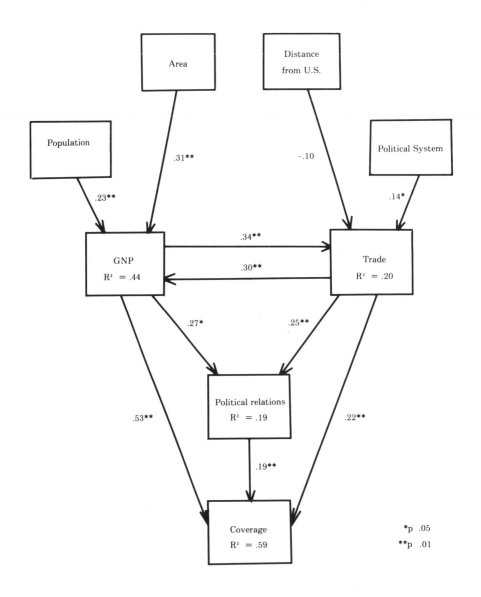

Fig. 14.2: **Structural model of national variable influence on news flow** (standardized coefficients)

DISCUSSION AND CONCLUSIONS. Third World dissatisfaction with the Western focus of international coverage has been a driving force in the decade-old debate in UNESCO and other international forums. Basing their critique on the North-South population disparity, representatives of the developing nations have charged that the developed nations of Western Europe and North America receive an inordinate share of foreign coverage in the world's news media (Aggarwala 1978; Masmoudi 1979).

Two methods for reducing this Western focus frequently advanced in UNESCO policy debate are the expansion of news values to encompass the slow, massive social change underway in developing countries, and the transfer of communications technology and expertise to the Third World. The findings in this study bear directly on these proposals.

The redefinition of news is clearly a gatekeeper oriented approach. It assumes an accessible, reasonably comprehensive universe of events from which news is selected on the basis of perceptual factors. To alter coverage in such a model, it is necessary only to adjust perceived news values to shift emphasis to other sectors of the event universe.

At the primary newsgathering level, however, the universe of events is not a worldwide panorama to be passively scanned, but rather a limited affair brought into being by the assignment of a small number of correspondents to a few overseas locations. Within its narrow thematic and geographic extent there is little scope to alter coverage on the basis of redefined news values. Redefinition of news values at this level implies redeployment of resources.

Wire services currently deploy their correspondents in response to market forces, which are in turn conditioned by general economic and political factors. Redeployment of resources on the basis of factors unrelated to political and economic structure is unlikely, under the model proposed. While the present political and economic order persists, the universe of events passed over the wires will continue to offer limited selection, and the ability of media gatekeepers to alter their editorial product in accordance with revised news values will be correspondingly restricted.

The structural coefficients of the model proposed here are unlikely to change while the major Western agencies supply the vast majority of foreign news. Providing advanced communications technology to the developing world, however, raises the possibility of alternate sources of coverage. A number of regional agencies have already commenced operation. If successful, these agencies will expand coverage from areas remote from the major centers of political and economic power. In terms of the model advanced, technology transfer could be expected to weaken the relations between GNP, trade, and political relations and news coverage, and thus reduce the Western emphasis in foreign news coverage.

REFERENCES

Adams, John B. 1964. A qualitative analysis of domestic and foreign news on the AP-TA wire. *Gazette* 10:285–95.

Aggarwala, Narinder K. 1978. News with Third World perspectives: a practical suggestion. In *The Third World and press freedom*, ed. Philip C. Horton, 187–208. New York: Praeger.

Azar, Edward E. 1980. Codebook of the conflict and peace data bank (COPDAB). Computer reproduced. Chapel Hill, N.C.: University of North Carolina.

Bass, Abraham Z. 1969. Refining the "gatekeeper" concept: A UN radio case study. *Journalism Quarterly* 46:69–72.

Boyd-Barrett, Oliver. 1980. *The international news agencies*. Beverly Hills, Calif.: Sage Publications.

Casey, Ralph D., and Thomas H. Copeland. 1958. Use of foreign news by 19 Minnesota dailies. *Journalism Quarterly* 35:87–89.

Charles, Jeff, Larry Shore, and Rusty Todd. 1979. The *New York Times* coverage of equatorial and lower Africa. *Journal of Communication* 29(2):148–55.

Cherry, Colin. 1971. *World communication: threat or promise?* New York: Wiley.

Cooper, Anne. 1981. News from the Third World. Unpublished paper prepared at the University of North Carolina at Chapel Hill.

Cutlip, Scott M. 1954. Content and flow of AP news. *Journalism Quarterly* 31:434–46.

De Verneil, A. J. 1977. A correlation analysis of international newspaper coverage and international economic, communication, and demographic relationships. In *Communication Yearbook I*, ed. B. D. Rubin. New Brunswick, N.J.: Transaction Books.

Dupree, J.D. 1971. International communication: view from a "window on the world." *Gazette* 17:224–35.

Epstein, Edward Jay. 1973. *News from nowhere*. New York: Random House.

Freedom House. 1978. *Comparative survey of freedom*. New York: Freedom House.

Galtung, Johan, and Mari Holmboe Ruge. 1965. The structure of foreign news. *Journal of Peace Research* 2:64–91.

Gieber, Walter. 1956. Across the desk: a study of 16 telegraph editors. *Journalism Quarterly* 33:423–32.

Hart, Jim A. 1966. Foreign news in U.S. and English daily newspapers: a comparison. *Journalism Quarterly* 43:433–48.

Heise, David R. 1975. *Causal analysis*. New York: Wiley.

Hendrix, H. 1962. The news from Latin America: the Associated Press. *Columbia Journalism Review* 1(3):50–51.

Hester, Al. 1971. An analysis of news flow from developed and developing nations. *Gazette* 17:29–43.

——————. 1973. Theoretical considerations in predicting volume and direction in international information flow. *Gazette* 19:239–47.

——————. 1974. The news from Latin America via a world news agency. *Gazette* 20:82–91.

Hicks, Ronald G., and Avish Gordon. 1974. Foreign news content in Israeli and U.S. newspapers. *Journalism Quarterly* 51:639–44.

International Press Institute. 1953. *The flow of the news*. Zurich: International Press Institute.

Larson, J.F. 1979. International affairs coverage on U.S. network television. *Journal of Communication* 29(2):136–47.

Lent, John A. 1977. Foreign news in American media. *Journal of Communication* 27(1):46–51.

Lewin, K. 1947. Channels of group life. *Human Relations* 1:143–53.

Lewis, P. 1981. Gloves come off in struggle with UNESCO. *New York Times*, May 24, E3.

MacLean, Malcolm, Jr., and Luca Pinna. 1958. Distance and news interest: Scarperia, Italy. *Journalism Quarterly* 35:36–48.

Marlens, A. 1962. The news from Latin America: United Press International. *Columbia Journalism Review* 1(3):51–54.

Masmoudi, Mustapha. 1979. The new world information order. *Journal of Communication* 29:172–85.

McNelly, John T. 1959. Intermediary communicators in the international flow of news. *Journalism Quarterly* 36:23–26.

——————. 1962. Meaning intensity and interest in foreign news topics. *Journalism Quarterly* 39:161–68.

Namboodiri, N. Krishnan, Lewis R. Carter, and H. M. Blalock, Jr. 1975. *Applied multivariate analysis and experimental designs*. New York: McGraw-Hill.

Ostgaard, Einar. 1965. Factors influencing the flow of news. *Journal of Peace Research* 1:39–63.

Peterson, Sophia. 1979. Foreign news gatekeepers and criteria of newsworthiness. *Journalism Quarterly* 56:116–25.

Righter, Rosemary. 1979. Who won? *Journal of Communication* 29:192–95.

Rosengren, Karl Erik. 1974. International news: methods, data, and theory. *Journal of Peace Research* 11(2):145–56.

——————. 1977. Four types of tables. *Journal of Communication* 27:67–75.

Rubin, Barry. 1977. *International news and the American media*. Beverly Hills, Calif.: Sage.

Sande, Oystein. 1977. The perception of foreign news. *Journal of Peace Research* 3–4: 221–37.

Sasser, Emery L., and John T. Russell. 1972. The fallacy of news judgment. *Journalism Quarterly* 49:280–84.

Schwartz, H. 1970. Covering foreign news. *Foreign Affairs* 48:744–57.

Semmel, Andrew K. 1976. Foreign news in four U.S. elite dailies: some comparisons. *Journalism Quarterly* 53:732–36.

Smith, A. 1980. *The geopolitics of information*. New York: Oxford University Press.

Smith, Raymond F. 1969. On the structure of foreign news: a comparison of the *New York Times* and the Indian *White Papers*. *Journal of Peace Research* 6:23–36.

Snider, Paul B. 1967. "Mr. Gates" revisited: a 1966 version of the 1949 case study. *Journalism Quarterly* 44:419–28.

Sparkes, Vernone, and J.P. Winter. 1980. Reader interest in foreign news. *ANPA research report no. 28*. Sept., 7–10.

Stevenson, Robert L., and Richard R. Cole. 1980. Foreign news and the "new world information order" debate. Parts I and II. U.S. International Communication Agency report R-10-80. Washington, D.C.

Tunstall, Jeremy. 1977. *The media are American*. New York: Columbia University Press.

United Nations. 1978. *World economic survey—1977*. New York: United Nations.

U.S. Arms Control and Disarmament Agency. 1978. *World military expenditures and arms transfers: 1966-1975*. Washington, D.C.: Government Printing Office.

U.S. Bureau of the Census. 1978. *Statistical abstract of the United States—1978*. Washington, D.C.: Government Printing Office.

White, D.M. 1950. The "gate keeper": a case study in the selection of news. *Journalism Quarterly* 27:383–90.

Wilhelm, J. 1966. The overseas correspondents. In *1966 directory of the Overseas Press Club of America*. New York: Overseas Press Club of America.

World Almanac and book of facts: 1980. New York: Newspaper Enterprise Association.

Yu, F. T. C., and J. Luter. 1964. The foreign correspondent and his work. *Columbia Journalism Review* 3(1): 15-22.

Zipf, G. 1946. Some determinants of the circulation of information. *American Journal of Psychology* 59:401-21.

About the Contributors

Thomas J. Ahern, Jr., works for the Department of Defense in Washington. He was in the master's degree program at the University of North Carolina at the time of this study.

Richard R. Cole is professor and dean of the School of Journalism at the University of North Carolina.

Anne M. Cooper is assistant professor at Mary Baldwin College, Staunton, Virginia. She was formerly a doctoral student in the mass communications research program at the University of North Carolina.

Gary D. Gaddy, School of Journalism and Mass Communications at the University of Wisconsin, was formerly in the doctoral program at the University of North Carolina.

Robert D. Haynes, Jr., is a doctoral student in political science at the University of North Carolina.

Jere H. Link, a doctoral student in history at the University of North Carolina, was in the journalism master's degree program at the time of the study.

Emmanuel E. Paraschos is associate professor of journalism at the University of Arkansas at Little Rock.

Donald Lewis Shaw is professor of journalism and director of the Media and Instructional Support Center at the University of North Carolina.

J. Walker Smith is director of market research for the Friendly Ice Cream Corporation in Massachusetts. He was formerly in the doctoral program in mass communication research.

Robert L. Stevenson is associate professor of journalism at the University of North Carolina.

Kirstin D. Thompson is a public affairs specialist with Philip Morris U.S.A. in New York City. She was formerly in the master's program at the University of North Carolina.

David H. Weaver is professor of journalism at Indiana University.

G. Cleveland Wilhoit is professor of journalism at Indiana University.